E SQUADRONS

No 3

No 4

No 11

No 12

No 14

No 15

No 16

No 23

No 24

No 25

No 27

No 28

No 41

No 42

No 43

No 45

No 47

No 63

No 64

No 65

No 70

No 72

No 100

No 101

No 111

No 115

No 120

No 216

No 230

No 234

No 360

No 617

ENCYCLOPAEDIA OF
MODERN
ROYAL AIR FORCE
SQUADRONS

CHRIS ASHWORTH

Patrick Stephens Limited

Title page *The Aden Strike Wing (Hunters of Nos 8 and 43 Squadrons) led by a Shackleton of No 42 Squadron (RAF Khormaksar).*

First published in 1989

British Library Cataloguing in Publication Data

Ashworth, Chris
   Encyclopaedia of modern Royal Air Force Squadrons
   1. Great Britain. Royal Air Force. Squadrons, to 1987
   I. Title
   358.4'131'0941

   ISBN 1-85260-013-6

Patrick Stephens Limited is part of the Thorsons Publishing Group, Wellingborough, Northamptonshire, NN8 2RQ, England.

Printed in Great Britain by Butler & Tanner Limited, Frome, Somerset
Typeset by MJL Limited, Hitchin, Hertfordshire.

10 9 8 7 6 5 4 3 2 1

Contents

Foreword

by Air Vice Marshal
G.A. Chesworth CB OBE DFC

This work is effectively a pocket history of the Royal Air Force and, at the same time, an up-to-date order of battle of the Service today.

More importantly, the Encyclopaedia gives an insight into the way the organisation of the 'sharp end' of the Royal Air Force has developed, and the contribution the Squadron structure has made in the past, makes now, and will undoubtedly make in the future, to the spirit and fighting efficiency of the Air Force.

Since its formation on 1 April 1918, the RAF has capitalised on the inherent sense of pride and belonging to the Squadron to maximise the effectiveness of the individual unit and the collective formation. The pride of the squadron members in their unit has always generated an *esprit de corps* which, through competition and rivalry in peace and war, enhances the value of the force. The value of this dedication and spirit has become increasingly important as high technology has brought increasing demands on the levels of skill and professionalism of all members of the Royal Air Force.

The reduction in numbers of aircraft and personnel has also added significantly to the burdens of commanders and has brought into focus the importance of maintaining morale. The integrity of the Squadron's identity is a major contribution to this cause.

Chris Ashworth's book provides students of air power in general, and the Royal Air Force in particular, with a useful reference. For those with a general interest in the Royal Air Force, this will provide fascinating and authoritative reading.

Introduction

My dictionary states that an encyclopaedia is a book giving information on all branches of knowledge or of one subject. This encyclopaedia attempts to tackle just one subject, that of modern Royal Air Force Squadrons, and confines itself almost exclusively to operational flying squadrons. A complete book could be written on each of the 67 squadrons covered — indeed, some of them have already had this treatment and nearly all have had long articles devoted to them. I have provided a short history of each squadron, with particular emphasis on its role and the aircraft employed during its active years, but have concentrated on the aspects which make each unique. It is this uniqueness which differentiates an operational squadron from other units, and in my view engenders the intense loyalty which both past and present members almost invariably feel towards it.

As already stated, this book is basically about current front-line flying squadrons, but for the sake of completeness it also includes the shadow units and two surface-to-air missile (SAM) units. It does not include the recently strengthened RAF Regiment and its squadrons, operational though they most certainly are, because they have already been described very adequately in the *Encyclopaedia of the Modern Royal Air Force* also published by Patrick Stephens.

Few books other than novels can be written entirely unaided, and this book is no exception. I have received generous assistance from many sources and am profoundly grateful. Particularly patient in answering seemingly pointless questions or providing essential photographs have been the staffs of the Air Historical Branch, MoD (Air); British Aerospace plc; Command PRO, RAF Germany; Mod P1B (Cer), Public Records Office, Kew; RAF Museum; the Commanding Officers/Historians of Nos 4, 9, 14, 23, 24, 25, 28, 47, 51, 54, 56, 78 and 84 Squadrons; and J.A. Bartholomew, M.J. Burrow, Chaz Bowyer, G.S. Leslie, M.W. Payne, B. Pickering (MAP), Flt Lt N. Roberson, B. Robertson, and Flt Lt A.S. Thomas.

R.C.B. Ashworth   *Padstow, Cornwall*

The Squadron

The squadron is the basic unit of the Royal Air Force. Now widely used for all sorts of formations on an RAF station, it has been the name employed for front-line fighting units since the birth of the Force on 1 April 1918, despite the tremendous changes in equipment, role and complement which have taken place over the past 70 years.

Of Italian derivation, a squadron was originally a square battle formation consisting of companies of infantry or mounted troops in close order. In the British Army, however, the squadron was almost exclusively used as the title for a mounted cavalry fighting unit, the equivalent infantry unit being the battalion. In the early days of military flying, the ability to ride a horse was seen as an important guide to a man's likely piloting skills, and this may have had some bearing on the choice of 'squadron' as the basic Royal Flying Corps (RFC) unit, though the titles 'company' and 'group' had both been considered and rejected before a sub-committee chaired by Captain Frederick Hugh Sykes finally approved the title early in 1912.

The original RFC squadrons consisted of three Flights of four aircraft and appropriate numbers of flying and technical personnel, an organization which stood the ultimate test when war came in August 1914, proving both manageable and flexible. The Naval Wing, independently spirited as ever, flirted with a number of different titles for their flying units, but by 1916 had also settled on the squadron as the most conveniently sized and named unit, a choice perhaps made easier by its long-standing use for a group of warships.

The RAF retained the general squadron organization which had proved so successful in France with the RFC. Commanded by a Major, a pilot not normally allowed to take part in operations over the lines, and easily controlled through a sensible rank pyramid, the standard fighter squadron of 33 officers, 8 Senior NCOs and 122 men was self-contained and capable of being mobile at short notice. Any maintenance required by the 25 aircraft beyond squadron capability was dealt with by the Air Depot/Park. Army co-operation squadrons were of roughly the

No 85 Squadron on the Western Front in 1918, the SE 5As identifiable by the already famous 'hexagon'. The number of pets is interesting — as is the flying kit (RAF Museum P1038).

Left *A formal photograph of No 3 (Fighter) Squadron in November 1937 showing off the unit silver and the 'spearhead' on the fins of the Gladiators.*

Left *What the best-dressed fighter pilot is wearing! No 19 Squadron pilots at West-hampnett in 1940.*

Below right *For the unit record. The officers and aircrew NCOs of No 51 Squadron pose in front of a York at Bassingbourne in the late 1940s (RAF Bassingbourne).*

same size, while day bomber and reconnaissance units had an average of 18 aircraft, and night bombers and flying boat squadrons, ten.

The now familiar RAF ranks were introduced in August 1919, but following the unpopularity of the original light (powder!) blue uniform colour, khaki for ex-RFC and dark blue for ex-RNAS personnel were permitted until 1922, by which time the present shade of blue had gained approval and was widely available.

After the First World War, fighter squadrons, now commanded by a Squadron Leader, continued to have three authorized Flights (each of three aircraft, with three more in immediate reserve and a further three in storage, a total of 15), while bomber, army co-op and coastal reconnaissance units had two Flights. Many home-based squadrons were seriously under strength until the mid-1920s, and all relied heavily on the back-up services provided by the sta-

tion organization. Overseas, the squadrons did retain a greater element of self containment and had much more transport.

By the mid-1930s, wholesale expansion was under way, a situation particularly noticeable in home-based bomber units on which cohesion was difficult because whole Flights were frequently hived off to form the nucleus of a new squadron. Throughout this period of upheaval, the authorized aircraft establishment stayed constant at 12 plus reserves for all except general reconnaissance flying boat units which rarely had more than four aircraft on strength.

During the Second World War, establishment of both men and aircraft fluctuated wildly (and strengths even more so). Most fighter squadrons continued with the basic 12 aircraft and about 16 pilots, but 16 and even 24 aircraft were not unusual in the latter stages of the war, especially on the Continent. Main force bomber squadrons steadily increased in size from the peacetime 12, each manned by two to four men, to 20 or more with crews of seven or eight. Coastal Command flying boat squadrons had an average of six aircraft, but crews were large, up to 12 in number, while landplane units numbered up to 18 aircraft with crews ranging from two in Beaufighter/Mosquito strike aircraft to eight aboard Liberators.

In 1939, all squadrons were commanded by a Squadron Leader, but as the numbers of personnel on the unit increased it became standard practice for COs to be Wing Commanders on all but single-engined fighter and army co-operation squadrons. All squadrons started the Second World War with their own groundcrew for first-line maintenance and turn-round duties — indeed, most fitters and riggers had their own aircraft, but the large-scale Exercise 'Spartan' held in 1943 revealed how unwieldy this practice had become. Many of the more mobile units lost their dedicated groundcrew, the men being formed into Servicing Echelons. In theory, these echelons could be transferred between squadrons as required, and, while this did happen occasionally, it was fiercely resisted by both groundcrew and aircrew, and usually they stayed with a particular unit and had an associated number. Despite this, the servicing echelons were not popular amongst tradesmen, and even less so were the various forms of Wing or Station servicing introduced on some of the more static bases operating large multi-engined aircraft.

During 1945-46, squadrons were not only drastically reduced in number but also in size, most units having an establishment of eight aircraft, except for flying boat squadrons which had six. They did however regain their groundcrew, except for long-range

transport squadrons which became involved in a highly centralized servicing system which, in various forms, has been in operation ever since. It spread temporarily to Bomber Command but more permanently to the maritime-reconnaissance elements of Coastal, and later Strike Command.

The Korean War, and the 'Cold War' which accompanied it, resulted in considerable expansion of the RAF, not only in the number of active squadrons, but also in the authorized strength of some units. The establishment of fighter units, for instance, doubled from eight to sixteen in February 1950. The mobility of squadrons in Germany was also increased and they became almost self-sufficient, reminiscent of Western Front squadrons in 1918 and Second Tactical Air Force units in Normandy during 1944.

Amongst personnel, a major change over the past 30 years has been the reduction in the number of NCO aircrew. Except for maritime, where most of the air engineers, winchmen and air electronic operators are NCOs, and transport, where air engineers and loadmasters are usually Master Aircrew, Flight Sergeants or Sergeants, flying personnel are now all commissioned. Most squadrons are commanded by a Wing Commander and have establishments for at least two Squadron Leaders, often more, while Flight Lieutenants abound. Fighter, strike and army support units still retain their own groundcrew, but the larger and more static maritime, tanker and transport units have their servicing, and often their aircraft, provided from Station resources.

In Germany, and occasionally at home, squadrons are accompanied by RAF Regiment contingents when they disperse, this attachment being particularly close with the two Chinook units (Nos 7 and 18

Left *No 120 Squadron's competition crew with their specially marked Nimrod ready for the start of the 1980 Fincastle Trophy contest, and illustrating the comparatively comfortable garb of the modern maritime reconnaissance crew.*

Right *Badges appear in many places. On aircraft — such as No 32 Squadron's badge on a Vampire FB9 in 1952; on buildings — the Headquarters of No 8 Squadron at Khormaksar (both R.B. Trevitt); on menu cards — for a No 6 Squadron dinner; and on people — Air Vice Marshal Dermot Boyle, AOC No 1 Group, at Binbrook before leaving on a tour of South America with four No 12 Squadron Canberras in 1952.*

Sqns) which have permanent Regiment elements. Some tactical squadrons, in particular those involved in reconnaissance, have a small Army photo-interpretation cell and any unit, large or small, may have personnel from NATO or Commonwealth air forces on strength under the highly successful, and popular, exchange scheme.

The steady withdrawal of British forces from the Middle and Far East since the Second World War has resulted in a complete re-organization of the RAF into three basic Commands, only two of them involved with operational flying. The resultant cutbacks in strength, some savage like those which followed the infamous 1957 White Paper, have stretched the remaining squadrons during periods of heightened tension and when extra commitments have suddenly been forced upon them; but without exception they have risen to the challenge, a tribute to the basic squadron concept and to the men themselves.

Human beings have a strong desire to *belong*, and the squadron has proved an ideal vehicle for the development of camaraderie and 'identity'. Desirable in peacetime, this almost indefinable *esprit de corps* is vital during war. It is rightly fostered by the squadron system which provides so well a simple command structure which everyone can understand, and a feeling of being part of a team and 'special'. It is helped by distinctive badges and aircraft markings, competition between *friendly* rivals, and by the Squadron Standard, even in these days when it is considered smart in some circles to sneer at such 'elitism'. These, and other factors, are detailed in the chapters which follow.

It is a maxim that, almost without exception and regardless of how many squadrons a man has served on, the current one is best! Long may it remain so.

Squadron badges

Heraldic devices embodied in coats of arms, crests and badges have been used as means of identification for centuries. Coats of arms were granted by the Sovereign to knights and noblemen in recognition of favours or important deeds, and were worn on the surcoat of the holder and emblazoned on his battlefield shield. Crests were worn on the knight's helmet and coat badges identified servants and retainers.

Subsequent rewards by the Sovereign, known as Augmentations of Honour, were incorporated into coats of arms, and military badges are thought to have developed from the similar Honourable Distinctions granted to army regiments to commemorate distinguished service. From the inception of the Standing Army in 1661, such badges were borne on the Regimental Colours, a traditional way of promoting pride in the unit as well as identification with it.

Heraldry was not long in appearing in military flying circles. In the First World War, some pilots distinguished their particular aircraft by painting devices or emblems on them, while unofficial shields and badges began to appear in messes. During the 1920s, such badges began to be used on aircraft in a semi-official way to identify them as belonging to a particular squadron, the form they took being very much the personal whim of the commanding officer. With

the rapid expansion of the 1930s, the situation started to get out of control, and it was decided to regularize matters; on 1 March 1935, the Chester Herald was appointed as Inspector of RAF Badges and the use of unofficial emblems was brought to an abrupt end.

The official badge was now to be surrounded by a standard frame, which had the squadron motto enclosed by a scroll below it, and was surmounted by a crown. The squadron number was set into the frame on both sides of the badge and the current role was also included. Squadrons were invited to submit their own ideas for a suitable badge, most choosing designs which alluded to particular events in their past, to aircraft equipment, birds and animals, or incorporated the coats of arms of counties or neighbouring towns. All were checked for heraldic suitability, mottos coming in for particular scrutiny, but most were accepted with small alterations, and provide a fascinating insight into the histories of the units. A few mottos used Arabic, others English, Malay and French, but the majority employed Latin and provide scholars with endless opportunity for argument over precise meanings!

Instructions covering the uses of the official badge on aircraft were issued on 16 January 1936. Operational squadrons were to use it without number or any inscription on a white background shaped to indicate the unit's function and outlined in the major colour of the badge. The first badges accepted by the Chester Herald (later renamed Clarenceux King of Arms) were approved by HRH King Edward VIII in May 1936 and included those of Nos 2, 15, 18, 19, 22 and 216 Squadrons. Other followed rapidly, but the majority received their royal assent under the signature of HRH King George VI, leaving just one of the current units, No 360 Squadron, to be confirmed by HRH Queen Elizabeth II.

During 1939, badges were removed from aircraft, in theory at least, for a few units managed to retain them during the early years of the Second World War. They returned in strength after the war, usually in the form of large transfers of the complete badge including the frame, motto and number; but with the advent of more colourful unit markings during the 1950s, they again largely disappeared on fighter and strike aircraft. Complete badges were retained on bomber, transport and maritime aircraft except when they were drawn from a station pool under the various centralized servicing schemes which have been tried since the Second World War. Nimrods and Hercules still operate on a Wing basis and carry Station badges, but most other aircraft carry some form of squadron badge, either complete or making use of the centrepiece.

Squadron badges are often used to identify head-quarters buildings and also appear at the Station entrance. They adorn squadron letterheads and the commanding officer's official car. They are worn on flying suits, and on groundcrew overalls. They are a source of pride in the unit, often avidly collected in the form of a plaque by ex-members.

The badges of all current operational flying and missile squadrons are depicted alongside each squadron's entry together with their heraldic descriptions and mottos.

Squadron Standards

Identification of friend and foe has always been a problem in battle, and from the very earliest days men have used some form of distinguishing sign. The badge or sign of a tribal chief was placed on a pole and carried aloft to enable opposing sides to recognize each other, and it also came to indicate a rallying point when an army was hard-pressed. In time, the badge came to symbolize past triumphs in battle, and successful tribes associated their victories with the power of these 'badges on a pole', or banners.

When knights went into battle dressed overall in armour, the need for recognition became even more important and coats of arms were devised and worn over the armour. The same insignia was used on rallying banners which gradually evolved as 'Colours'. These were carried by every company in an English regiment until 1707 when official control was exercised and the number of Colours was cut drastically, first to three per battalion and later to two.

In 1751, a distinction was made between the 'King's Colour' and a 'Regimental Colour', and it is the latter, emblazoned with the unit's battle honours and badges and regarded as the symbol of the spirit of a regiment, that an RAF Squadron Standard closely resembles in both appearance and meaning. It is called a 'Standard' rather than a 'Colour' because it is capable of free standing and is not always carried aloft.

HM King George VI signified his intention to award a ceremonial flag, or standard, to operational RAF squadrons on 1 April 1943, the 25th anniversary of the formation of the Royal Air Force. Air Ministry Order A.886/43 subsequently announced that squadrons would qualify in one of two ways, either by 'Completion of 25 years of service in the Royal Air Force, the Royal Air Force Regiment, the Royal Auxiliary Air Force, the Royal Flying Corps, or the Royal Naval Air Service', or by 'Earning the Sovereign's appreciation following specially outstanding operations'.

The expression 'operational squadron' included

No 100 Squadron Standard showing the arrangement of the eight Honours scrolls, the intricate embroidering of the badge and the tasselled surround.

photographic reconnaissance, air/sea rescue, meteorological and RAF Regiment squadrons, and the Standard consists of a rectangular silk flag in Royal Air Force blue, measuring 2 ft 8 in (0.8 m) by 4 ft (1.2 m), fringed and tasselled. The squadron's badge is centred on the flag, flanked by up to eight scrolls containing battle honours. Each flag originally had a border of embroidered roses, thistles and shamrocks, the traditional emblems of England, Scotland and Ireland, but understandably it was not long before the Welsh complained and in 1953 the leek was added. The staff of the Standard is 8 ft 1 in (2.4 m) in length and is surmounted by a gilt eagle with wings outstretched.

Thirty squadrons were qualified to receive the award of a Standard in 1943, and as additional units became eligible they made their claim for Royal approval, resulting in the promulgation of further lists from 1950 onwards. When a squadron qualifies for the award of a Standard, a list of Battle Honours to which it is entitled is prepared by the Air Historical Branch and agreed within the Ministry of Defence. Entitlement is restricted to units which engaged in active operations in a combat zone, the first list of battles, promulgated in February 1947, covering 35 First World War engagements, (two more were added retrospectively in 1964), 26 inter-war engagements and 56 Second World War engagements. Since then, the three Sunderland Squadrons which flew patrols in Korean waters during 1950-53 have become eligible, as have a further fifteen squadrons for operations in the South Atlantic between 2 April and 14 June 1982.

Up to eight Battle Honours can be emblazoned on the Standard, the final choice being made by the Squadron Commander of the day. Until 1982, only Battle Honours gained during First and Second World War operations were eligible for emblazonment, but following the Falklands conflict it was decided that the three RAF units which had direct contact with Argentinian forces, Nos 1, 18 and 63 (Regiment) Squadrons, had the right to have 'South Atlantic 1982' on their Standards. The maximum number of Battle Honours so displayed was, however, still limited to eight until August 1987, when 'by Royal Command', Nos. 1 and 18 Squadrons were allowed to add 'South Atlantic 1982' as a ninth scroll — a signal honour.

Only two Standards have been awarded for specially outstanding operations, the units so honoured being Nos 120 and 617 Squadrons. The reason for the latter's inclusion, despite its comparatively short history, is well known to anyone with the slightest interest in aviation history, but the former's exploits against German U-boats in mid-Atlantic at a critical stage of the war when they single-handedly 'closed the gap' have not had the same dramatic impact on the general public or even within the Royal Air Force.

Presentation of Standards to squadrons was delayed until after the war, No 1 Squadron receiving the first on 24 April 1953. The Standard epitomizes the service and deeds of a squadron and is regarded with veneration, receiving a religious blessing when presented. The first two RAF Standards were consecrated in a similar ceremony to that employed for Colours, but it was then decided that dedication was more appropriate and this form of service was first used on 9 October 1953 when No 7 Squadron was presented with its Standard.

The Standard is usually presented by the

Above left *The Governor of Aden presents No 8 Squadron's Standard at Khormaksar in 1954* (via H. Galloway).

Above right *No 7 Squadron's old Standard is paraded for the last time on a chill day in June 1978 at St Mawgan, on the occasion of the presentation of the new colour by Princess Alice, Duchess of Gloucester.*

Commander-in-Chief of the Command in which the squadron serves, or by a distinguished past member of the unit. There is no fixed rule, however, and members of the Royal Family, including the Queen, have presented Standards, as have governors of Colonies and other dignitaries.

On disbandment, permanent or temporary, the Squadron Standard is laid up in a church or chapel. Despite the great care taken with Standards, deterioration due to age and environment is inevitable and many squadrons have had new Standards presented. The old ones are then laid up in a place of the squadron's choice, many choosing the RAF Church, St Clement Danes. Built by Sir Christopher Wren in 1682 on the foundations of even older churches, St Clement Danes was reduced to a charred ruin by incendiary bombs on 10 May 1941. After the war,

monies raised by the Royal Air Force, Commonwealth and Allied Forces enabled the church to be restored and it was reconsecrated on 19 October 1958 during a ceremony attended by HM Queen Elizabeth II and HRH The Duke of Edinburgh. More than 700 squadron and unit badges made of Welsh slate have been let into the floor, together with a memorial to Polish squadrons. Beneath the north gallery is a memorial to the 19,000 members of the United States Army Air Force who gave their lives while flying from British soil. The Church of St Clement Danes is a fitting memorial to the men and women of many countries who fought and flew with the RAF during the Second World War, but it is also a living church and therefore a marvellous place for squadron Standards to rest.

Information on the Standards and Battle Honours

of individual squadrons are included in their histories, while Appendix III lists the Battle Honours which can be awarded.

Affiliations

During the First World War, organizations of all sorts, and even individuals, were encouraged to raise money for the nominal purchase of an aircraft. In most cases, a machine was selected and suitably inscribed with the name of the donors. It was then known as a 'presentation' aircraft. At least one donor, the Nizam of Hyderabad, gave sufficient money to 'purchase' a whole unit, and No 110 Squadron was thereafter unofficially referred to as the 'Hyderabad' Squadron. This was the first rather tenuous affiliation — an idea taken up officially when Reserve and Auxiliary squadrons were formed in the 1920s, such units having a definable connection with a particular town or county. This affiliation was embodied in the squadron's official title and very close ties were developed.

In April 1939, the Air Ministry sought to extend the ties between the Royal Air Force and the public by approving the affiliation of regular units, including squadrons, to 'principal cities and towns in the United Kingdom'. The object was to foster the public's interest and increase the ordinary airman's feeling of *esprit de corps*. Usually the affiliation was between a unit and a town close to its base, examples being No 43 Squadron (at Tangmere) and Chichester and No 51 (Driffield) and York.

Some of the liaisons were very successful and long-lasting, though the start of the Second World War within a few months of the scheme being launched inevitably broke some links. Often such affiliations were kept alive by the 'Wings for Victory' campaign, even when the unit was posted far away. To coincide with a 'Wings Week', local newspapers were provided with press releases describing the exploits of 'their' squadron and, as in the First World War, individual aircraft were inscribed with names of cities, boroughs and towns.

These affiliations were not considered significant enough to embody in the squadron's official title, but under another Air Ministry scheme Dominions, Colonies, Indian States and other organizations contributing sufficient funds to 'purchase' a complete squadron were allowed that privilege. A total of 49 squadrons were so named, only seven of which are extant. Confusingly, other units, notably Nos 44 and 266 (Rhodesia) Squadrons, adopted the names of territories in recognition of the large number of personnel from that country serving in them rather than being 'gift' squadrons. Following changed attitudes towards, and by, Dominions and ex-colonies, such

No 42 Squadron's Standard on parade at the Freedom of the Borough of Restormel, Cornwall, in 1987.

titles have been allowed to lapse in recent years.

In February 1949, the Air Ministry announced that certain disbanded squadrons which had a distinguished past would be linked on a 'number only' basis with existing front-line units. The scheme was not very popular, however, and had fallen into disuse by the end of the 1950s.

In 1959, another attempt was made to involve stations and squadrons with the local community under the Municipal Liaison Scheme and this has been reasonably successful over the years. It is perhaps really more appropriate for stations than for squadrons because, despite the comparative stability of the modern RAF, squadrons do still move, detach for long periods or disband, and this makes boroughs and town councils reluctant to become too involved with them. There are notable exceptions however, one of them being No 201 Squadron's long-standing close association with Guernsey. Such contacts are undoubtedly very worthwhile, for anything that increases understanding and a feeling of belonging is invaluable for any military organization.

Mascots

Mascots, animal or bird (and even human on occasion), have long formed part of Army Regimental tradition. Their very presence on the battlefield has proved an inspiration to troops, and in barracks a focus for humour and relaxation during quieter periods. Some were officially presented to a unit, others just attached themselves or had been personal pets which were adopted by the Regiment.

This tradition has been carried over into the Royal Air Force, though on a much smaller scale. Perhaps the most famous mascots have been the series of goats named 'Lewis' at the Apprentices' School, Halton. Some squadrons have managed to maintain a mascot despite the problems engendered by a constant turn-over of personnel and sudden movement of the whole unit, often by air. Thus the popularity of live animals, reptiles and birds has waxed and waned, and with a few notable exceptions most of those that remain are being cared for in zoos or are stuffed! Known examples of squadron mascots are listed with the unit information in the main section of this book.

Trophies

Sports trophies and Station cups made an early appearance in the Royal Air Force and squadrons soon collected an incredible variety of trophies, some extremely disreputable, but it was 1925 before the first presentation was made for an inter-squadron flying competition. This was the Ellington Cup provided by Sir Edward Ellington, Air Officer Commanding RAF India, for award to the squadron winning a local bombing competition. In the same year, Sir Phillip Sassoon, Bart, presented a trophy to HQ Fighting Area, Air Defence Great Britain, for competition between fighter squadrons — not for air firing, but for team map-reading ability!

In 1926, the most impressive and one of the longest lasting of the pre-1939 trophies, the Lawrence Minot, was given anonymously, followed by the Armament Officer's and Salmond Trophies in 1930, all for bombing competition. Sir Phillip Sassoon, a long-serving Under Secretary of State for Air and a great friend of the Royal Air Force, presented more trophies in 1932 and 1933 for army co-operation and bomber competition respectively.

There were other competitions organized on a local

Above *The 'grand daddy' of them all — the Salmond Bombing Trophy was first awarded in July 1930 and is still current.*

Below *The stylish Dacre Trophy awarded annually to the Strike Command fighter squadron judged the best all-round unit (RAF Leconfield).*

basis, and the Auxiliaries competed for the Esher Trophy, but those listed above remained the premier trophies for permanent pre-Second World War squadrons. Competition was intense, for there was prestige to be gained by winning, not only for the Commanding Officer but for everyone involved, right down to the orderly room clerk.

The Munich Crisis of 1938 saw the end of such competitions, and they were not generally re-introduced until the 1950s. Rapid advances in aircraft and techniques resulted in the original competitions being out-moded, and new rules had to be drafted and agreed. Some of the trophies were re-allocated to new Commands and roles, only those presented for aspects of bombing broadly continuing their original purpose. At the same time came a surge of new trophies, some very specialized and confined to squadrons employing the same type of aircraft or engaged in a particular role.

While squadrons were numerous, such trophies were welcome, but with the steady contraction of the RAF during the late 50s and 60s they had to be rationalized. The various 'bomber' trophies became part of the annual Bomber Command Bombing Competition, while those awarded for ground attack/ photo reconnaissance were awarded for elements of the 2/4 ATAF competitions in Germany. Competition amongst fighter units was sustained by the Dacre Trophy in 11 Group and the Duncan in Germany, while Coastal/18 Group maritime reconnaissance squadrons competed for the Aird-Whyte, and Transport/Air Support Command units for the Lord Trophy.

The demise of the Vulcan resulted in the withdrawal of the Strike (ex-Bomber) Command Bombing & Navigation Competition and associated trophies, and both the Duncan and Lord Trophies have been suspended. No 11 Group has, however, gained two new trophies and the Salmond has been re-instated for competition amongst strike units.

It would be impossible within the confines of this book to adequately cover all the trophies which have been presented to the RAF over the years, but a representative selection of current trophies showing all the winners is included in Appendix IV.

Squadron markings

British aircraft entered the First World War with no internationally accepted markings, but some pilots had Union Jacks painted on their machines after a few days in France. On 26 October 1914, the Admiralty made the Union Jack compulsory on the underside of its aircraft's mainplanes, though the RFC had already banned such markings because the only part which stood out was the white cross, and that was being confused with the standard German insignia.

The RFC in the field decreed on 11 December that a roundel based on the French marking, but with the red and blue reversed, was to be painted on all aircraft in France. Eight days later, the Admiralty followed suit by issuing instructions that a red ring with a white centre was to be used under the wings, while the Union Jack was retained on the fuselage sides and rudder. Further refinements followed in May 1915 when the RFC introduced rudder stripes, the sequence from the rudder post being blue, white and red, and the following month made roundels mandatory on the aircraft sides as well as underwing on all machines with covered fuselages.

So far these decrees had all involved national markings, but early in 1916 the need to identify corps recce BE 2Cs by unit became evident. Distinctive coloured shapes or bars painted on fuselage sides were authorized for artillery observation/reconnaissance squadrons and introduced on 23 April 1916. Gradually, such markings also spread to fighter scout and day bomber squadrons, while personal markings also made their appearance — and were firmly stamped on by Colonel Hugh Trenchard in August 1917. Some changes were made to officially authorized markings in December, but more radical were orders issued on 22 March 1918 requiring the removal of all unit markings from bomber and corps recce aircraft and to change those on fighter machines. The object was to confuse enemy intelligence during preparations for the Allied spring offensive when units were to be reshuffled.

It was at this point that the RAF was born, but the order was not rescinded, all aircraft other than fighters carrying only a single letter or numeral as distinguishing marks for the rest of the war. This situation continued into the 1920s, aircraft becoming if anything more nondescript following the general adoption of overall silver as a paint scheme when fighter units also lost their individual markings. They soon re-appeared, however, though reversion to wartime symbols, advocated in September 1924, was not adopted because fighter squadrons were already designing their own much more flamboyant schemes. Such markings remained the privilege of fighter units, however, the rest having to make do with individual flight colours on wheel discs, introduced universally during December 1924. The discs on 'A' Flight aircraft were red, 'B' Flt yellow, and, if the squadron had a 'C' Flt, its machines carried blue as the distinguishing colour. Commanding Officer's and Flight Commander's aircraft often had painted fins.

Squadron individuality inevitably reared its head, for members were, and are, proud of their unit iden-

Left *No 17 Squadron's famous zigzag which first appeared in 1924. This Woodcock at Upavon in 1926 has the marking on the fuselage sides and upper wing, the standard layout of the time (A.V. Gladstone).*

Right *Lancaster B1 ME 844 in 1944 carrying the wartime 'LS' code of No 15 Squadron.*

Left *The 'spearhead' device of 1936 enclosed the Squadron emblem, here superimposed on a black triangle on a No 25 Squadron Fury II in May 1937 (C.E. Sergeant).*

Right *The two-letter codes were retained after the war but often applied more artistically. This Mosquito FB VI of No 84 Squadron at St Thomas Mount, India, in 1946 has them 'highlighted' (R.H. Dargue).*

tity and wanted to demonstrate it. Additional markings gradually appeared even on such soberly coloured aircraft as night bombers in their drab 'Nivo' dark green. Often the markings took the form of unofficial squadron badges, and sometimes aircraft were individually named. Standard national markings also slowly changed. From March 1927, large-sized aircraft serials were painted under the wings — in black on silver machines and white on 'Nivo' — and between August and October 1930 the colour order of the rudder stripes was revised. In August 1934 they were removed altogether and wing roundels were reduced in size to prevent overlap on to ailerons following the discovery that the additional paint thickness was affecting control as speeds increased.

Various forms of squadron emblems and crests mushroomed during the early 1930s, only to be cut back savagely during February 1936 when the Air Ministry ordered such markings to be strictly limited to a unit symbol (intended to be the centrepiece of the authorized squadron badge) set in a standard frame painted on both sides of the fin. The frame was in the form of a 'spearhead' for fighters, a 'grenade' for bombers and a 'six-pointed star' for army co-operation and reconnaissance units (including flying boats). This scheme had been implemented almost universally by the time of the 1938 Munich Crisis. Hasty camouflaging then became the order of the day and code letters, one set for peacetime and another in the event of war, were issued. The codes took the

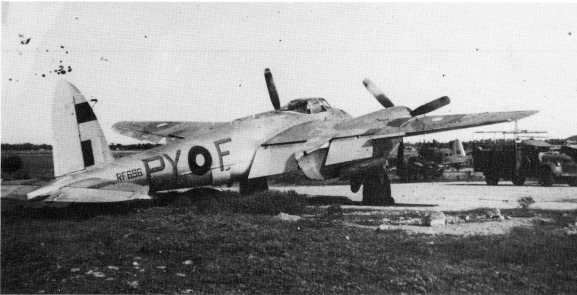

form of a two-letter identification for the unit painted on the left-hand side of the fuselage roundel, and a single letter denoting the individual aircraft to the right, and were intended to replace all other indentifying markings apart from roundels and serials. The peacetime codes could be applied from 25 September onwards and some squadrons adopted the scheme with alacrity and exactly as specified. A few wrongly used their wartime allotment and others retained their spearhead, grenade or star symbols which rather destroyed the object of the exercise. A number, particularly overseas, did nothing until the system became mandatory following the publication of Air Ministry Order A 154/39 dated 27 April 1939.

In September 1939, the application of the wartime codes was ordered and adopted universally at home and in France, but rather patchily further afield. A few squadrons still clung to their symbols, a well-known example being 85 Squadron which continued to put its hexagon on the tails of its Hurricanes. As the war progressed, some squadrons, particularly in the Middle and Far East, gave up the use of unit codes favouring single letter (and occasionally number) aircraft identification only, while others were allocated new codes in an attempt to confuse the enemy, or because the unit became so large (usually Bomber Command squadrons) that two sets of codes had to be used at the same time. For a period during 1943, Coastal Command adopted a numeral unit identification system and in general mixed letter/numeral

This Canberra B 2 of No 100 Squadron being 'bombed-up' illustrates well the large serials introduced in Bomber Command in the late 1950s, and the yellow and blue check fin markings adopted by the Wittering Wing, with a green disc for No 100 Squadron.

In May 1950, fighter 'bars' were re-introduced in a standard size and format. This Hunter of No 54 Squadron carried its blue and yellow checks on the nose on each side of the badge — other units chose the roundel as the centrepiece.

Similarly styled 'bar' markings were later applied to helicopter rotor mountings, as here on a Wessex HC 2 of No 72 Squadron in June 1976.

More recently, the 'bar' markings have been miniaturized, as on this Phantom FGR 2 of No 23 Squadron at Mount Pleasant, Falkland Islands — the aircraft also carries the colony badge (D. Burrows).

Right *Tails have always been a popular place for markings, like this intricate representation of the No 3 Squadron badge on the tail of a Tempest V in September 1945. The pilot is Sqn Ldr R.B. Cole DFC, the Commanding Officer (F.L. Pitt).*

Below *Markings on the tail of a No 47 Squadron Beverley in September 1966 and on the dielectric fin panel of a Canberra PR 7 of No 100 Squadron in 1956 (M. Retallack).*

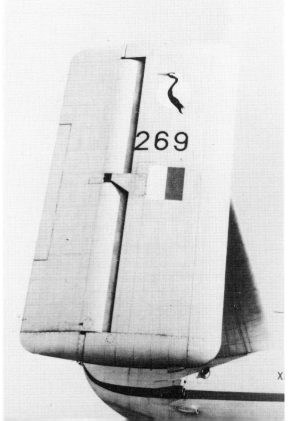

This Canberra B(I)8 of No 16 Squadron has the 'cross keys' emblazoned on the nose. . . (M. Muttitt)

. . . while this Tornado F 3 has the three 'X's of No 29 Squadron on the engine intake.

combinations became common in the latter stages of the conflict.

After the Second World War, the letter/numeral codes remained in use accompanied from 1948 onwards by coloured noses, propeller spinners or engine intakes. Inevitably, fighter squadrons tried to go further but anything more colourful was frowned on by higher authority until May 1950 when 'fighter bars' on either side of the fuselage roundel or flanking a squadron badge on the nose were authorized.

The Germany-based Second Tactical Air Force squadrons adopted similarly distinctive markings, but Bomber, Coastal and Transport Command aircraft

remained comparatively sober in appearance, though Canberra units did employ 'lightning flashes' on the sides of the noses of their aircraft to denote the squadron.

Fighter squadrons have long spawned unofficial aerobatic teams, but in the 1950s and 60s the 'official' team scheme was revived and their markings became more flamboyant year by year. Aped by other units, such markings were retained until 1966 when the order to cut back on special paint schemes was enforced. In 1970 came a general tone-down in gloss finishes, followed during 1974 by a reduction in the size of squadron markings, subsequently to be con-

An almost unidentifiable Jaguar GR 1A of No 41 Squadron specially painted with whitewash for Arctic operations...

...and a Puma HC 1 of No 230 Squadron at the 1982 'Tiger Meet' (Military Aircraft Photographs).

tained in an 18 in (0.46 m) diameter white disc on the fin.

All these moves were intended to make RAF aircraft less conspicuous, this principle being taken much further in 1981 with the widespread introduction of 'low visibility' all-grey camouflage and 'washed-out' national and unit markings on fighter aircraft. The success of such schemes encouraged the general adoption of the 'hemp' colour on maritime and flight refuelling aircraft, and various shades of grey on tactical transports, leaving strike aircraft clinging to their traditional dark grey/dark green disruptive pattern camouflage, and strategic transports

and communications types their attractive white/grey or white/natural metal schemes. At the same time, however, there has been a welcome return to brighter, and in many cases, larger squadron markings on all but the largest aircraft — a sign that individualism is still very much with us, and just cannot be suppressed for long.

Detail on the markings of individual squadron aircraft can be found in the unit entries in this book. For more information on the general subject of aircraft markings, the reader should consult one of the excellent reference books available.

The modern Squadrons

No 1 Squadron

Badge

A winged numeral '1' — approved by HRH King Edward VIII in July 1936 as the authorized version of an unofficial badge which originated during the First World War as a wreathed roundel from which sprouted a pair of RFC wings and on which the figure '1' was superimposed.

Motto

In omnibus princeps — 'First in all things'

History

As befits its motto, No 1 Squadron was one of the three squadrons formed on 13 May 1912, the day the Royal Flying Corps (RFC) officially came into being. The Squadron took over the balloons, airships and man-carrying kites of No 1 Airship Company, Air Battalion, Royal Engineers, at Farnborough and operated these lighter-than-air craft until 1 May 1914 when the unit was redesignated the Airship Detachment, RFC. The same day, a new No 1 Squadron, RFC, was formed at Brooklands, equipped with a motley collection of aircraft most of which were taken over by other RFC units and went to France with the British Expeditionary Force (BEF) when war was declared in August.

New aircraft were painfully gathered together and training resumed at Netheravon in November 1914. Early in March of the following year, No 1 moved to France as a reconnaissance unit and continued to operate a hotch-potch of aircraft until January 1917 when it was completely equipped with Nieuport Scouts and assumed the 'fighter' role. Despite heavy losses, the Squadron was soon showing its mettle, the 200th German aircraft being claimed on 9 October 1917.

Re-equipped with SE 5As in January 1918, the pilots of No 1 played a full part in repelling the March offensive launched by the Germans, making repeated low-level strafing attacks on their forward troop positions. Redesignated No 1 Squadron, RAF, on 1 April 1918, the unit remained in the thick of the action on the Western Front, close support operations being replaced by fighter patrols and finally bomber escort. Following the Armistice, the Squadron busied itself ferrying aircraft back to the United Kingdom before reduction to cadre and then disbandment on 20 January 1920. The next day it reformed in India, equipped with Sopwith Snipe biplanes which it took to Iraq in May 1921 to become the sole fighter squadron in the whole of the Middle East.

Disbanded in November 1926, the Squadron was again reborn the following February as part of the slowly expanding United Kingdom air defence force, receiving the nimble Siskin at Tangmere. For 12 golden years, No 1 remained on the Sussex coast, re-equipping with the superlative Fury biplane in February 1932. These aircraft, and the Squadron, became famous for their formation aerobatic displays at Hendon, and also further afield during visits to Canada and Switzerland.

The first Hurricanes arrived in October 1938 shortly after the Munich Crisis, and No 1 was ready for France when the call came nine months later. The odd combat during the 'Phoney War' period suddenly mushroomed into full-scale action in May 1940, but by mid-June the Squadron was back in the United Kingdom preparing for the inevitable Battle of Britain. After more fierce fighting during the summer,

Above *A late series Fury 1 K8276 carrying the red stripes and 'spearhead' badge of No 1 Squadron in 1937* (RAF Museum P2673).

Right *Hunter FGA 9 XE651 of No 1 Squadron at Luqa in 1968* (D. Lawrence).

No 1 went north in September 1940 for a rest before returning to Tangmere to take part in 'intruder' flights over France during 1941-42. In July 1942 the venerable Hurricanes were exchanged for Typhoons, and, after another spell of inaction, 'intruding' started again and continued through D-Day until the unit was withdrawn for 'anti-diver' operations during the Summer of 1944, during which 39 V1s were destroyed.

No 1 Squadron was back at Tangmere yet again in 1946 to fly Meteors, but in August 1947 the unbelievable happened when, despite all protests, the unit was redesignated a Group Instrument Training Squadron and equipped with Harvard and Oxford dual trainers. After ten months of this indignity, common sense prevailed and the premier RAF squadron returned to the front line to operate with Meteors until September 1955 when the first Hunters were delivered. In August 1956 the Squadron went to Cyprus to fly alongside No 34 during the ill-fated Suez campaign, but was back at Tangmere by Christmas. Disbanded on 23 June 1958, the unit was reformed seven days later at Stradishall by renumbering 263 Squadron, and spent another two years with No 11 Group, Fighter Command, before joining 38 Group, Transport Command, still with Hunters but now on strike duties!

After nine years with 38 Group's 'rapid response' force, No 1 started to receive operational Harriers and gained another 'first' by pioneering this revolutionary V/Stol aircraft in service. Since then, the Squadron has taken part in countless Air Sup-

A Harrier GR 3A of No 1 Squadron lurks in its 'hide', armed and ready to go (MoD/PRB 4447/136).

port/Strike Command exercises and has operated lengthy detachments in Belize, Central America. During the 1982 Falklands campaign, elements of the Squadron flew non-stop from the United Kingdom to Ascension, a record distance of 3,670 miles (5,905 km), courtesy of Victor tankers, a feat which has received scant recognition. They continued down into the South Atlantic by ship before flying operations from HMS *Hermes* against the Argentinians.

Based at Wittering since receiving Harriers, the Squadron was eagerly awaiting delivery of the updated and much improved GR5 variant in 1988.

Standard

Granted by HRH King George VI and promulgated on 9 September 1943. Presented by Air Vice Marshal Sir Charles Longcroft KCB CMG DSO AFC at Tangmere on 24 April 1953 — the first Squadron Standard presentation. Sir Charles was the Commanding Officer when No 1 reformed as an aeroplane unit in 1914.

A new Standard was presented by Marshal of the Royal Air Force Sir Dermot Boyle GCB KCVO KBE AFC at Wittering on 21 June 1983.

Battle Honours

*Western Front 1915-1918
Neuve Chappelle
*Ypres 1915
Loos
*Somme 1916
Arras
Ypres 1917
Somme 1918
Lys
Amiens
Hindenburg Line
*Germany 1918
Kurdistan 1922-1925
Iraq 1923-1925

*France & Low Countries
*Battle of Britain
Channel & North Sea 1941-1945
Home Defence 1940-1945
*Fortress Europe 1941-1944
Biscay 1944-1945
Normandy 1944
*France & Germany 1944-1945
Arnhem
Rhine
South Atlantic 1982

*Denotes Honours emblazoned on Standard

Affiliations

Brighton, Sussex — originally under the Air Ministry liaison scheme of April 1939 but revived in 1957 when the Squadron was again at Tangmere.

Nicknames

'Brighton's Own' — used unofficially during the Second World War.

Aircraft insignia and markings

No official markings were carried until 1917 when Nieuport Scouts started carrying large individual aircraft letters and a vertical red stripe aft of the fuselage roundel. The latter was changed to a sloping white line on each side of the roundel on SE 5As, but within a month these were replaced by a hollow white circle aft of the roundel.

In the early 1920s, no markings were carried on Snipes but when reformed with Siskin IIIs in 1927, two horizontal red stripes, parallel in front of the fuselage roundel but tapering to a point aft, were introduced, and were retained on the famous Furies. Similar stripes were painted across the full span of the upper mainplane. Propeller bosses and the main wheel centres were painted in standard Flight colours. Later, the fins of the Flight Commander's aircraft were also painted in Flight colours and a squadron badge was painted on a white 'spearhead'.

Late in 1938, the aircraft were camouflaged and all markings obliterated. Soon after the Hurricanes were received, the unit code 'NA' was applied, each aircraft also having an individual letter. In September 1939, the unit code became 'JX', these letters being used throughout the war and into the Meteor era. In 1950, a modernized version of the colourful pre-war markings replaced the codes, standardized as a red-edged white rectangle on each side of the fuselage roundel.

When Hunters replaced the venerable Meteors in 1955, the markings were moved to the sides of the nose and consisted of a white disc on which was painted a winged '1' flanked by red-outlined white triangles. Aircraft code letters were painted on the fin in white. The same nose markings have been retained on Harriers, but individual aircraft identification has alternated between numerals and letters and is now much toned down in colour. For exercises in Norway, the aircraft periodically appear in white and grey matt emulsion paint which provides very effective Arctic camouflage.

No 2 Squadron

Badge

Three concentric circles over all a Wake Knot — approved by HRH King Edward VIII in May 1936. A version of the unofficial badge first adopted in 1931, the circles represent the RAF and the Wake Knot is derived from the arms of Hereward the Wake and indicates the basic role of the unit as a guardian of the Army.

Motto

Hereward

History

Formed at Farnborough on 13 May 1912 as one of the original squadrons of the RFC, No 2 became well known before the First World War for a number of epic long-distance flights around the United Kingdom. At the outbreak of war, No 2 Squadron went to France with the BEF claiming the honour of being the first RFC unit across the Channel. The Squadron concentrated on reconnaissance and artillery spotting but did some bombing. It was on 26 April 1915 during one of the latter operations that Second Lieutenant W. B. Rhodes-Moorhouse won the first Victoria Cross awarded to an airman by pressing home an attack on Courtrai railway station despite accurate return fire which seriously wounded him. At base he insisted on making his report before treatment, and died the next day.

The BE 2 variants which had formed the main equipment since the unit arrived in France were finally replaced by the tough and reliable Armstrong Whitworth FK 8 in April 1917, and it was on this aircraft that the second Squadron VC was won on 27 March 1918 during a low-level strafing attack on advancing German troops. Second Lieutenant A. A. MacLeod and his observer Lieutenant A. W. Hammond were engaged by eight Fokker triplanes, and although Hammond destroyed three of them, the FK 8 was set on fire. MacLeod had to stand on the wing to fly it and somehow managed to crash-land between the lines and pull his observer out of the wreckage.

Reduced to cadre in February 1919, the Squadron was disbanded on 20 January 1920 but reformed eleven days later in Ireland equipped with Bristol F2Bs for army co-operation duties. Moved to England early in 1922, No 2 was back in Ireland within three months on standby in case of trouble during partition. In September of that year, the Squadron headquarters was transferred to Farnborough, leaving a detachment at Aldergrove until February 1923, and it was at about this time that the unofficial title 'II (AC) Squadron' was adopted. For the next five years No 2 engaged in routine army co-operation work with the Aldershot garrison until in April 1927 it suddenly left for China aboard HMS *Hermes*. Unrest in that vast country was threatening lives in the International Settlement at Shanghai and the Squadron was disembarked on the racecourse to provide a 'presence'.

Returning to the United Kingdom in September, the Squadron re-assembled at Manston and at the end of 1929 started receiving the AW Atlas, the first aircraft to go into RAF service actually designed for army co-operation work. Remaining in southern England, No 2 Squadron gradually worked its way through Audax and Hector biplanes and was at Hawkinge with Lysander monoplanes when war was declared.

The Squadron returned to France in October 1939 as part of the Air Component of the BEF, but did little except exercise until the German breakthrough in May 1940 when it was heavily engaged in fruitless

efforts to stem the tide. Back in the United Kingdom, No 2 carried out coastal patrols and army exercises, receiving Tomahawks in August 1941, then, for its new fighter-reconnaissance role, the much more effective Mustang in April 1942. Joining the Second Tactical Air Force, the Squadron was again back in France in July 1944, five months later re-equipping with the Spitfire XIV. With these aircraft it moved to Celle in Germany as part of the British Air Forces of Occupation (BAFO), still on fighter recce to which was added photo-reconnaissance when PR XI Spitfires joined the Mk XIVs in September 1945.

In December 1950, Meteors started to replace the Spitfires, and they remained in use until the first Swift FR5s entered service in March 1956. A nightmare to keep serviceable, the Swifts were replaced by Hunter FR10s with which the unit built up an enviable reputation in NATO, winning many competitions. Though a fine aircraft, the Hunter was outdated by the late sixties, and in March 1971 was finally relinquished in favour of a version of the Phantom FGR2 fitted with a multi-purpose reconnaissance pod.

After frequent moves around the British Zone of West Germany, No 2 settled in at Laarbruch in April 1971 and, with a change to recce-podded Jaguar GR1s five years later, has remained there ever since. The Squadron is due to re-equip with specially-equipped Tornado GR1s and maintain its traditional reconnaissance role into the foreseeable future.

Standard

Granted by King George VI and promulgated on 9 September 1943. Presented at Wahn by Air Chief Marshal Sir Robert Foster KCB CBE DFC on 31 October 1953.

A new Standard was presented by Air Chief Marshal Sir Alasdair Steedman GCB CBE DFC FRAeS CBIM, Controller of the RAF Benevolent Fund, at Laarbruch on 30 May 1984.

The old Standard was laid up in the Church of St Peter & St Paul, Courteenhall, Northants.

Battle Honours

*Western Front 1914-1918
Mons
*Neuve Chappelle
*Ypres 1915
Loos
*Somme 1916
Lys
*France & Low Countries 1939-1940
*Dunkirk
Fortress Europe 1942-1944
*Normandy 1944
*Arnhem
Walcheren
Rhine
France & Germany 1944-1945

*Denotes Honours emblazoned on Standard

Affiliations

Twinned with Goch, a town near Laarbruch, in 1984.

Aircraft insignia and markings

The BE 2C was the first No 2 Squadron aircraft type to carry unit markings, a triangle aft of the roundel appearing in April 1916. The triangle was black on clear doped machines and white on others. Soon after the introduction of the AW FK 8, it was replaced by

Left *With its prominent 'recce' pod under the fuselage, Jaguar GR 1A XZ108 of No 2 Squadron waits on the flight line for the weather to clear. The 'wake knot' emblem is just visible on the intakes* (Military Aircraft Photographs).

Right *A 'recce-podded' Phantom FGR 2 of the Squadron, a type replaced in 1976 by the current Jaguars* (D. Lawrence).

a white zigzag stripe between the roundels and the tailplane.

In Ireland during 1920, the Squadron's Bristol F2Bs were distinguishable by two red stripes around the rear fuselage, the space between them being filled by Flight colours, white for 'A', yellow for 'B' and blue for 'C' Flight. Later, the original First World War marking, the black triangle, was revived on the F2B, but when the Atlas entered service the markings disappeared, to be re-introduced on the rear fuselage of the Audax, often with the aircraft serial superimposed on the triangle. The Squadron badge was carried on the fin of late service Audax and the same markings were retained on Hectors, the last pre-war Squadron aircraft to be painted all-over silver.

Lysanders were camouflaged green/brown with silver undersides and initially carried the unit code 'KO', replaced in 1941 by 'XV' which was used until late 1943. No codes were carried by No 2 Squadron's aircraft after it joined the Second Tactical Air Force until after the war when the new code 'OI' was adopted. By 1951, some of the Spitfires were over-all silver, a colour retained by Meteors which at first used the unit code 'B' plus an individual aircraft letter. In 1952, the Meteors were camouflaged but retained the codes until squadron markings were re-introduced and the famous triangle resurrected, in white on a black rectangle on each side of the fuselage roundel.

Retained through the Swift and Hunter eras, the unit marking was moved to the nose of the Phantom, the space between the triangles being occupied by the Wake Knot on a white disc. This device, together with a white triangle with the superimposed aircraft code letter/numeral introduced on the fins of Hunters, has been retained on the Jaguars.

No 3 Squadron

Badge

On a monolith, a cockatrice — approved by HRH King George VI in September 1937. It was developed from the original unofficial badge which depicted five monoliths to commemorate the unit's connection with Stonehenge. The cockatrice was chosen because in mythology it was the first creature to fly.

Motto

Tertius primus erit — 'The third shall be first'.
The motto is a reference to the fact that No 3 Squadron, RFC, was the first to be equipped with heavier-than-air machines.

History

No 3 Squadron was formed at Larkhill on 13 May 1912 from No 2 (Aeroplane) Company with a motley collection of aircraft, the most airworthy of which went to France with the BEF in August 1914. After 18 months on reconnaissance duty, the Squadron finally received a full complement of Morane Parasols in December 1915 and these were used for artillery

A Bulldog IIA of No 3 Squadron at Halton showing off its broad green stripe which stretches the length of the fuselage (W.H. Christmas via A.W.P. Spears).

spotting. Late in 1917, Camels were received and No 3 Squadron was designated a fighter scout unit; it had accounted for 59 enemy aircraft by the Armistice. Reduced to cadre in February 1919, the Squadron was disbanded on 27 October 1919.

Reformed in India on 1 April 1920 from 'A' Squadron with Sopwith Snipes, it only lasted 20 months, but was immediately reborn on 1 October 1921 when the Mobile Flight of 205 Squadron, Leuchars, was redesignated. Equipped initially with special three-seat DH 9As, these had been replaced by the time the unit reached Gosport a year later by the even more ungainly Westland Walrus, and on 1 April 1923 the Squadron was disbanded after division into two independent Flights.

Reformed yet again on 1 April 1924 and equipped with Sopwith Snipes, the Squadron moved to Upavon a few weeks later for what proved to be a ten-year stay. Woodcocks, Gamecocks and Bulldogs were flown in succession, the latter being taken to the Sudan in October 1935 during the Abyssinian crisis. Returning to the United Kingdom in August 1936, the Squadron re-assembled at Kenley and in March 1937 introduced the Gladiator to front-line service. After briefly converting to Hurricanes, they reverted to Gladiators for a year while Kenley was extended, finally receiving Hurricanes at Biggin Hill just before the war started.

After a quiet time as part of Fighter Command, No 3 Squadron was sent to reinforce the Air Component of the BEF following the German breakthrough into France, but had to retire after ten days confused fighting during which it claimed 60 enemy aircraft for the loss of 21. Banishment to Scotland for 18 months monotonous patrolling was followed by equally fruitless night sorties co-operating with 'Turbinlite' Havocs over East Anglia. Conversion to Typhoons started in February 1943, these hefty aircraft being used for fighter bomber intruder and anti-shipping strikes. In March 1944, the Squadron became one of the first Tempest units, flying them over the Normandy beach-head and against the V1 flying bombs (of which it destroyed 288). It resumed armed reconnaissance in September when it moved on to the Continent with the Second Tactical Air Force for the advance through the Low Countries into Germany.

The Squadron remained in Germany with BAFO, converting to Vampires in April 1948, Sabres in May 1953 and Hunters in May 1956, but disbanded on 15 June 1957 as part of the reduction in the day fighter force. Reformed on 21 January 1959 by renumbering 96 Squadron, for two years it formed part of the all-weather fighter force in Germany with Javelins before disbandment once again on 31 December 1960. Reformed the next day by renumbering No 59, it flew Canberra B(I)8 low-level tactical bombers for eleven years from Geilenkirchen and Laarbruch before moving to Wildenrath and converting to Harriers in the tactical reconnaissance and strike role. Since March 1977 No 3 Squadron has been at Gutersloh, and is still equipped with up-dated Harriers.

Standard

Granted by HRH King George VI and promulgated on 9 September 1943. Presented by Air Chief Marshal Sir Philip Joubert de la Ferte KCB CMG DSO at Geilenkirchen on 11 December 1953. The Standard was temporarily laid up in St Boniface Church, Monchen Gladbach, on 15 September 1957, remaining there until 1959.

A new Standard was presented by Air Marshal Sir Patrick Hine KCB FBIM, C-in-C RAF Germany, at Gutersloh in June 1983.

The old Standard was permanently laid up in St Clement Danes church on 27 November 1983.

Battle Honours

*Western Front 1914-1918
*Mons
Neuve Chappelle
Loos
Somme 1916
Cambrai 1917
*Somme 1918
Hindenburg Line
*France & Low Countries 1940
*Battle of Britain 1940
Home Defence 1940-1945
Fortress Europe 1942-1944
Channel & North Sea 1943-1945
*Normandy 1944
*Arnhem
Rhine
*France & Germany 1944-1945

*Denotes Honours emblazoned on Standard

Aircraft insignia and markings

No unit markings were carried by No 3 Squadron aircraft until it re-equipped with Sopwith Camel scouts in October 1917. They had two vertical white

bars just aft of the roundel as distinguishing marks, changed in December 1917 to one on each side of the roundel, and again in March 1918 to two bars just forward of the tailplane.

After the war, the Squadron's aircraft carried no special markings until 1924 when the silver-painted Snipes appeared at Upavon with a broad green stripe down each side of the fuselage from propeller to rudder post, and also across the upper mainplane. These markings were retained on subsequent aircraft until the arrival of camouflaged Hurricanes. When the unit reverted to Gladiators in July 1938, these aircraft also adopted camouflage and were subsequently coded 'OP' to designate the unit, individual aircraft letters being carried as well. Replacement Hurricanes also used 'OP', changing to 'QO' in August 1939, which code was used until June 1944 when the Tempest Vs then on strength were re-coded 'JF'.

The code changed again in 1946 to 'J5' when some aircraft carried a badge on the fin. Silver-painted Vampire 1s and 5s also used 'J5', the former on the the nose, the latter on the booms. In 1950, the unit code was deleted and the individual aircraft letter was repeated on the nose. Later still, the fin 'acorn' fairings were painted the traditional leaf-green colour,

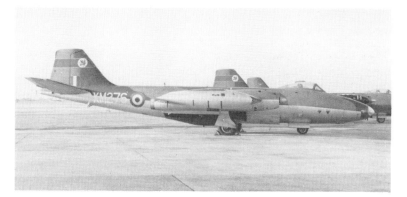

Canberra B(I)8s of No 3 Squadron in their attractive camouflage top and silver undersides. The Squadron 'cockatrice' is boldly painted on a green stripe across the tail.

Harrier GR3 XZ129 of No 3 Squadron awaits its pilot (MAP B03823).

and finally the Second Tactical Air Force Squadron code 'A' was added on the booms, this being retained on camouflaged aircraft.

When the unit received Sabres, markings were confined to leaf-green engine intakes, then later, on camouflaged aircraft, they changed to green rectangles edged in gold on each side of the fuselage roundel with individual aircraft letters on the fin, also gold lined. Hunters were similarly marked, but the Javelins wore a red and grey cockatrice on a white disc superimposed on a green band across the upper fin, the individual code being in white. Canberras and Harriers retained this format, though the green band and individual letters were not applied until the Canberras had been in service for several years; on the Harrier, the device was moved on to the sides of the nose.

No 4 Squadron

Badge

A sun in splendour divided per bend by a flash of lightning — approved by HRH King Edward VIII in May 1936. The red and black segmented sun suggests 'round-the-clock' operations, while the lightning flash indicates speed and is also a reference to the unit's early use of wireless telephony for artillery co-operation.

Motto

In futurum videre — 'To see into the future'

History

Formed at Farnborough in September 1912 from a nucleus provided by No 2 Flight of No 2 Squadron, No 4 Squadron flew the usual motley collection of aircraft, taking the more capable of them to France on 16 August 1914 to provide part of the air reconnaissance element of the BEF. This role occupied the Squadron for the whole of the First World War, the unit standardizing on BE 2Cs in April 1915, and RE 8s from June 1917. 'A' Flight was redesignated 4A Squadron for two months following detachment

in January 1918 to work with the Portuguese Corps.

Returning to the United Kingdom in February 1919, the unit disbanded the following September but reformed on 30 April 1920 equipped with Bristol Fighters. 'A' Flight went to Ireland later in the year but returned to Farnborough in January 1922, only to be sent out to Turkey aboard HMS *Ark Royal* in August as part of the reinforcement of British forces during the Chanak crisis. Transferred to the 'flat-topped' HMS *Argus* by crane, the F2Bs were assembled and flown off the carrier to Kilia airfield on 11 October.

Back at Farnborough a year later, the unit settled into a peacetime army co-operation routine working with the Aldershot Command, receiving Atlas aircraft in October 1929 followed by Audax in December 1931. The Squadron moved to Odiham early in 1937 and re-equipped with Hectors, exchanging these obsolescent biplanes for Lysander monoplanes in January 1939.

No 4 Squadron returned to France in October 1939, again in support of a BEF, but was forced out in May 1940 following a hectic period of operations flown in an attempt to stem the German breakthrough. After coastal patrol and air-sea rescue work, replacement of the Lysanders by Tomahawks and Mustangs was completed in August 1942, when tactical reconnaissance in support of the Army became the main role. Soon standardized on the excellent Mustang, No 4 Squadron joined the Second Tactical Air Force in August 1943 and in the following January changed roles, becoming a photographic reconnaissance unit equipped with Mosquito PR XVIs and Spitfire PR XIs for work in connection with the forthcoming invasion of Europe. The Mosquitos left in June, but a few Typhoons were added to the complement in the autumn by which time No 4 Squadron had been on the Continent for two months.

Disbanded in Germany on 31 August 1945, No 4 reformed the next day when No 605 Squadron was renumbered at Celle. Mosquito light bombers were flown until July 1950 when Vampire 5 fighter bombers were received at Wunsdorf. Becoming a day fighter unit, No 4 Squadron received Sabre 4s in October 1953 and Hunters in July 1955 at Jever. With the Second Tactical Air Force day fighter establishment savagely cut, the Squadron was disbanded on 31 December 1960, re-appearing the following day at Gutersloh when 79 Squadron, operating Hunter 10s in the fighter-reconnaissance role, was renumbered. These aircraft were flown for the next 9½ years, joined by a UK echelon in September 1969 using ex-54 Squadron Hunter FGA 9s while working up on Harriers at Wittering. When fully converted, the detached echelon moved to Wildenrath

Picking up a message. The Army Co-op 'six-point star' badge on the fin and the '4' on the fuselage leave no doubt as to the 'owner' of this Audax (M.J. Smith via A.S. Thomas).

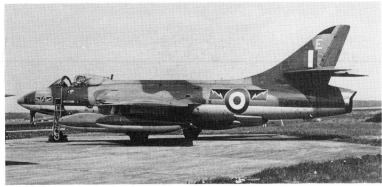

A Hunter FR 10 colourfully displaying No 4 Squadron markings both fore and aft.

as No 4 Squadron and the Gutersloh element disbanded on 28 May 1970.

Eighteen years later, No 4 Squadron was still at Gutersloh operating the versatile Harrier GR 3 in the tactical strike role. The up-dated Harrier GR 5 is due in 1989.

Standard

Granted by HRH King George VI and promulgated on 9 September 1943. Presented by Marshal of the Royal Air Force Sir John Slessor GCB DSO MC at Jever on 20 November 1953.

A new Standard was presented by Air Marshal Sir Patrick Hine KCB FBIM, C-in-C RAF Germany, at Gutersloh on 6 July 1984.

The old Standard was laid up in Wittering Church on 6 November 1984.

Battle Honours

*Western Front 1914-1918
*Mons
Neuve Chappelle
Somme 1916
*Ypres 1917
Lys
*Somme 1918
*France & Low Countries 1939-1940
Fortress Europe 1942-1944
*France & Germany 1944-1945
*Normandy 1944
*Arnhem
Rhine

*Denotes Honours emblazoned on Standard

Aircraft insignia and markings

During 1916, the Squadron's BE 2Cs had a white band around the fuselage forward of the roundels. The replacement RE 8s were similarly marked, except for those of 'A' Flight during the early months of 1918 when they operated independently and sported three white bands on the underside of the rear fuselage.

The post-war Bristol F2Bs initially appeared with the white band painted aft of the roundels, but when over-all silver was adopted in place of the olive drab all unit markings were deleted until the arrival of Audax in February 1932. These aircraft carried a

Carrying its recce pod on the centre-line mounting, Harrier GR 3A XV738 hurries on its way to the 'target' (No 4 Squadron).

large red figure '4' on the fuselage sides between the gunner's cockpit and the roundel. Replacement Hectors employed the unit badge superimposed on a six-point star as a fin marking, and Lysanders were similarly embellished but also carried the unit code 'TV', changed to 'FY' in May 1939. In September 1939, the code reverted to 'TV', but from 1943 no unit identification was carried. The Mosquito PR XVIs and the Spitfire PR XIs which arrived in January 1944 were painted over-all PR blue with small white serials and individual aircraft code letters.

When the unit took over 605's Mosquito FB VIs at Celle in September 1945, the latter's 'UP' code was retained. First painted a dull red, the codes were later in royal blue with a gold outline. Vampire FB5s also briefly carried the code 'UP' on the booms but this was soon replaced by the Second TAF unit code 'B' and individual letters. Replacement Sabres were similarly marked, the letters in white flanking the fuselage roundel. A stylized unit badge was also painted on the fin, consisting of a black eight-pointed star on which a red '4' was superimposed. By 1955, squadron markings had been introduced, these being rectangles on each side of the roundel painted black and red, the colours divided by a yellow lightning flash. The aircraft code letter was moved forward of the unit markings, the fin badge being retained.

Hunters used the same format, the stylized badge being moved to the sides of the nose and white individual aircraft codes being applied to the fin. Shortly before disbanding, the large markings on each side of the roundel were removed and similar, but smaller, rectangles displayed on either side of the nose emblem. This version of the markings was retained on the Harrier, the fin code letter being in yellow.

No 5 Squadron

Badge

A maple leaf — approved by HRH King George VI in June 1937 as the authorized version of a badge long used by the Squadron. It commemorates the Squadron's close association with the Canadian Corps during 1917-18, in particular during the Battle of Vimy in April 1917 and at Amiens in August 1918.

Motto

Frangas non flectas — 'Thou mayst break but shall not bend me'

History

Formed at Farnborough on 26 July 1913 by detaching a Flight from No 3 Squadron, No 5 Squadron flew the usual variety of types, going to France on 15 August 1914 for reconnaissance duties in support of the BEF. Operational on 21 August, the Squadron had the dubious distinction of recording the RFC's first war casualties the next day when an aircraft was hit by rifle fire and two officers were killed. The

Tempests carrying the wartime code 'OQ' of No 5 Squadron are fairly common, but a Hart (India) is rarer (via E.A. Harlin).

Squadron took a leading role in the development of aerial photography and of wireless for artillery observation during the early war years.

By 1916, the unit was entirely equipped with BE 2Cs and added night bombing to its repertoire, though 'art obs' remained the main task throughout the First World War. In May 1917 came re-equipment with the more effective RE 8, and co-operation with the Canadian Corps was fostered, the Squadron moving into Germany with them after the Armistice as part of the Army of Occupation. Bristol Fighters joined the Squadron in March 1919, but the RE 8 remained active until the unit returned to the United Kingdom in September as a cadre.

Disbanded on 20 January 1920, No 5 was reformed at Quetta, India, on 1 April for army co-operation work on the North-West Frontier by re-numbering 48 Squadron. Its venerable Bristol Fighters were retained for eleven years, general purpose Wapitis finally arriving in May 1931. These large biplanes also soldiered on well past their prime, only being replaced after the Squadron became a light bomber unit on 10 June 1940 and received Harts! These were supplanted by equally out-dated Audax in February 1941 when No 5 became a fighter squadron.

Following the Japanese attack on Malaya in December 1941, No 5 Squadron was moved to Calcutta to provide what little defence could be mustered, the aircraft becoming single-seaters with increased forward-firing armament. Mohawks appeared at the end of the year, however, and operating from Assam they escorted Blenheims attacking targets in northern Burma during 1942. Escort and ground attack work gradually increased, especially after the arrival of Hurricanes in May 1943, these being replaced by

the mighty Thunderbolt a year later. Operations ceased in May 1945 in preparation for the planned invasion of Malaya, a requirement forestalled by the Japanese surrender.

The Squadron remained in India, converting to Tempest IIs in March 1946, but disbanding on 1 August 1947. Eighteen months later, on 11 February 1949, No 595 Squadron was re-numbered No 5 Squadron at Pembrey, South Wales, and for 2½ years the unit was engaged on mundane target towing over the firing ranges of Wales and South-west England. Again disbanded on 25 September 1951, No 5 soon reformed, this time in Germany with Vampire 5 fighter-bombers as part of the Wunsdorf Wing of the Second Tactical Air Force. Re-equipped with Venom FB1s in December 1952 and Venom 4s in July 1955, it disbanded on 12 October 1957 as part of the defence cuts being made at that time.

No 5 Squadron was reborn on 20 January 1959 when 68 Squadron was re-numbered at Laarbruch and flew Meteor 11 night fighters until re-equipped with Javelins a year later. No 5 continued as part of the all-weather fighter force in Germany until disbanded on 7 October 1965. The following day, a new No 5 Squadron formed at Binbrook with the first Lightning F6s to enter front-line service. The Lightnings survived several planned retirement dates and served 22 years with the Squadron as a component of Britain's air defence organization before being withdrawn from NATO tasking on 1 November 1987. The Squadron returned to the front line on 1 May 1988 at Coningsby flying Tornado F3s.

Standard

Granted by HRH King George VI and promulgated

Above *Javelin FAW 9* XH905 *in August 1963 using its broad fin to advantage to display the unit markings.*

Left *Tornado F3* ZE760 *of No 5 Squadron at Waddington on 30 April 1988 in its striking markings — a red arrowhead surrounding the fuselage roundel and a broad red stripe across the fin outlining the famous green maple leaf* (J.A. Todd).

on 9 September 1943. Presented by Air Chief Marshal Sir Leslie Hollinghurst GBE KCB DFC at Wunsdorf on 24 April 1954.

The Standard was temporarily laid up in the Church of St Boniface, Monchen Gladbach, on 12 October 1957 until January 1959, then permanently laid up in Binbrook village church on 14 August 1983.

A new Standard was presented by Air Vice Marshal G. A. White AFC LLB, Deputy Commander RAF Germany, on 11 August 1983 at Binbrook.

Battle Honours

Western Front 1914-1918
*Mons
Neuve Chappelle
*Ypres 1915
*Loos
*Arras
*Somme
*Amiens
Hindenburg Line
Waziristan 1920
North West Frontier 1930-1931
Mohmand 1927
North West Frontier 1935-1939
*Arakan 1942-1944
Manipur 1944
*Burma 1944-1945

*Denotes Honours emblazoned on Standard

Aircraft insignia and markings

The unit's BE 2Cs were the first Squadron aircraft to carry markings, consisting of two bands around the fuselage, one forward of the roundel and the other immediately forward of the tailplane. The bands were painted black on clear doped aircraft and white on khaki drab machines. Similar markings were used on RE 8s, but post-war no insignia was carried until silver-painted Bristol fighters entered service in India. These carried individual aircraft letters forward of the fuselage roundel, and for a time a black '5' on the fin.

Replacement Wapitis had the aircraft letter painted on the nose side panels and a black band around the rear fuselage; some carried a maple leaf emblem on the fin. The Wapiti was still in service when the code letters 'QN' were allotted but, as yet, there is no published evidence that they were carried, and when Harts started to be coded in 1941, 'OQ' was used.

Mohawks were also coded until late 1942 then, as on the Hurricanes and Thunderbolt 1s which followed, only individual aircraft letters were carried. The unit code 'OQ' re-appeared on Thunderbolt IIs and subsequently on post-war Tempest IIs, some of which had the maple leaf motif on the sides of the engine cowling.

In Germany, Vampire FB5s had the Second TAF unit code 'B' and an individual letter painted in white on either side of the boom roundel, and carried a badge on the nose. Similar markings were used on Venoms until replaced by red rectangles on the booms and red flashes on white wing-tip tanks. The same fuselage marking was retained on Meteor NF11s, but moved to the fin on Javelins when a maple leaf badge superimposed on a white disc replaced the roundel as the centrepiece. The red stripe was edged with pale blue while the individual code letter on the fin and the serial on the engine intakes were in white.

When the Squadron reformed with Lightnings, the red rectangles re-appeared on each side of the fuselage roundel, now on the sides of the nose. The maple leaf was retained on the fin which also carried the individual aircraft letter and, for a visit to Malta on Exercise 'Sunfinder' in November 1974, large 'dayglo' Maltese Crosses adorned the fins of the Lightnings, but were removed soon after return to Binbrook. Camouflaging in 1976 made little difference to the unit markings, but the general tone-down and introduction of the low-visibility grey scheme in the early 1980s resulted in their reduction to small red bars on each side of the maple leaf badge and two-letter aircraft codes in white on the fin.

On Tornado F3s, a red arrowhead on the nose and a similarly coloured tail band both outline the green maple leaf emblem.

No 6 Squadron

Badge

An eagle, wings elevated, preying on a serpent — approved by HRH King George VI in January 1938 as the authorized version of an unofficial badge consisting of an eagle perched on the lower part of a figure '6'.

Motto

Oculi exercitus — 'The eyes of the Army'

History

Formed at Farnborough on 31 January 1914, No 6 Squadron, RFC, worked up with the usual odd collection of aircraft types and also found itself responsible for the Kite Flight, transferred from No 1 Squadron. The useful aircraft on strength went to France with No 2 Squadron in August 1914, and the Commanding Officer, Major J. H. W. Becke, had to rebuild his squadron from scratch. It was decimated again to provide casualty replacements, but he persevered and No 6 crossed the Channel to France on 7 October 1914. Corps Reconnaisance duties were started immediately and proved to be the Squadron's main role for the rest of the war, though occasional bombing was tried, and for about a year a Scout Flight using Martinsyde S1s and Bristol Scouts was attached. It was on 25 July 1915 in one of the latter that Captain L. G. Hawker DSO fought the action following which he received the VC, though it was awarded in recognition of his outstanding courage and determination demonstrated throughout eleven months of continuous operational flying.

By the end of 1915, the Squadron was largely equipped with BE 2Cs, these being replaced by the 'improved' BE 2E in October 1916. Real re-equipment followed in May 1917 with the RE 8, and it was with this comparatively successful aircraft that No 6 finished the war. After a spell on the Continent as a communications unit, No 6 Squadron was sent to Iraq in April 1919, still equipped with the faithful RE 8s.

Officially an army co-operation unit, the Squadron was employed on general duties, patrolling dissident areas of Northern Iraq. After re-equipping with Bristol Fighters, the unit undertook the bombing of Turkish-backed rebels and the policing of large areas of desert to subdue marauding tribesmen. In October 1929 the unit moved to Egypt (with a detachment at Ramleh in Palestine) and when Fairey Gordons were received two years later, No 6 was re-designated a bomber squadron. The Gordons were replaced by Harts and Demons in October 1935, the latter being transferred to 29 Squadron four months later.

Following increasing tension between Jews and Arabs, the whole Squadron moved to Ramleh in November 1937 where it was re-equipped with the general-purpose Hawker Hardy early in 1938. These were supplemented by Gauntlets and Lysanders in 1939, the latter becoming the sole equipment in April

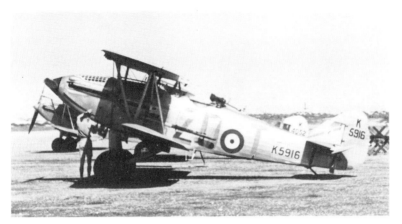

1940, shortly after the unit had again been designated an army co-operation squadron.

Detachments were provided for operations against the Italians in the Western Desert from September 1940, but the headquarters remained in Palestine until February 1941 when a Hurricane Flight was established. The Lysanders were completely replaced in June and the whole squadron was soon back in Palestine for a six-week rest. Returning to the Western Desert, the Squadron flew a mixed bag of Lysanders, Gladiators, Blenheims and Hurricanes until January 1942, when pioneering preparations for anti-tank operations were started. Hurricanes equipped with 40 mm 'S' guns arrived in April when No 6 Squadron became a fighter unit, and a very satisfying 'tank busting' period commenced which, apart from a dreary three-month interlude on convoy protection duties, continued until the end of the North African campaign. Converting to rocket-firing Hurricanes, the Squadron went to Italy in February 1944 and flew operationally over the Balkans for the remainder of the war.

Returning to Palestine in July 1945, the Squadron received some Spitfire IXs but was destined to be the last front-line unit to operate Hurricanes, only relinquishing them in December 1946 when re-equipped with Tempest VIs at Nicosia, Cyprus. The unit moved to the Sudan in November 1947 and to Egypt in May 1948 where conversion to Vampire fighter-bombers was completed at the end of 1949. These were replaced by Venoms four years later, and after a series of moves around the Middle East the Squadron settled down at Akrotiri in April 1956 just in time for the Suez operation. A year after Operation 'Musketeer' (Suez) came a complete upheaval when all the 'fighter' men were posted and the nucleus of a 'new' Squadron arrived from the United Kingdom with Canberra B 2s. No 6 was re-designated a bomber unit, and Canberra B 6s were received in December 1959. A year later, the role changed from high-level bombing to low-level interdiction, a task continued with the specialized Canberra B 16s which arrived in January 1962 and remained until disbandment of the Squadron on 13 January 1969.

This was the end of nearly 50 years continuous service in the Middle East, but No 6 is able to claim that the disbandment was on paper only, because it was reformed at Coningsby the next day in cadre from. Re-activated on 7 May 1969 as the first RAF Phantom squadron, No 6 was declared operational as a tactical reconnaissance and ground attack unit the following August. The Squadron disbanded once more on 1 October 1974, but again this was purely administrative, for a Jaguar-equipped echelon was already in being, and it reformed with these ground attack aircraft the following day. In November, the Squadron moved to Coltishall and still forms, with Nos 41 and 54 Squadrons, the Air Element of the United Kingdom Mobile Force.

Standard

Granted by HRH King George VI and promulgated on 9 September 1943. Presented by Air Marshal Sir Claude Pelly KCB CBE MC, Air Officer Commanding Middle East Air Force, at Amman on 31 January 1954.

A new Standard was presented by Air Chief Marshal Sir Keith Williamson GCB AFC ADC at Coltishall on 31 October 1980.

The unit is unique amongst serving squadrons in having two Standards, the second presented by King Abdullah of Jordan on 15 October 1950 following a visit he made to Mafraq. The standard is of silk in the Jordanian colours of black, white, green and red, with the Royal Crest in gold as the centrepiece.

Battle Honours

*Western Front 1914-1918
*Neuve Chappelle
*Ypres 1915

Loos
*Somme 1916
Ypres 1917
Amiens
*Hindenburg Line
Iraq 1919-1920
Kurdistan 1922-1924
Palestine 1936-1939
*Egypt & Libya 1940-1943
*El Alamein
El Hamma
*Italy 1944-1945
South-East Europe 1944-1945

*Denotes Honours emblazoned on Standard

Nicknames

'The Flying Tin-openers' — from Hurricane IID anti-tank operations in the Western Desert.

'Shiny Six' — used before the Second World War in the Middle East.

Aircraft insignia and markings

BE 2Cs started to carry officially authorized markings in 1916, No 6 Squadron being allocated three fuselage bands, one on each side of the roundel and one immediately forward of the tailplane. They were black on clear doped aircraft and white on khaki drab painted machines. Similar markings adorned the Squadron's RE 8s until March 1918 when reconnaissance aircraft again became anonymous.

Post-war Bristol Fighters carried a white '6' on the fin superimposed on a pointed star, later modified to an eagle preying on a serpent shaped like a '6', this unofficial unit badge later appearing with a red shield as a background. Much later, a 'gunners' stripe' was added, painted diagonally across the fin, replacement Gordons being similarly marked. Some aircraft, probably the COs' and Flight Commanders', had coloured fins.

Markings on Harts were more restrained, being reduced to the badge and shield on the fin, while Demons and Hardys featured no unit insignia at all until after the Munich Crisis when the code letters 'ZD' appeared on Hardys. 'XE' was allotted in April 1939 but probably not used, and 'JV', introduced at the outbreak of war, was carried intermittently on Lysanders and Hurricanes until July 1943. For the remainder of the war, only individual aircraft letters were used, but the 'JV' code re-appeared on Hurricane IVs, Spitfires and Tempests, the 'gunners' stripe' flanking a Squadron badge being introduced in 1949 on the fins of the latter aircraft.

On Vampires, the insignia was retained but moved to the sides of the nose, the unit code was deleted, and the individual letter painted on the rear of the booms just below the tailplane 'acorn.' A small representation of the 'flying tin-opener' motif was painted on the rudders. Camouflaged Venoms sported the Royal Artillery 'gunners' stripe' (light blue with a red zigzag) as rectangular-shaped markings on each side of the fuselage roundel, a squadron badge on the nose and, from January 1957, the 'tin-opener' motif on the tip tanks in red.

Canberras retained the 'tin-opener' emblem and proudly carried the 'gunners' stripe' on the fin. When Phantoms first appeared they had the 'tin-opener' emblem superimposed on a white disc painted on the fin together with the aircraft's 'last three' (the numerals of the serial), but by 1971 the 'gunners' stripe' was back on the fin and the emblem had moved to the nose. With the introduction of low-visibility camouflage, both serials and national markings were toned down.

Jaguars were similarly marked until 1981 when two-letter identification codes were introduced, the suffix 'E' indicating No 6 Squadron. Currently the aircraft are matt camouflaged overall, the familiar 'gunners' stripe' is painted across the fin-mounted rear warning radar antennae and the 'flying tin-opener' motif on the engine intake sides is coloured a dull red.

No 7 Squadron

Badge
On a hurt, seven mullets of six points forming a representation of the constellation Ursa Major — approved by HRH King George VI in June 1939 as the authorized version of an unofficial badge devised in 1926 which depicted the constellation Ursa Major against the moon.

Motto
Per diem, per noctem — 'By day and by night'

Detached for 'Operation Firedog', Lincoln B 2 of No 7 Squadron flies over Malaya in March 1954 (M. Retallack).

In pristine condition, Canberra TT 18 WJ721 prepares to stream a flare target for the benefit of naval gunners.

History

Formed at Farnborough on 1 May 1914, No 7 Squadron, RFC, had hardly started its work up on Sopwith Tabloids and a single BE 8 when it was disbanded, the personnel being used to bring other squadrons up to strength before going to France. Reformed on 28 September, 1914, it was used as a training and experimental unit until April 1915 when No 7 also went across the Channel and was immediately thrown into the Second Battle of Ypres using RE 5s for reconnaissance and Vickers FB 5s for escort work.

On 31 July 1915, Captain J.A. Liddell MC and his observer, Lientenant R.M. Peck, were on patrol over Belgium when both crew and aircraft were hit by heavy ground fire. Liddell suffered a broken thigh but insisted on continuing his reconnaissance for another 30 minutes before struggling back home with a badly damaged aircraft and injured observer. Tragically, Liddell died four weeks later from septic poisoning, but his determination and gallantry undoubtedly saved the life of his observer and he was awarded the Victoria Cross.

The Squadron standardized on the BE 2C/E during the summer of 1916, these aircraft being replaced by RE 8s in July 1917 to continue the corps-recce role for the rest of the war. Then came a spell with the occupation forces before No 7 returned to the United Kingdom in September 1919 and disbanded at the end of the year.

Reformed at Bircham Newton on 1 June 1923, No 7 Squadron started with a single Flight of Vickers Vimy, but was joined by 'D' Flight of No 100 Squadron in July and designated a heavy bomber unit. At the end of the following year, Virginias were received and the unit moved to Worthy Down in April

1927 to fly the aircraft until it was fully re-equipped with Heyfords in April 1935. Monoplanes, in the form of Wellesleys, briefly equipped one flight in 1937 but it was March 1938 before the Squadron's first Whitleys arrived and the impressive but antiquated biplanes were fully supplanted.

In April 1939 the Squadron converted to Hampdens, but the beginning of the Second World War found the unit in the training role and on 4 April 1940 it amalgamated with No 76 Squadron to form No 16 Operational Training Unit. A new No 7 Squadron formed with Hampdens on 30 April, but disbanded within a month, and it was with the task of working up the new Stirling four-engined bomber that the unit was again formed on 1 August 1940. There were serious problems, however, and it was to be 10 February 1941 before the first operational sortie was flown. In October 1942, the Squadron transferred to the Pathfinder Force and, converting to Lancasters during July 1943, marked targets for Bomber Command's main force for the rest of the war.

Remaining in Bomber Command, the Squadron re-equipped with Lincolns in August 1949, these aircraft taking part in Operation 'Firedog' (against terrorists in Malaya) and provided a detachment in Aden from August 1955, the latter becoming 1426 Flight when the Squadron disbanded on 2 January 1956. Eleven months later, No 7 reformed with Valiants as part of the V-Force, flying them until 1 September 1962 when it disbanded following the Vulcan/Victor take-over of the strategic bomber role.

After lying dormant for nearly eight years, No 7 Squadron reformed once more on 1 May 1970 as a second line unit in No 18 (Maritime) Group, Strike Command, in the target facility role. Equipped mainly with Canberra TT 18s which towed special

Chinook HC 1 ZA710 'EY' awaits its load of troops during an exercise in October 1987. The 'Ursa Major' badge shows up clearly in the early morning sunshine.

Rushton gunnery targets, the unit's total of 18 aircraft also included other Canberra variants for use as so-called 'silent' targets. A detachment left St Mawgan for India in 1973 to work with the Indian Air Force and Navy for a couple of months; other less exotic places were frequently visited, the aircraft becoming a common sight over ranges in Scotland, England and Wales.

On 5 January 1982 the Squadron disbanded, its task absorbed by No 100 Squadron, but on 1 September that same year it re-appeared with Chinook heavy lift helicopters and a new role of tactical support for the Army. Currently it remains at Odiham with these highly versatile helicopters.

Standard

Granted by HRH King George VI and promulgated on 9 September 1943. Presented by Marshal of the Royal Air Force Sir John Salmond GCB CMG CVO DSO at Upwood on 9 October 1953. Sir John was the Squadron's first commanding officer and No 7 was the first bomber squadron to receive a Standard.

A new Standard was presented by Air Marshal HRH Princess Alice, Duchess of Gloucester, GCB CI GCVO GBE at St Mawgan on 8 June 1978.

The old Standard was laid up in Truro Cathedral on 4 February 1979 and the new Standard was placed in the RAF College, Cranwell, for safe custody on 4 January 1982 while the Squadron was temporarily disbanded, remaining until September of the same year.

Battle Honours

*Western Front 1915-1918
*Ypres 1915
Loos
*Somme 1916
Ypres 1917
*Fortress Europe 1941-1944
*Biscay Ports 1941-1944
*Ruhr 1942-1945
German Ports 1942-1945
*Berlin 1943-1945
*France & Germany 1944-1945
Normandy 1944
Rhine

* Denotes Honours emblazoned on Standard

Affiliations

Linked as 7/76 Sqn, February 1949 - December 1953.

City of Truro — freedom of the city was received on 14 February 1979, and a Canberra TT 18 was named 'City of Truro'.

Aircraft insignia and markings

Unit markings were first applied in April 1916 when No 7 Squadron was allotted two coloured bands around the rear fuselage, black on clear doped aircraft and white on khaki drab BE 2Cs. When RE 8s replaced the BEs in July 1917, two white bands were standardized, painted slightly further forward on the fuselage, completely clear of the fin.

When reformed in 1923, the silver-painted Vimys were initially unmarked except for a black '7' in a circle on the sides of the nose, and replacement Virginias were similarly marked until dark green (Nivo) night camouflage was applied in 1926. Then individual aircraft letters in white on a black panel were painted on the nose and repeated on the rear fuselage. Some aircraft also had the name of a star applied to the nose. Variations on this theme continued into the Heyford era, including a representation of the unofficial Squadron badge on the tip of the nose during most of the 1930s.

The Whitleys initially carried the figure '7' on one side of the fuselage roundel with an individual aircraft letter on the other, but after the 1938 Munich Crisis period the unit code 'LT' replaced the Squadron numeral. The code was changed to 'MG' in September 1939 and at one stage was applied in a uniquely small size on the Stirlings. The 'MG' code continued in use after the war on Lancasters and Lincolns until 1951, when all codes were removed and squadron identity reduced to the badge already applied under the pilot's cockpit-side windows and the colour of the propeller spinners, blue denoting No 7 Squadron. In March 1952, Bomber Command aircraft started sporting enlarged aircraft serials on the fuselage sides.

Valiants displayed the centre portion of the Squadron badge on the tail fin, seven white stars on a blue disc background, and this marking was retained on Canberra TT 18s and the Chinooks, the latter also having a two-letter unit/aircraft code in black on the rear rotor mounting.

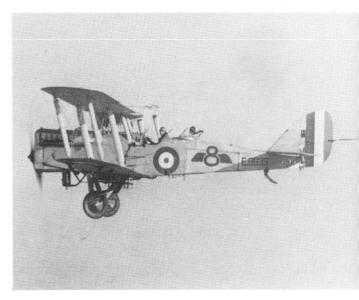

The markings of No 8 Squadron aircraft varied considerably in the 1920s, but usually featured a winged '8', as on this DH 9A (G.S. Leslie/J.M. Bruce collection).

current in the 1920s and early 1930s was a winged numeral '8'.

Motto

Uspiam et passim — 'Everywhere unbounded'

History

Formed at Brooklands on 1 January 1915, No 8 Squadron immediately moved to Gosport and became the first RFC unit to be equipped from the start with one type of aircraft, the BE 2C. These were taken to France in April and were used for both bombing and recce flights until the Squadron was designated a dedicated corps reconnaissance unit. Artillery spotting and tactical recce were then the primary tasks. The BEs were replaced by AW FK 8s in August 1917, and the following year the Squadron started to specialize in the spotting of anti-tank guns, being allocated to the Tank Corps in June 1918 for this purpose. It was after just such a sortie that Captain F.M.F. West, the 'B' Flight Commander, was awarded the Victoria Cross for his outstanding dedication and bravery in pin-pointing enemy concentrations in the face of intense opposition and severe injury.

The rugged but outdated 'Big Acks' were supplanted by Bristol Fighters in December 1918 when the Squadron was preparing to move into Germany as part of the occupation forces. This did not last long, for No 8 returned to the United Kingdom in July 1919 and disbandment on 20 January 1920.

The Squadron reformed at Helwan, Egypt, on 18

No 8 Squadron

Badge

A sheathed Arabian dagger — approved by HRH King George VI in December 1943, and adopted in recognition of the unit's long association with Arabia. The weapon is sheathed to symbolize the guardian duties of the Squadron. An unofficial badge

October 1920 in the day bomber role, using DH 9As for the policing of Iraq and, from 1927, the Aden Protectorate. General-purpose Fairey IIIFs replaced the venerable 'Ninaks' in January 1928, and in April 1935 the capable Vickers Vincent arrived in Aden to help in the continuing task of keeping the more belligerent tribesmen in check.

Blenheims were received in April 1939, but a Flight of Vincents remained until March 1942 for operations into the interior of the Protectorate, while the twin-engined monoplanes flew coastal reconnaissance and went into action against the Italians in Somaliland. In May 1942, No 8 became a general reconnaissance squadron equipped with Blenheim IVs, supplemented in September by the Mk V (Bisley) variant. Anti-submarine and convoy patrols were flown with these aircraft over the Indian Ocean and Red Sea, though little was achieved until Hudsons arrived in February 1943. Soon afterwards, the Squadron could at last claim a sighting, and a U-boat 'kill' came in July. During January 1944, general reconnaissance Wellingtons replaced the Hudsons on the endless round of monotonous patrolling which continued until 1 May 1945 when the Squadron disbanded.

Ten days later, No 8 Squadron reformed at Jessore, India, by the simple expedient of re-numbering the Liberator-equipped No 200 Squadron. Almost immediately the unit moved to Ceylon for 'special duties', which meant supply dropping to guerilla forces in Malaya until the Japanese surrender. On 15 November 1945, the Squadron again disbanded, only to reform back in Aden on 1 September 1946 by re-numbering No 114 Squadron; it thus became a light bomber unit flying Mosquitos.

Again Aden's garrison squadron, No 8 received Tempest VIs in April 1947 for fighter ground attack work, these aircraft being replaced by Brigand light bombers in July 1949. The Brigand was not a great success, and Vampire fighter-bombers arrived in December 1952, followed in turn by Venoms in 1955. The latter spent some time in Cyprus during Operation 'Musketeer', the Franco-British attack on Egypt, which was followed by increased unrest throughout southern Arabia. This necessitated long detachments at Sharjah for which the Venoms were joined by Meteor FR 9s, added to the strength in January 1958 for reconnaissance work.

Hunter FGA 9s replaced the Venoms in January 1960, followed by the Meteors giving way to FR 10s in April 1961. Both went to Bahrein in June when Iraq threatened the tiny oil-rich State of Kuwait. The threat subsided but other detachments followed, reduced in scope after another upsurge in activity in the Protectorate and the arrival of No 43 Squadron in March 1963 to form with No 8 (and the Shackle-

tons of No 37 Squadron) the Aden Strike Wing. The Hunter FR 10s were hived off to form 1417 Flight in April, but were back with the Squadron in September 1967 when the unit moved to Bahrein, transferring to Sharjah for its final three months in southern Arabia before disbandment on 15 December 1971.

On 8 January 1972, No 8 Squadron reformed for yet another very different role, that of airborne early warning using Shackletons! The first of the specially-equipped AEW variant of the aircraft arrived at Kinloss during the Spring of 1972, and in August 1973 the unit moved the short distance to Lossiemouth. Halved in size in 1981, the unit has had to soldier on with the ageing and completely outdated Shackletons, firstly because of delays in the introduction of the replacement, and then its cancellation. Boeing AWACS have been ordered but will not enter service until 1991, so No 8 Squadron crews are forced to fill the gap with inadequate equipment, only their expertise and determination enabling them to perform the difficult air control task allotted to them by the air defence organization.

Standard
Granted by HRH King George VI and promulgated on 9 September 1943. Presented by His Excellency the Governor of Aden, Sir Tom Hickbotham at Khormaksar on 9 April 1954.

No 8 Squadron became the first RAF unit to receive a replacement Standard, presented by His Excellency the Governor of Aden, Sir Richard Turnbull, at Khormaksar on 25 February 1967.

The old Standard, badly damaged by the effects of heat and high humidity, was laid up at St Clement Danes Church on 12 March 1967.

Battle Honours
*Western Front 1915-1918
*Loos
*Somme 1916
*Arras
*Cambrai 1917
Somme 1918
Amiens
Hindenburg Line
Kurdistan 1922-1924
Aden 1928
Aden 1929
Aden 1934
*East Africa 1940-1941
*Eastern Waters 1942-1945
*Burma 1945

* Denotes Honours emblazoned on Standard

Mascots
Tortoise — for a time in Aden.

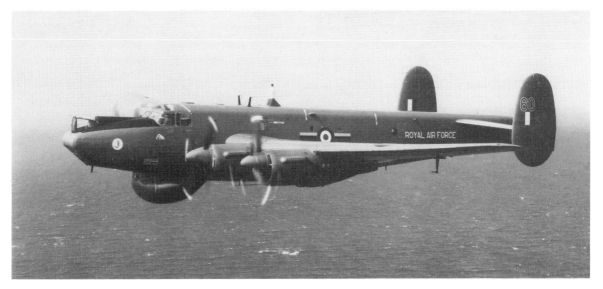

Dougal over the North Sea. An evocative view of Shackleton AEW 2 WR960 showing off its 'fighter-type' 'bar' markings, and the Arabic dagger emblem on the nose.

Owl — named 'Bubo' at Lossiemouth in the early 1980s.

Nicknames

'Aden's Own' — in general usage when at Khormaksar, Aden.

Aircraft insignia and markings

No unit markings were applied until April 1916 when a stripe, black on clear doped and white on khaki drab aircraft, was painted along the line of the top longeron from the rear (observer's) cockpit to the rudder post. This marking was invariably in white on FK 8s, but Bristol Fighters were unmarked apart from those aircraft received from other units which kept their previous symbols.

The DH 9As initially carried no unit markings apart from a large individual aircraft letter, but later a winged '8' was painted on the rear fuselage of some aircraft, and during the mid-1920s the CO's aircraft sported a winged emblem on the fin and centre section of the upper mainplane while the wing and tailplane tips were painted red. Fairey IIIFs also used a winged '8' on the fins during the late 1920s, but this had changed to a large individual aircraft letter by the 1930s.

Silver-painted Vincents also carried individual letters but painted in Flight colours. After the Munich Crisis, unit code 'YO' was allotted but not carried. In September 1939 it was changed to 'HV', and this was applied to the hastily camouflaged Vincents, but the Blenheims continued unmarked except for aircraft letters on the fuselage forward of the roundel. The replacement Hudsons followed the same scheme as did the Wellingtons until late in their service with the Squadron when the unit code 'A' was introduced.

The Liberators retained the No 200 Squadron aircraft letter code applied to the rear fuselage and repeated in miniature on the sides of the nose. It is probable that the short-lived Mosquitos also kept their previous markings.

With the introduction of the Tempest came more flamboyant insignia. They carried a large red individual code letter aft of the fuselage roundel and some of them a winged figure '8', also in red, on the lower portion of the Sabre engine cowling.

When Brigands first joined the Squadron, they were in standard temperate climate camouflage, individual aircraft codes being applied in white immediately aft of the roundel, but when fuselage sides and top surfaces were painted white to lower temperatures inside, the codes became black and a Squadron badge was painted on the nose. Ansons were similarly marked during their stay with the unit, the code being repeated on the nose cone, but the Vampires remained unmarked until late in 1953 when the Squadron's first really colourful markings appeared on the tail booms. These consisted of bars of 'sand' (uppermost), blue (central) and red (lower) colour, 'fish-tailed' fore and aft. Venom 1s continued this vogue, but the Mk 4s had the same colours applied to the nose in the form of an arrowhead which Meteors carried on the rear fuselage with the roundel superimposed during 1958 and 1959. The bar

Left *Hunter FGA 9s of No 8 Squadron bank over scrub country. Note the Squadron 'bars' and the 'dagger' on the nose* (No 8 Squadron).

Right *Wellington 1s of No 9 Squadron carrying the pre-war code 'KA' and the unit badge on the forward fuselage* (RAF Museum P3357).

markings then re-appeared together with the Squadron badge on the nose and were retained on the Hunters and on the Shackletons! The latter also carried the 'last two' of the aircraft serial on the fins and for a period were also individually named after *Magic Roundabout* characters. These names, painted under the cockpit side windows until frowned on by 'higher authority', were as follows:

WL741	*PC Knapweed*	WL790	*Mr Machenry*
WL745	*Sage*	WL753	*Ermintrude*
WL747	*Florence*	WL795	*Rosalie*
WL754	*Paul*	WR960	*Dougal*
WL756	*Mr Rusty*	WR963	*Ermintrude*, later *Parsley*
WL757	*Brian*	WR965	*Dill*
WR967	*Zebedee*	WL787	*Machenry*, later *Dillon*
	(MR2)		(MR 2)

No 9 Squadron

Badge

A bat — approved by HRH King Edward VIII in November 1936 as the authorized version of an unofficial badge produced in 1927 to highlight the Squadron's night bombing activities.

Motto

Per noctum volamus — 'Throughout the night we fly'

History

Formed on 8 December 1914 from the Wireless Flight attached to the RFC Headquarters at St Omer, France, No 9 Squadron continued the task of developing wireless for corps reconnaissance duties using BE 2As, soon joined by Maurice Farmans and Bleriot XIs. Three Flights were formed and attached to other squadrons, which absorbed them during February/March 1915 resulting in the disbandment of 9 Squadron.

Reformed on 1 April at Brooklands, No 9 became, in effect, the RFC Wireless School, but after a spell at Dover the unit returned to France on 12 December with 11 BE 2Cs and a Bristol Scout to carry out recce and bombing until the end of 1916. A reorganization then resulted in No 9 concentrating on corps reconnaissance for which it re-equipped with RE 8s during May 1917. In July 1918, a few Bristol Fighters were received but the unit did not have its full complement until May 1919 when in Germany as part of the occupation forces. It was reduced to cadre on 30 July and disbanded in the United Kingdom on 31 December.

The Squadron reformed at Upavon on 1 April 1924 with Vimy night bombers, but at the end of the month swopped places with No 3 Squadron at Manston because the Upavon hangars had proved too small! The first Virginias arrived in January 1925 and variants of this aircraft remained with the unit until May 1936, by which time the Squadron was at Aldergrove. Replacement Heyfords had begun to arrive two months earlier, but it was February 1939 before monoplanes in the form of the sturdy Wellington finally reached the Squadron.

Following the declaration of war, the Squadron

engaged in anti-shipping sweeps, but after the Norwegian campaign increasingly turned its attention to targets in Germany. Conversion to Lancasters came in August 1942, the Squadron continuing strategic bombing until the end of the war, specializing in operations using large bombs, in particular the 12,000lb (5,440 kg) 'Tallboy'. It was during a 'Tallboy' attack on the Dortmund-Ems canal on the night of 1-2 January 1945 that Flying Officer H. Denton's Lancaster was hit by flak and caught fire. The wireless operator, F/Sgt G. Thompson, dragged the unconscious dorsal gunner from his turret amid exploding ammunition, and then pulled the rear gunner from his blazing position, beating out flames before reporting to the captain. Badly burnt and frost-bitten, Thompson was taken to hospital but died three weeks later. He was posthumously awarded the Victoria Cross for his gallant actions.

No 9 Squadron was scheduled for 'Tiger Force', the heavy bomber organization, in preparation for the final assault on Japan, but the sudden end to the war in the Pacific cancelled the plan. The Squadron still went East, however, spending the first three months of 1946 in India before returning to the United Kingdom to re-equip with Lincolns as part of Bomber Command's much reduced peacetime force. Canberras replaced the Lincolns in May 1952 and also went east to Malaya in March 1956, where, during a three-month detachment, they took part in the bombing of communist insurgents. In October of the same year, the Squadron was in Malta for Operation 'Musketeer', the Suez affair, during which it took part in attacks on Egyptian airfields.

Disbanded at Coningsby on 13 July 1961, the Squadron reformed at the same airfield on 1 March 1962 and joined the V-Force with Vulcans. In February 1969, the unit was transferred from Strike Command to the Near East Air Force (NEAF) with No 35 Squadron, to replace a four-squadron Canberra Wing at Akrotiri in Cyprus. With the general run-down of British forces in the area, No 9 Squadron returned to the United Kingdom in January 1975 and settled down at Waddington as part of No 1 Group, Strike Command, remaining there until disbanded on 9 April 1982.

Reformed on 1 June 1982 as the first Tornado strike squadron, No 9 stayed at Honington until 1 October 1986 when it transferred to RAF Germany to complete the Bruggen Wing, flying alongside Nos 14, 17 and 31 Squadrons.

Standard

Granted by HRH King George VI and promulgated on 27 March 1953. Presented by Air Chief Marshal Sir Hugh Lloyd KCB KBE CB MC DFC at Binbrook on 9 October 1956.

A new Standard was presented by Air Chief Marshal Sir David Craig KCB OBE MA, Air Officer Commanding-in-Chief Strike Command, at Honington on 23 May 1984.

The old Standard was laid up in St Edmundsbury Cathedral, Bury St Edmunds, on 21 October 1984.

Battle Honours
*Western Front 1915-1918
*Somme 1916
*Ypres 1917
Amiens
Hindenburg Line
Channel & North Sea 1939-1945
Norway 1940
Baltic 1939-1945
France & Low Countries 1940
German Ports 1940-1945
*Fortress Europe 1940-1944
*Berlin 1941-1945

Vulcan B 2 XM648 at Mildenhall in May 1981. The shield above the unit 'bat' on the fin is the Waddington station badge.

Tornado GR 1 ZA457 'AJ' of No 9 Squadron outside its Hardened Aircraft Shelter (HAS) in 1986 (Military Aircraft Photographs).

Biscay Ports 1940-1945
*Ruhr 1941-1945
France & Germany 1944-1945
*Tirpitz
*The Dams
Rhine

* Denotes Honours emblazoned on Standard

Mascot

Live fruit-bat — presented to the Squadron at Lagos, Nigeria, in February 1956. Named 'Niger Gambia', it had a wing span of 15 inches and was blind in one eye. Its fate is unknown.

Affiliation

Ipswich — under the Municipal Liaison Scheme, March-May 1939 (then transferred to No 110 Squadron).

Nickname

'Ipswich's Own' — Unofficial name during part of the Second World War despite transfer to No 110 Squadron.

Memorial

In the centre of Bardney village, a Lancaster propeller mounted on a brick base was dedicated as a memorial to No 9 Squadron on 19 October 1980. A plaque carries the Squadron badge and the inscription 'IX Squadron, RAF, in memory of all ranks killed or missing 1939-1945. The Squadron flew from Honington, Suffolk, 1939-1942, Waddington 1942-1943 and from Bardney 1943-1945'.

Aircraft insignia and markings

When unit markings were first introduced in April 1916, No 9 Squadron was allotted a single broad band around the rear fuselage just aft of the roundel. It was painted black on clear doped aircraft and white on khaki drab machines. RE 8s were similarly marked, but Bristol Fighters apparently carried no unit insignia.

Silver-painted Vimys were also devoid of identifying markings except for a 'diving bird' badge on the nose, but soon after the dark green (Nivo) Virginias arrived, they carried a single distinguishing numeral on the sides of the nose. These were replaced by Flight-coloured identification letters on nose and mid-fuselage. In 1927, each aircraft received a name associated with Wessex and the code letters were highlighted.

Heyfords also had Flight-coloured individual letters — in addition to wheel spat trim — but the naming ceremony was dropped and it was the Wellington which introduced night bomber camouflage and the Squadron code 'KA' painted in white aft of the fuselage roundel with an individual aircraft letter forward of it. A large unit badge adorned the sides of the aircraft's nose. Following the outbreak of war, the Squadron code was changed to 'WS' and moved forward of the roundel on the port side. No 9 Squadron used 'WS' throughout the war, and on post-war Lancasters and Lincolns.

The markings on Canberras were more restrained, limited initially to a blue lightning flash on the nose. A unit badge was added when silver-painted Mk 6 aircraft were received, these aircraft also carrying a grey-green bat symbol surmounted by 'IX' in yellow on the fin. Later light blue tip tanks were introduced for a time, some aircraft having a '9' flanked by bat's wings superimposed. Fins were also painted blue and had a white disc carrying the grey-green bat and the Roman numerals 'IX' in red or yellow superimposed.

The markings on Vulcans also varied considerably during the 20 years they were in service with the Squadron. The white 'anti-nuclear flash' painted aircraft had gained a large bat symbol on the upper fin by late 1963 together with a Squadron badge between the fuselage roundel and the wing. With the introduction of camouflage, such markings were removed but re-introduced at Waddington when a Wing badge (City of Lincoln arms) and the green bat (now on a yellow disc) adorned the fins of the aircraft.

The Tornadoes are decorated with the green spread-eagled bat symbol on the fin and a green chevron forms the background for the fuselage roundel, both emblems being thinly edged in yellow. Since joining the Bruggen Wing, the individual aircraft code letter has been suffixed with an 'A' to indicate the unit.

No 10 Squadron

Badge

A winged arrow — approved by HRH King George VI in September 1937 as the official version of a badge devised by Wing Commander A.T. Whitelock, the Commanding Officer 1929-30, while watching archery practice at Oxford. It occurred to him that the bomb was the modern equivalent of the medieval arrow, the wings being added to indicate great speed.

Motto

Rem acu tangere — 'To hit the mark'

History

Formed on 1 January 1915 at Farnborough from a nucleus provided by No 1 Reserve Squadron, No 10's variety of aircraft were gradually replaced by BE 2Cs, the RFC's standard corps-reconnaissance aircraft. No 10 Squadron went to France in July 1915 and a month later was flying in support of the Indian Corps during the Battle of Loos. For the Battle of Arras (April 1917), the Squadron added bombing to its repertoire and it was with considerable relief that the sturdy AW FK 8 was received in July. They were supplemented by Bristol Fighters during the summer of 1918 but it was with FK 8s that the Squadron spent some time in Germany after the Armistice. The personnel returned to the United Kingdom in February 1919 and the Squadron disbanded at the end of the year.

The Squadron reformed on 3 January 1928 as a night bomber unit based at Upper Heyford and equipped with Hyderabads. An updated version, the Hinaidi, supplemented them from December 1930, but full re-equipment was delayed until March 1931. In September 1932, the unit converted to Virginia Xs, but in less than two years Heyfords started arriving at Boscombe Down for No 10, and it was these large biplanes which were taken to Dishforth in January 1937. Two months later, Whitley monoplanes were received and 10 Squadron took these lumbering, but reliable machines into action on 8 September 1939 — on a leaflet raid! With the abrupt end of the 'Phoney War', night raids began in earnest and the Squadron converted to Halifaxes in December 1941, variants of this aircraft serving No 10 for the rest of the war in Europe on intensive 'main force' Bomber Command operations.

The impressive Heyford — K4037 of No 10 Squadron sports the unit badge on the nose (RAF Museum P17996).

Halifax B II Series 1 BB324 *of No 10 Squadron, named* Wings for Victory *(Real Photographs/MAP).*

VC 10 C 1 XV105 Albert Ball VC *flies over Abingdon in September 1979* (J. Bartholomew).

No 10 Squadron transferred to Transport Command on 7 May 1945 and converted to Dakotas during August, flying out to India three months later for army support and trooping duties within the subcontinent. Disbanded on 20 December 1947, the unit reformed at Oakington on 5 November 1948 by renumbering No 238 Squadron, and flew Dakotas during the Berlin Airlift (Operation 'Plainfare').

When the blockade was lifted, Transport Command was savagely cut, and on 20 February 1950 No 10 was again disbanded. Three years later it was reborn to fly Canberra light bombers, and during October-November 1956 the unit was in Cyprus for the ill-starred Suez campaign (Operation 'Musketeer'). The unit returned to Honington where it disbanded on 15 January 1957 after exactly four years of Canberra operations.

On 15 April 1958 the Squadron reformed at Cottesmore with Victors as part of the V-Force, lasting nearly six years before disbanding again on 1 March 1964. Its current role, as a long-range strategic transport squadron, started on 1 July 1966 when No 10 reformed at Brize Norton to fly the mighty VC 10, its fleet of 14 aircraft still in operation over 20 years later — and still popular. In addition to regular route

flying, the Squadron is on standby for emergencies anywhere in the world and is active in the VIP and VVIP roles, used for long-distance flights by Her Majesty the Queen, other members of the Royal Family, Government Ministers and military chiefs.

Standard

Granted by HRH King George VI and promulgated on 27 March 1952. Presented by HRH The Princess Margaret at Cottesmore on 21 October 1958.

Battle Honours

*Western Front 1915-1918
Loos
Somme 1916
*Arras
*Somme 1918
Channel & North Sea 1940-1945
Norway 1940
*Ruhr 1940-1945
*Fortress Europe 1940-1944
German Ports 1940-1945
Biscay Ports 1940-1945
*Berlin 1940-1945
*Invasion Ports 1940

France & Germany 1944-1945
*Norway 1944
Rhine

* Denotes Honours emblazoned on Standard

Affiliation

Blackburn — Municipal Liaison Scheme, March 1939.

Nicknames

'Shiny Ten' — probably originated with the expression '10 out of 10'.

'Blackburn's Own' — used unofficially during the Second World War, largely by newspapers.

Aircraft insignia and markings

A disc painted on the fuselage sides aft of the roundel was the Squadron's identification when such markings were first introduced in 1916. The disc was black on clear doped BE 2Cs and white on khaki drab aircraft. The same markings were initially applied to FK 8s but changed to a horizontal white bar painted along the lower fuselage longerons. In March 1918, squadron markings were removed from corps recce aircraft and not re-applied before disbandment.

On reforming, the Squadron's dark green (Nivo) camouflaged Hyderabads carried individual aircraft letters on each side of the nose in white and a representation of the unofficial 'winged arrow' badge on the nose and tail. The same markings appeared on Hinaidis and Virginias, but Heyfords had the aircraft code repeated aft of the fuselage roundel and the unit badge on both sides of the nose with Flight colours on the wheel spats.

Night bomber camouflaged Whitleys initially sported a large white '10' forward of the roundel and the individual code letter aft until the Munich Crisis of 1938 when the unit code 'PB' was applied in place of the '10'. Following the outbreak of war, the code was changed to 'ZA' which continued into the Dakota era. During the Berlin Airlift, only aircraft code letters were carried and Canberras were even more nondescript, markings being confined to the Scampton Wing 'speedbird' in red on the nose, changed during 1955 to the Honington Wing 'pheasant' in white on the tail. By the time of Suez, the fuselage serial had been enlarged and a 'winged arrow' symbol appeared in red on the tip tanks. Yellow and black stripes were painted around the fuselage and across the wings during the detachment to Cyprus for 'Muskateer'.

The Victors carried no individual markings, but a Squadron badge embellished the nose just forward of the entrance door and a representation of the 'winged arrow' adorned the fin above the fin stripes. VC 10s have also remained free of individual iden-

tity except for the name of an RAF VC painted on each side of the nose from 1968. Above the standard royal blue 'transport' cheat line, the ownership of the aircraft, successively RAF Transport Command, RAF Air Support Command, RAF Support Command and now just RAF, has appeared in large black letters on the fuselage, while the 'last three' of the serial is painted on the fin and a Squadron badge on each side of the nose.

The VC 10s were named on Armistice Day 1968 as follows:

XR806 *George Thompson VC*
XR807 *Donald Garland VC & Thomas Gray VC*
XR808 *Kenneth Campbell VC*
XR809 *Hugh Malcolm VC*
XR810 *David Lord VC*
XV101 *Lance Hawker VC*
XV102 *Guy Gibson VC*
XV103 *Edward Mannock VC*
XV104 *James McCudden VC*
XV105 *Albert Ball VC*
XV106 *Thomas Mottershead VC*
XV107 *James Nicolson VC*
XV108 *William Rhodes-Moorhouse VC*
XV109 *Arthur Scarf VC*

No 11 Squadron

Badge

Two eagles volant in pale — approved by HRH King George VI in May 1937. The badge commemorates the unit's First World War operation of two-seater fighter-recce aircraft, eagles being chosen to symbolize speed and strength.

Motto

Ociores acrierosquaquilis — 'Swifter and keener than eagles'

History

Formed at Netheravon on 14 February 1915 from a nucleus provided by No 7 Squadron, No 11 Squa-

Two Hart (India) of No 11 Squadron under guard on a landing ground on the North-West Frontier in the 1930s. In addition to the two red identification bands around the fuselage, the aircraft carry the unit badge on the fin (E.A. Harlin).

dron lays claim to being the first RFC squadron specifically equipped as a scout unit. Two-seat Vickers FB 5 pusher biplanes, universally known as the Gunbus, arrived in June, and on 25 July the Squadron went to France and was quickly in action. Amongst many combats, the action by Second Lieutenant G.S.M. Insall on 7 November 1915 stood out. He attacked and forced down an Aviatik two-seater, destroying it on the ground by a well-aimed incendiary bomb. His aircraft damaged by ground fire, Insall had to force-land, but helped his observer/gunner, Air Mechanic T.H. Donald, to repair the leaking fuel tank overnight and flew the Vickers back to base the following morning. He received the Victoria Cross for this determined effort in the face of the enemy.

In June 1916, FE 2Bs replaced the obsolete Gunbus and the Squadron was relegated to long-range reconnaissance until Bristol Fighters were received a year later. Offensive patrols became the main task but the Squadron also joined in ground strafing of front-line troops. After the war, the Squadron moved into Germany as part of the occupation forces but returned to the United Kingdom in September 1919 and was disbanded at the end of the year.

Reformed at Andover on 13 January 1923 from personnel of the Air Pilotage School, the Squadron looked after the Group communications aircraft until it moved to Bircham Newton and received DH 9A day bombers. These were replaced by the ungainly Fairey Fawn in April 1924, the unit taking them to Netheravon the following month and forming a second Flight in June. In November 1926, Horsley day bombers were received, but these were passed to No 100 Squadron two years later following receipt of overseas movement orders. The Squadron embarked immediately after Christmas, arriving at Risalpur,

India, on 22 January 1929 for North-West Frontier duty with Wapiti general-purpose aircraft. In February 1932, the special Indian version of the Hart day bomber began to replace the Wapitis, army co-operation continuing to be relieved at intervals by punitive bombing raids on the villages and forts of rebel tribesmen.

Modern equipment in the form of Blenheim Is arrived during July 1939 and the following month these were taken to Kallang, Singapore. In June 1940, the Squadron transferred to Aden and took an active part in the early stages of the East African campaign. Six months later the unit was in Egypt operating in support of General Wavell's advance into Cyrenaica, and was then sent to Greece with Blenheim IVs late in January 1941 as part of the abortive attempt to stem the occupation of the country by Axis forces.

Retiring to Crete during April, and Palestine early in May, the Squadron took part in the Syrian campaign against Vichy French forces two months later, and became involved in operations in Iran before returning to the Western Desert late in September for Operation 'Crusader'. In January 1942, preparations began for a move to Ceylon, the Squadron re-assembling on Colombo racecourse early in April. An attempt to bomb an approaching Japanese fleet on 5 April was unsuccessful, as was a repeat performance on the 10th when five Blenheims were lost.

A very dull period of garrison duty followed, lasting until January 1943 when the Squadron moved to India and began bombing raids on the Arakan. In September, the unit re-armed with Hurricane IICs for ground attack work in support of the XIVth Army, remaining in Burma until June 1945. Re-equipped with Spitfires in Southern India, the Squadron embarked on HMS *Trumpeter* and on 9 September flew off the carrier to Kelanang. The unit stayed in Malaya until May 1946 when it was transferred to Japan as part of the Commonwealth occupation forces. The Squadron disbanded in Japan on 23 February 1948.

No 11 Squadron reformed in Germany on 4 October 1948 by re-numbering 107 Squadron; it was equipped with Mosquito fighter-bombers, subsequently receiving Vampire 5s, Venom 1s and Venom 4s before disbanding again on 15 November 1957, a victim of defence cuts.

A little over a year later, on 21 January 1959, No 256 Squadron was re-numbered No 11 at Geilenkirchen, Germany, its Meteor NF 11s being replaced by Javelin 4s, 5s and finally 9s in December 1962. On 12 January 1966, the Squadron disbanded yet again but was soon the 'shadow' number for 228 OCU, flying Javelins and Canberras. No 11 (Shadow) Squadron disbanded during December 1966 but on 1 April 1967 the unit reformed at Leuchars as a front-line squadron equipped with Lightning F 6s as part of the United Kingdom air defence forces. The Squadron moved to Binbrook on 22 March 1972 and continued to fly Lightnings for the next 17 years, its stand-down on 1 May 1988 completing the phase-out of this very impressive, but now obsolescent, interceptor. After conversion to Tornado F3, the Squadron moved to Leeming on 1 July 1988 and became operational in November as the first unit in a new interceptor fighter wing.

Standard

Granted by HRH King George VI and promulgated on 9 September 1943. Presented by Air Marshal Sir Owen Jones KBE CB AFC BA FRAeS at Wunsdorf on 28 August 1954.

A new Standard was presented on 17 August 1984 by Air Vice Marshal P.S. Collins AFC BA FBIM, Director General Communications Information Systems and Organisation (RAF), at Binbrook. AVM Collins was the Squadron Commanding Officer in 1967.

The old Standard was laid up in Binbrook village church on 19 August 1984.

Battle Honours

Western Front 1915-1918
*Loos
Somme 1916
Arras
*Cambrai 1917
*Somme 1918
Amiens
*Hindenburg Line
North-West Frontier 1930-1931
North-West Frontier 1935-1939
East Africa 1940
*Egypt & Libya 1940-1942
Greece 1941
Syria 1941
Ceylon April 1942
*Arakan 1943-1944
*North Burma 1943-1944
Manipur 1944
*Burma 1944-1945

* Denotes Honours emblazoned on Standard

Aircraft insignia and markings

No unit markings were carried by No 11 Squadron aircraft until Bristol Fighters arrived in June 1917. These had sloping white bars painted on the fuselage on each side of the roundel. The silver-painted DH 9As, Fawns and Horsleys carried no Squadron insignia, but in India a broad vertical black stripe was painted around the fuselage forward of the roundel, accompanied by a large individual aircraft numeral. Later the Harts sported a representation of the badge painted on a white disc on the fin, and carried two red bands around the aft fuselage and a small individual numeral on the top coaming just to the

A couple of Lightning F 6s in 1974, when natural metal finish was in vogue and unit markings were larger (RAF Lossiemouth).

Tornado F3 ZE785 at Coningsby on 11 June 1988 soon after application of the finalised No 11 Squadron markings which are almost identical to those so familiar on Lightnings.

rear of the gunner's cockpit. The code 'OY' was allocated in 1938 but probably not carried.

Blenheims were coded 'YH' from September 1939 whilst in the Far East, but were using 'AD' in the Western Desert and Greece. Hurricanes and replacement Spitfires only carried individual aircraft letters and SEAC white bands across wings, tailplane, fins and rudders, but Mosquito FB VIs wore the official 'EX' code introduced after the war. The 'EX' code also appeared on Vampire FB 5s until the Second TAF adopted a single letter unit code and allocated 'L' to No 11 Squadron. This was painted on the booms forward of the roundel with a similarly sized aircraft letter aft in black, outlined in white on camouflaged aircraft. The same system was employed on Venoms which also sported black and yellow 'candy bar' striped tip tanks and later had the letter code replaced on the booms by black rectangles on which a yellow triangle was superimposed on each side of the roundel. The fuselage marking was retained on Meteors, and transferred to the fin of the early Javelins on which the centrepiece was a white disc carrying the aircraft's letter in black. On Javelin FAW 9s, this motif was replaced by a broad black stripe with a tapering yellow flash superimposed, painted immediately below the tailplane. While No 11 Squadron was their 'shadow', 228 OCU aircraft featured two buff-coloured eagles with yellow beaks and feet painted on a white disc, positioned on the fin.

Lightning unit markings reverted to black rectangles and yellow triangles on each side of the roundel, but with the 'eagle' badge on a white disc on the tail together with the aircraft's individual letter in black. By the mid-1970s, the 'eagle' badge had been enlarged and painted directly on to the fin in dark brown, with yellow beaks and talons. With the general tone-down in markings, miniaturized black rectangles appeared on each side of a small Squadron badge on the fin, and in the 1980s the individual aircraft letter was prefixed by the letter 'B' to indicate the squadron.

No 12 Squadron

Badge

A fox's mask — approved by HRH King George VI in February 1937. The badge was based on a suggestion by LAC T.A. Rees late in the 1920s when the Squadron was equipped with the Fairey Fox, an aircraft of which they were proud and also the sole operators. The actual design of the original unofficial badge was by Mr V.R. Godfrey, the Fairey representative at Andover.

Motto

Leads the field — suggested by the use of the fox as the Squadron emblem and its reputation for daylight bombing development work.

History

No 12 Squadron formed on 14 February 1915 from a nucleus provided at Netheravon by No 1 Squadron, and started training on a variety of aircraft types; by April it had a full complement of BE 2Cs. No 12 went to France in September and settled in at St Omer as the HQ long-range reconnaissance squadron. A few bombing raids were also mounted, but in February 1916 the Squadron transferred to VI Corps as a dedicated corps recce unit, and by the end of the year was using the slightly improved BE 2E. These were replaced by the much more effective RE 8 in August 1917, and night bombing was added to the repertoire followed by extremely dangerous ground strafing of front-line troops during the desperate days of the last German offensive in March 1918. In May, the first Bristol Fighters were received for long-range artillery spotting, but the RE 8 remained the Squadron's main equipment until the Armistice. No 12 Squadron was then moved into Germany with the Army of Occupation and by December had 24 'Brisfits' and a number of RE 8s on strength, the latter finally leaving in July 1919. By November, No 12 was the sole remaining operational squadron in Germany, and the unit soldiered on until 22 July 1922 when it disbanded at Bickendorff.

The Squadron reformed for day bombing on 1 April 1923 with a single Flight of DH 9As at Northolt. The first Fairey Fawns to enter service were received in March 1924 just before the unit moved to Andover to start an 11 year association with that pleasantly situated airfield. Operating as a semi-trials unit, No 12 Squadron was engaged in the development of bombing techniques during the 1920s, and in June 1926 was re-equipped with the Fairey Fox, an aircraft which outpaced contemporary fighters and revolutionized tactics. The Squadron converted to Hawker Harts in January 1931 and took these to Aden in October 1935 during the Abyssinian crisis. Back at Andover the following August, the Squadron re-equipped with Hinds in October 1936 and entered the monoplane era with Battles during February 1938.

On 2 September 1939, the Squadron's 16 Battles crossed the Channel to France as part of the Advanced Air Striking Force, BEF. On 12 May 1940, during desperate efforts to stop the German advance through Belgium into France, Flying Officer D.E. Garland and his observer, Sergeant T. Gray, led two

other Battles in an attack on a vital bridge over the Albert Canal. All were shot down by withering ground fire, but the western end of the bridge was destroyed and both Garland and Gray were posthumously awarded the Victoria Cross.

The remnants of the Squadron were withdrawn from France in June and commenced night bombing of barge and shipping concentrations in the Channel ports. In November 1940, the unit began re-equipment with Wellingtons and resumed operations during April 1941, spending the rest of the war as a 'main force' Bomber Command unit, having received Lancasters in November 1942. After the war, No 12 Squadron converted to Lincolns in August 1946, flying them until the arrival of Canberra B 2s in April 1952. Following the work-up, a 24,000 mile (38,625 km) round trip to South America was undertaken by four Squadron crews, one of the first of many Canberra 'flag waving' tours. The much-improved B 6 version of the aircraft was in service for the first 'Firedog' detachment by the Squadron to Malaya. Six months later, the unit was at Hal Far, Malta, for the Suez campaign, making the first bombing attack on the Cairo area on 31 October, and continuing operations into November.

Back in the United Kingdom early in December, the Squadron resumed its normal low-level bombing role until disbanded at Coningsby on 13 July 1961. No 12 reformed, again at Coningsby, on 1 July 1962 equipped with Vulcan B 2s, and flew these mighty aircraft for 5½ years, disbanding at Cottesmore at the end of 1967. It was not long absent from the Battle Order, however, for on 1 October the Squadron reformed at Honington with Buccaneers for maritime strike operations. Becoming the first operational unit equipped with Martel missiles, the Squadron moved to Lossiemouth during November 1980 and is still there as part of No 18 (Maritime) Group, Strike Com-

A Hart formation carrying both the '12' identification on the fuselage and the 'fox' mask on the fin (RAF Museum P13767).

Top *Vulcan B 2 XM597 in nuclear anti-flash paint scheme and 'washed-out' markings, but with the 'mask' on the fin and a large No 12 Squadron badge on the forward fuselage.*

Above *Buccaneer S 2 XW527 of No 12 Squadron in July 1987 — the 'fox' mask and 'XII' markings show up well on the engine nacelle.*

mand. Frequent detachments are made to bases in Europe and the Mediterranean, but the practice reinforcement of the Falkland Islands defence force by two Buccaneers in March 1983 is likely to retain the longest distance record.

Standard

Granted by HRH King George VI and promulgated on 9 September 1943. Presented by Marshal of the Royal Air Force, The Lord Newall GCB OM GCMG CBE MM at Binbrook on 23 June 1954. As Major C.L.N. Newall, he had been the first Commanding Officer of the Squadron.

The Standard was temporarily laid up at the RAF College, Cranwell, from July 1961 to July 1962.

A new Standard was presented by Air Marshal Sir Nigel Maynard KCB CBE DFC AFC, Commander-in-Chief, RAF Germany, at Honington on 21 December 1975.

Battle Honours

Western Front 1915-1918
*Loos
Somme 1916
Arras
*Cambrai 1917
*Somme 1918
Hindenburg Line
*France & Low Countries 1939-1940
*Meuse Bridges
Fortress Europe 1940-1944
German Ports 1941-1945
Biscay Ports 1940-1945
*Berlin 1941-1945
*Ruhr 1941-1945
France & Germany 1944-1945
*Rhine

* Denotes Honours emblazoned on Standard

Mascot

Fox — given the honorary title APO 'Freddie Fox', the animal was presented to the Squadron on 8 June 1956. 'Freddie' escaped on 23 August but was replaced by APO 'Swift Fox'.

Affiliation

Borough of Grimsby — under the Municipal Liaison Scheme of April 1939. The Freedom of Grimsby was received on 11 September 1954.

Nickname

'Shiny Twelve' — from the highly polished engine cowlings of the Fairey Fox during the 1926-1931 era.

Memorial

At the entrance to Wickenby airfield is a memorial stone and the badges of Nos 12 and 626 Squadrons, dedicated to the memory of the 1,080 men from the two Squadrons who gave their lives on operations from the airfield during 1942-1945.

Aircraft insignia and markings

No official unit markings were authorized until April 1916 when the BE 2Cs of No 12 Squadron started to appear with two horizontal bars painted on the fuselage, black on clear doped and white on khaki drab machines. The same marking was used on BE 2Es, but when RE 8s arrived in August 1917 a white strip along the lower longeron from roundel to rudder was substituted. All unit markings were removed in March 1918 and only returned after the Armistice when No 12 Squadron started to paint large white Flight letters and aircraft numerals aft of the fuselage roundel.

DH 9As remained unmarked except for national insignia, but Fawns employed a small black '12' in a circle on the fin. Early Foxes used the same unit symbol, later replaced by the 'fox's mask' badge in a circle with the Roman numerals 'XII' above it. The colour of the ring denoted the Flight, red for 'A', yellow for 'B' and blue for 'C'. By 1930, the number '12' was being painted in black forward of the fuselage roundel in addition to the fin marking, and this scheme was retained on Harts and Hinds except during the 'Abyssinian' detachment. Camouflaged Battles also carried the numerals '12', replaced by the unit code 'QE' following the 1938 Munich Crisis, and changed to 'PH' at the beginning of the war. The 'PH' code was used throughout the Wellington, Lancaster and early Lincoln eras, the additional code 'GZ' being allocated and occasionally used on Lancasters. In 1952, Lincolns sported enlarged serials in place of codes, No 12 Squadron being identifiable by the aircraft's yellow propeller spinners.

Canberras initially employed the Binbrook 'flash' on the nose, painted in gold on No 12 Squadron air-craft. With the arrival of the B 6s, a 'leaping fox' was painted in red on the fin, but by 1958 the aircraft had green fins with the 'masked fox' emblem superimposed on a white disc. The Vulcan 2s featured pale anti-flash national markings and the Squadron 'fox' markings on an over-all white finish when No 12 Squadron first received the aircraft, but camouflage schemes took over in 1964 as the low-level role was introduced. Central servicing was the vogue at this time, and no squadron markings were applied to the aircraft at either Coningsby or Cottesmore.

The first of the Squadron's Buccaneers carried no unit markings, but the 'masked fox' badge soon appeared on the sides of the engine intakes, usually on a white background. Later, individual aircraft letters were painted in black on the fin, changed to a two-letter code at Lossiemouth, the unit letter 'F' (for Fox) being preceded by the aircraft letter, both outlined in white. Hunter T 7s used for training and instrument flying checks are similarly marked.

No 14 Squadron

Badge

A winged plate charged with a cross throughout and shoulder pieces of a suit of armour — approved by HRH King George VI in May 1937, and based on an unofficial badge depicting a winged cross of St George shield surmounted by a tower with 'XIV' on a scroll beneath the shield. The official badge represents a crusader in association with the Cross of St George because of the Squadron's close First World War ties with the reputed burial place of the Saint at Diospolis, Palestine, and its location in the Middle East at the time of submission to the Chester Herald.

Motto

Arabic — 'I spread my wings and keep my promise' (An extract from the Koran suggested by the Emir of Transjordan)

History

Formed at Shoreham on 3 February 1915 from a

nucleus provided by No 3 Reserve Squadron, the unit trained on Farmans and Martinsydes before working up on the BE 2 variants it took to the Middle East in November. The Squadron task was to co-operate with the Army in Egypt, Palestine, Arabia and the Western Desert, by sending detachments to trouble spots as they arose. This was no small task and it was with relief that No 14 found itself concentrated in Palestine by the summer of 1917, and able to remain in the area for the rest of the war. A Fighter Flight equipped with Vickers FB 19, Bristol Scouts and M 1C monoplanes was operated for a time but transferred to No 111 Squadron in August 1917. No 14 received RE 8s in November for reconnaissance work, retaining them until January 1919 when the unit left for the United Kingdom and was disbanded the following month.

Reformed on 1 February 1920, again in Palestine, by renumbering No 111 Squadron at Ramleh, the unit was destined to stay in the area for the next 20 years. Some DH 9As complemented the unit's Bristol Fighters in August 1924 and No 14 was completely re-equipped with the 'Ninak' in January 1926, transferring to the day bomber role in July. In practice, however, the traditional tasks of an overseas unit in the inter-war period, air policing, photo survey, training and long-distance 'showing the flag' flights, took up most of the time. Fairey IIIFs arrived in December 1929, replaced by Gordons during September 1932.

Modern equipment in the form of Wellesleys arrived in March 1938, and the Gordons left in June, No 14 taking its large single-engined monoplane bombers to Egypt at the outbreak of war, though they were soon back in Jordan. The anticipated entry of Italy into the war on the German side resulted in a move to the Sudan, and the Squadron commenced bombing raids on Eritrean targets on 11 June 1940. A Gladiator Flight was added in September, and Blenheims replaced the Wellesleys in December.

These were used for operations over the Western Desert and other Middle East trouble spots until the summer of 1942 when Marauders arrived; these were used mainly for anti-shipping operations from North Africa for the next two years.

In October 1944, the Squadron left its aircraft in North Africa and embarked for the United Kingdom, re-assembling at Chivenor for anti-submarine operations over the Bay of Biscay using Wellington XIVs. Disbandment came at Chivenor on 8 June 1945, but the next day No 14 re-appeared at Banff when No 143 Squadron was re-numbered. The Squadron was now a Coastal Command strike unit flying Mosquito VI fighter-bombers, and it continued in this role until the Banff Wing disbanded on 31 March 1946.

The following day, No 128 Squadron at Wahn, Germany, was re-numbered No 14 and Mosquito XVI light bombers, supplemented by B 35s from December 1947, were flown until the unit re-equipped with Vampire FB 5s in February 1951. In turn, these aircraft were supplanted by Venom FB 1s in May 1953, but two years later the Squadron was re-designated a day fighter unit and Hunter F 4s were received.

Disbanded at Gutersloh on 17 December 1962, the Squadron was immediately reformed by the re-numbering of No 88 Squadron, and flew Canberra B(I)8 bombers at Wildenrath until 30 June 1970. On the same day, a new No 14 Squadron was established at Bruggen with Phantom FGR 2 fighter/ground attack aircraft, replaced during the summer of 1975 by the single-seat Jaguar GR 1. Throughout this post-war period, No 14 Squadron remained in Germany and is still there, equipped since November 1985 with the very potent Tornado GR 1 as part of the Bruggen Wing.

Standard

Granted by HRH King George VI and promulgated on 9 September 1943. Presented by Air Vice Mar-

shal T.C. Traill CB OBE DFC at Fassberg on 21 August 1954.

A new Standard was presented by Air Chief Marshal Sir Keith Williamson GCB AFC ADC at Bruggen on 26 November 1982.

The old Standard was laid up in St Clement Danes Church on 22 January 1984.

Battle Honours
*Egypt 1915-1917
Gaza
Megiddo
*Arabia 1916-1917
*Palestine 1917-1918

Transjordan 1924
Palestine 1936-1939
*East Africa 1940-1941
*Mediterranean 1941-1943
*Egypt & Libya 1941-1942
*Sicily 1943
*Atlantic 1945

* Denotes Honours emblazoned on Standard

Mascot
Burmese rock python — named 'Fred Aldrovandi', it was taken over from No 88 Squadron in December 1962 and achieved some 50 hours flying and the

rank of Squadron Leader. In 1985, a 12-inch long replacement was obtained and named 'Eric'. In two years he had grown to over 7 feet (2.2 m) and is expected to reach 24 feet (7.4 m) when fully mature.

Nickname

'Crusaders' — derived from the Squadron's 'winged Crusader' badge.

Aircraft insignia and markings

No Squadron markings were carried during the First World War, but Bristol Fighters had a broad black band painted around the fuselage aft of the roundel during the mid-1920s when on army co-operation duty. The day bomber DH 9As sported a form of the unofficial badge on the fin, but marking of IIIFs and Gordons was confined to large individual aircraft letters on the tail. Perhaps surprisingly, the camouflaged Wellesleys were more flamboyantly attired, carrying the Squadron badge on the fin and large aircraft letters in white on the fuselage aft of the roundel. Blenheims and Marauders also used this form of identification — but without the badge!

Thus it was not until white and grey camouflaged Wellington GR XIVs equipped the Squadron that the unit code 'CX' was carried, the Mosquitos based in Scotland and Germany being similarly adorned. Unit and individual aircraft code letters of the Second TAF Mosquitos were yellow, outlined in black, and the Squadron badge was carried on the fin.

Ground attack Vampires carried the Fassberg 'lightning flash' on the nose and a Squadron badge on a white disc on the fins. The Venoms had the badge superimposed on the nose 'flash', the Second TAF code letter 'B' aft of the boom roundels and the 'lightning flash' repeated on the tip tanks. Replacement Hunters were given standard day fighter style markings, a white rectangle with three blue diamonds superimposed, painted on each side of the fuselage roundel. Later aircraft also had a unit badge on the nose and the aircraft letter in a black disc on the fin. The Canberra B(I)8s carried similar unit markings on the nose painted on each side of the unit badge, a version of the latter being repeated on the fin. Phantoms continued the nose markings but carried the 'last three' in white on the upper portion of the fin, while Jaguars had the now famous 'fighter style' markings on the sides of the engine intakes. Towards the end of the aircraft's service with the Squadron, they carried the unit code letter 'B' on the fin alongside the aircraft letter, both outlined in white.

The current Tornados carry similar markings, the 'Crusader' badge and white rectangles/blue diamonds being on the sides of the fuselage beneath the pilot's cockpit, the code letters in black-outlined silver on the lower fin, while in line with the RWR fairing is a row of nine blue diamonds.

No 15/XV Squadron

Badge

A hind's head affrontee erased at the neck between wings elevated and conjoined in base — approved by HRH King Edward VIII in May 1936. The badge was a modification of the hart emblem used previously, changed to highlight the fact that the Hind aircraft was in service when the badge was authorized.

Motto

Aim Sure

History

Formed at Farnborough on 1 March 1915 from a nucleus provided by No 1 Reserve Squadron and the Recruits Depot, the Squadron was soon at Dover training crews for operations while at the same time preparing itself for France. By November, almost a full complement of BE 2Cs had been gathered together, and it was with these aircraft that the Squadron crossed the Channel on 23 December 1915 for corps recce work with the 2nd British Army. Moving to the Somme in March 1916, No 15 concerned itself with artillery observation, but when ordered also took on ground strafing and bombing, for which the BE was manifestly unsuitable.

RE 8s were received in May 1917 and the Squadron continued its general-purpose work, even dropping ammunition to forward troops by parachute during the summer of 1918. The unit stayed on the Continent with V Corps until January 1919 when the 'Harry Tates' were disposed of and the Squadron returned to the United Kingdom for subsequent disbandment at the end of the year.

No 15 Squadron was reformed at Martlesham Heath on 20 March 1924 in a blatant attempt to disguise the puny strength of the home-based Royal Air Force. On paper it was a day bomber squadron, but in fact it was the Armament Flight of the A & AEE, its motley collection of trials aircraft supplemented by a few DH 9As. This charade continued for ten years during which the DH 9As were replaced by Horsleys, but it was not until a completely new No 15 Squadron formed at Abingdon on 1 June 1934 that the unit became effective. On the insistence of the new Commanding Officer, Squadron Leader T.W. Elmhirst DFC, the unit now became known officially as XV Squadron, and was soon showing its expertise with the Hart day bomber. Hinds replaced them in March 1936 followed by Battles in June 1938, and it was with these aircraft that the Squadron went to France in September 1939 as part of the Advanced Air Striking Force. Within four months, XV Squadron was back in the United Kingdom to re-equip with Blenheims and these were used to good effect in May 1940 during attacks on German troop columns advancing through the Low Countries.

During November 1940, the Squadron began conversion to Wellington night bombers, using them operationally for the first time on 21 December. In April 1941, XV became the second squadron with Stirlings and was operational with them on 30 April, when Berlin was attacked. Their most famous Stirling was N6086 *MacRobert's Reply*, a machine presented by Lady MacRobert during October 1941 in memory of her three sons, all killed on flying duties in the RAF.

The Squadron re-equipped with Lancasters during December 1943 and operated as a 'main force' bomber unit for the remainder of the war and into the aftermath, some of its aircraft being modified to carry 22,000 lb 'Grand Slam' bombs. During February 1946, Lincolns reached XV Squadron, a number having enlarged bomb doors to enable the 12,000 lb 'Tallboy' bomb to be carried — the big bomb tradition had been established and was hard to break!

The unit was declared non-operational in November 1950 when conversion to B 29 Washington bombers began, but they lasted only a little over two years, the first Canberras for XV Squadron arriving at Coningsby in April 1953. In October 1956, the Squadron deployed to Nicosia, Cyprus, for the Suez operation during which it dropped more bombs than any

of the other 14 Canberra squadrons involved. Back in the United Kingdom in November, the Squadron was disbanded at Honington on 15 April 1957.

It was not long out of the Battle Order, however, for XV reformed at Cottesmore on 1 September 1958 as the second Victor B 1 squadron. During the Indonesian 'confrontation', four Victors were sent to Malaya on a nine-month detachment to bolster the bombing forces, but this was a swan song, the whole Squadron being declared non-operational on its return at the end of September 1964; disbandment followed on 31 October.

Six years later, on 1 October 1970, XV Squadron reformed yet again, this time at Honington with Buccaneer S 2s which were taken to Laarbruch in January 1971 to form part of RAF Germany's interdictor/strike force. After 13 years of very successful operation of the robust Buccaneer, XV Squadron became the first of RAF Germany's Tornado GR 1 strike units on 31 October 1983. The Squadron is still at Laarbruch alongside Nos 2, 16 and 20 Squadrons.

Standard

Granted by HRH King George VI and promulgated on 27 March 1952. Presented by HRH The Duchess of Kent at Cottesmore on 3 May 1961. The Standard is unique in having the Squadron number embroidered in Roman numerals by special dispensation from the Chester Herald.

A new Standard was presented by Squadron Leader P. Boggis DFC RAF (Retd) at Laarbruch on 8 May 1981. A former Squadron member, Sqn Ldr Boggis was awarded his DFC for his part in a raid on the battle cruisers *Scharnhorst* and *Gneisenau* in Brest harbour while flying the Stirling *MacRobert's Reply*. He is the most junior officer to have performed the ceremony.

The old Standard was laid up in St John's Church, Beck Row, near Mildenhall, on 25 April 1982.

Hart K3972 with a tiny badge on the fin but 'XV' boldly painted on the fuselage (RAF Museum P12161).

Buccaneer S 2 XT287 turns over the Rhine while indulging in some contour flying (RAF Germany).

Tornado GR 1 ZA448 coded 'EB', and with 'XV' on the fin, displays its underbelly weapon beams (RAF Germany).

Battle Honours

*Western Front 1915-1918
*Somme 1916
Arras
*Cambrai 1917
Somme 1918
*Hindenburg Line
France & Low Countries 1939-1940
*Meuse Bridges
Dunkirk
Invasion Ports 1940
Fortress Europe 1941-1944
*Ruhr 1941-1945
*Berlin 1941-1945
Biscay Ports 1941-1945
France & Germany 1944-1945
*Normandy 1944

* Denotes Honours emblazoned on Standard

Affiliations

Oxford — under the Municipal Liaison Scheme, April 1939. Linked with No 21 Squadron — as XV/21, February 1949 to September 1953. Weeze — 'twinned' in 1984 with this town near Laarbruch.

Nickname

'Oxford's Own' — unofficially during the Second World War.

Aircraft insignia and markings

In company with other corps recce squadrons, No 15 did not display official unit markings until April 1916 when a single band, black on clear doped and white on khaki drab aircraft, was painted around the fuselage immediately forward of the tailplane. By the beginning of 1918, the unit's RE 8s were also carrying individual aircraft numerals aft of the fuselage roundel and also on the top decking behind the observer's cockpit. In March 1918, unit markings were removed and did not re-appear until Harts equipped the Squadron at Abingdon in 1934. These aircraft had the Roman numerals 'XV' forward of the fuselage roundel painted in red on 'A' Flt, yellow on 'B' Flt and blue on 'C' Flt aircraft. During the summer of 1935, a unit badge appeared on the fin and similar markings were retained on Hinds.

Presumably Battles also used the unique 'XV' marking at first, but after the Munich Crisis of 1938 the code 'EF' was adopted, painted on the rear fuselage with an individual letter forward of the roundel. In September 1939, the code was changed to 'LS', a combination which remained in use until March 1951, having been carried on Blenheims, Stirlings, Lancasters, Lincolns and Washingtons. For the rest of 1951, the only distinguishing mark was the colour of the nose wheel door — blue for XV Squadron.

At Coningsby, the Squadron's Canberras remained anonymous, but after moving to Cottesmore in May 1954 a form of the Station badge — a hunting horn and horseshoe — was painted in red on the fin, replaced at Honington by the Wing's 'pheasant', coloured white with red edging. During the Suez operation, roughly painted yellow and black stripes were painted around the rear fuselage and across the wings as identification marks.

White-painted Victors soon had a small stylized version of the unit badge — a black hind's head between yellow wings — on the upper portion of the fin together with the numerals 'XV', these being toned down in 1962 in concert with the general 'anti-flash' concept of pale roundels, fin flashes and serials. The Squadron markings were then a pale blue hind's head with black trim, pink wings and a pink 'XV', shadowed in pale blue!

Camouflaged Buccaneers and the Hunter T 7s used in Germany had 'XV' in white on the upper fin, these numerals being toned down by repainting in red as low-visibility markings became the vogue again in 1972. The rules were slightly relaxed in October 1974 when the 'XV' returned, and this form of Squadron marking was retained on the Tornado, this aircraft also having a single black-painted identification letter on the fin. From 1984, the aircraft letter was preceded by the unit code letter 'E'.

No 16 Squadron

Badge

Two keys in saltire — approved by HRH King Edward VIII in November 1936. The badge symbolizes the time spent on army co-operation duties, the keys indicating the unlocking of the enemy's secrets, the gold key by day, the black key by night.

Motto

Operta aperta — 'Hidden things are revealed' (a reference to the reconnaissance role of the Squadron)

History

No 16 Squadron was formed at St Omer on 10 February 1915 by the amalgamation of Flights detached from Nos 2, 5 and 6 Squadrons. The usual odd selection of aircraft types was flown on reconnaissance for the British Army, the Squadron pioneering the operational use of wireless to report troop movements during the Abures Ridge battle of May 1915. The unit standardized on the BE 2C in 1916 and the first RE 8s were received during April 1917, artillery spotting remaining the main occupation, though the Squadron joined in bombing raids when required. During the Battle of Vimy Ridge, an association was formed with the Canadian Corps which lasted until the Armistice. The unit remained on the Continent until reduced to cadre in February 1919, and returned to the United Kingdom for disbandment at the end of the year.

A formation of No 16 Squadron Lysanders carrying the pre-war code 'KJ' (RAF Museum P19163).

No 16 Squadron reformed at Old Sarum on 1 April 1924 with Bristol F2Bs, and for ten years was attached to the School of Army Co-operation. Re-equipped with the Atlas in January 1931, and the much more useful Audax during December 1933, the Squadron became truly independent the following June, though it continued co-operation with troops exercising on Salisbury Plain. Four years later, the Squadron was the recipient of the first operational Lysanders, but when war was declared found itself used in the training role until April 1940 when it moved to France and was immediately embroiled in the chaos which followed the German breakthrough.

Withdrawn to Lympne on 19 May, the Squadron flew recce and supply dropping sorties across the Channel, before commencing anti-invasion coastal patrols which lasted until March 1941. Army exercises were not neglected, however, and when the obsolescent Lysanders were supplemented by the excellent Mustang in April 1942, the Squadron was also used for shipping reconnaissance and 'Rhubarbs' against continental ports and coastal installations. In June 1943, the unit even got involved in the interception of German 'hit and run' fighter-bombers which were attacking South Coast towns.

Conversion to PR Spitfires commenced in September 1943 as part of the D-Day build-up, and a year later the Squadron was back on the Continent with the Second TAF carrying out both high-level and low-level photo reconnaissance. Following VE Day, the Squadron operated a high-speed mail service for three months, but in September 1945 it was split into three parts and absorbed by Nos 2, 26 and 268 Squadrons. Confusion then ensued, for while the ground echelon returned to the United Kingdom and was not officially disbanded until 20 October, both No 487 Squadron at Cambrai, France, and No 268 Squadron

at Celle, Germany, were informed on 19 September that they were to be re-numbered No 16 Squadron. The confusion was finally resolved by No 487 being retrospectively re-numbered No 268 Squadron, while the original No 268 officially became No 16 Squadron on 20 November 1945! The Squadron then flew fighter-reconnaissance Spitfire XIVs from Celle until disbanded on 31 March 1946.

The next day, No 56 Squadron, flying Tempests at Fassberg, was re-numbered No 16 Squadron, and after a move to Gutersloh, the unit re-equipped with Vampire 5s during December 1948. Now a dedicated ground attack unit, No 16 received Venom 1s in January 1954, but was disbanded in June 1957 as part of the wholesale cuts which took place in that year.

On 1 March 1958, the Squadron reformed as a Canberra B (1) 8 interdictor unit based at Laarbruch and flew this excellent aircraft for 14 years. It was finally displaced on 6 June 1972 when the newly-formed Buccaneer element of the Squadron was declared operational. The long-range strike/attack Buccaneer was to see 12 years of service in RAF Germany before the last of them left on 29 February 1984 with the arrival of a full complement of worked-up Tornado crews at Laarbruch. The Squadron now flies alongside Nos 2, XV and 20 Squadrons as the Laarbruch Wing — a very potent force.

Standard

Granted by HRH King George VI and promulgated on 27 March 1952. Presented by HRH The Duchess of Kent at Celle on 6 April 1956.

A new Standard was presented by Air Vice Marshal D. Parry-Evans CBE, Commander-in-Chief RAF Germany (designate), at Laarbruch on 12 July 1985.

The old Standard was temporarily laid up in the Church of St Boniface, Monchen Gladbach, on 15 September 1957 until the Squadron reformed in March 1958. It was permanently laid up in St Edmundsbury Cathedral, Bury St Edmunds, on 6 July 1986.

Battle Honours

Western Front 1915-1918
Neuve Chappelle
Loos
*Somme 1916
*Arras
*Ypres 1917
France & Low Countries 1940
*Dunkirk
Fortress Europe 1943-1944
France & Germany 1944
*Normandy 1944
*Arnhem
Ruhr 1944-1945

* Denotes Honours emblazoned on Standard

Affiliation

Kevelaer — twinned with this town near Laarbruch in 1984.

Nickname

'The Saints'—the Squadron was formed at St Omer in Northern France. The 'matchstick man' emblem on their aircraft indicates the unit pride in the nickname.

Aircraft insignia and markings

No markings were carried until April 1916 when the Squadron was allotted a vertical bar forward and a band to the rear of the roundel, black on clear doped aircraft and white on khaki drab machines. The markings were used on BE 2 variants and RE 8s until March 1918 when all unit identification was removed from corps recce aircraft. It is doubtful whether army co-operation F2Bs carried any markings, but the

Left *Buccaneer S 2 XV863 shows off its 'cross keys' badge and 'Saint' emblem to advantage* Military Aircraft Photographs).

Right *A well-loaded Tornado GR 1 of No 16 Squadron taxying at Binbrook in October 1985* (S. Scott).

Atlas had a single black band painted aft of the roundel. A similar marking was used on the Audax but moved forward of the roundel.

From 1937 onwards, the centrepiece of the Squadron badge was painted on the fin within a six-pointed star. Lysanders were coded 'KJ' after the Munich Crisis of 1938, these unit code letters being changed to 'EE' in April 1939. In both cases, the unit codes were forward of the roundel with a similarly sized individual letter aft. Shortly before leaving for France, the code was changed to 'UG' and this was carried on Lysanders until they were withdrawn in 1942.

It is possible that Mustangs also used 'UG', but with the Second TAF the Squadron carried no unit insignia until equipped with Tempests. These aircraft, and the Vampires which followed, carried the code 'EG'. When the Second TAF adopted single-letter codes, No 16 Squadron was allocated 'L' which was painted on the booms of Vampires. The pre-war black band, now edged in yellow, was re-introduced on Venoms and the same marking was retained on the Canberras, the band being broken by the fuselage roundel. Large serials were painted in white on the rear fuselage, and the black and yellow 'cross keys' insignia on a yellow-edged white disc appeared on the sides of the nose beneath the cockpit. With the general tone-down, the nose insignia was removed and the serials painted in black, but the now famous black band was retained and in the early 1970s the 'Saint' marking appeared on the fin.

With the introduction of the Buccaneer in June 1972, the band became a black arrowhead edged in yellow painted on the nose, but the 'Saint' was retained on the fin in yellow on a black disc, and the 'cross keys' insignia appeared on the sides of the engine intakes. On the Tornado, the same combination of markings was retained, yellow-edged black bars flanking the roundel on the nose, while the 'cross

keys' graced the sides of the engine intakes and the yellow 'Saint' adorned the tail on a black disc centred on a yellow-edged black stripe. The unit code letter 'F' together with the individual aircraft letter was also in yellow-edged black on the fin.

No 17 Squadron

Badge

A gauntlet — approved by HRH King Edward VIII in October 1936. The badge is indicative of armed strength, but also commemorates the Gloster Gauntlet in use by the Squadron when the badge was designed. Earlier, an unofficial emblem had been a shield cut diagonally by the famous zigzag and emblazoned with 'XVII', a turreted tower and a small winged shield.

Motto

Excellere contende — 'Strive to Excel'

History

Formed at Gosport on 1 February 1915, the Squadron was equipped with a variety of BE 2 variants and embarked for Egypt in November. Flying in support of troops fighting the Turks in the Sinai Desert in December, early in 1916 detachments went into

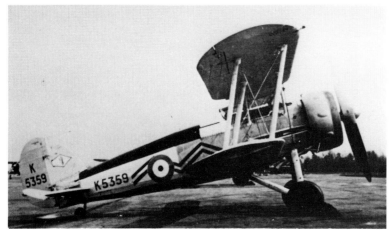

Left *Gauntlet II K5359 demonstrates the zigzag and 'gauntlet' markings during 1936* (RAF Finningley).

Right *With everything down, Tornado GR 1 ZD717 of No 17 Squadron approaches a landing in 1985* (Military Aircraft Photographs).

Left *Phantom FGR 2 XT901 shows off the stylized zigzags and the 'gauntlet' badge* (Military Aircraft Photographs).

Arabia on reconnaissance duty. In July, the Squadron was concentrated at Mikra Bay, Salonika, with 12 BE 2C and five DH2/Bristol Scout aircraft, the latter operating as a fighter component.

The Scouts were gradually updated but it was March 1918 before the sturdy AW FK 8 at last replaced the obsolete BE 2. The following month, the fighters, now Nieuport 17s and SE 5As, were handed over to No 150 Squadron, and for the remainder of the war No 17 Squadron was engaged in reconnaissance and artillery spotting on the Bulgarian border. After the Armistice, the Squadron remained in Turkey, re-equipping with 12 DH 9s and six Camels in December 1918 when 'A' Flight was sent to Batum in support of White Russian forces. The Squadron disbanded at Constantinople on 14 November 1919.

Reformed at Hawkinge on 1 April 1924 with the ubiquitous Snipe, the Squadron re-equipped with Woodcocks in March 1926, Gamecocks in January 1928, Siskin IIIAs later in the same year, Bulldog IIAs

in October 1929 and Gauntlet IIs in August 1936. Throughout this period, No 17 remained part of the United Kingdom fighter defence force, though most of its Bulldogs were allocated to other squadrons during the Abyssinian crisis and Hart (Specials) had to be used instead. Monoplanes, in the shape of Hurricanes, finally replaced obsolescent biplanes in June 1939, the Squadron flying defensive patrols over southern England from September until the German breakthrough into France during May 1940.

The Squadron went over to France early in June but was soon evacuated to the Channel Islands before returning to the mainland and preparing for the Battle of Britain. After a successful Battle and a brief spell in Scotland during 1941, the Squadron was sent to the Far East, arriving in Burma during January 1942 just as the Japanese advanced on Rangoon. Forced back into India, No 17 re-assembled at Calcutta and flew Hurricane IIs in defence of that city until converted to the ground attack role in Febru-

ary 1943. In August, the Squadron moved to Ceylon and in March 1944 received Spitfire VIIIs.

Returning to India in November, the Squadron was used for escort and ground attack work in Burma until June 1945 when withdrawn to prepare for the invasion of Malaya. This was cancelled following the Japanese collapse, and equipped with Spitfire XIVs the Squadron went to Japan in April 1946 as part of the occupation forces. It was disbanded on 23 February 1948.

A year later, No 691 Squadron, flying Spitfire XVIs, Oxfords and Beaufighter TT 10s on anti-aircraft co-operation duties, was re-numbered No 17 Squadron, this low-point in the unit's career lasting until disbandment on 13 March 1951. The Squadron reformed on 1 June 1956 and flew photographic reconnaissance Canberras in Germany for 13 years, before again disbanding on 12 June 1969.

Still in Germany, the Squadron reformed on 16 October 1970, this time as a fighter/ground attack unit flying Phantoms, and, from December 1975, Jaguar GR 1s. The first Tornado GR 1 was delivered in August 1984 and the following March No 17 was declared operational with the aircraft. The Squadron now forms part of the Bruggen Wing alongside Nos 9, 14 and 31 Squadrons.

Standard

Granted by HRH King George VI and promulgated on 27 March 1952. Presented by Marshal of the Royal Air Force Sir Dermot Boyle GCB KCVO KBE AFC at Wildenrath on 12 July 1960. No 17 Squadron had been Sir Dermot's first operational unit.

A new Standard was presented by Air Marshal Sir Patrick Hine KCB FBIM, Commander-in-Chief RAF Germany, at Bruggen on 8 February 1985.

The old Standard was laid up in St Clement Danes Church on 8 December 1985.

Battle Honours

*Egypt 1915-1916
*Palestine 1916
*Macedonia 1916-1918
*France & Low Countries
*Dunkirk
Home Defence 1940
*Battle of Britain 1940
*Burma 1942
Arakan 1943
*Burma 1944-1945

* Denotes Honours emblazoned on Standard

Affiliation

No 43 Squadron — linked as 43/17 Squadron from March 1951 to 1955.

Nickname

'Black Knights' — derived from the Squadron badge and in use at Bruggen during the 1980s.

Aircraft insignia and markings

As far as is known, unit markings were not carried during the First World War or up to disbandment in November 1919. After reforming in 1924, the Squadron adopted a double zigzag painted in black along the length of the fuselage and across the span of the upper mainplane of their Snipe, Woodcock, Gamecock, Siskin, Bulldog and Gauntlet aircraft, the latter also having a black fuselage top decking. After the Munich Crisis of 1938, the Gauntlets were camouflaged and coded 'UV' on the fuselage forward of the roundel, with an individual aircraft letter aft. In September 1939, the unit code changed to 'YB', a marking retained throughout the Second World War.

At Chivenor on anti-aircraft co-operation work, No 17 Squadron used 'UT' as the unit code, most aircraft also having an individual number painted forward of the fuselage roundel. On reforming with Canberra PR 7s, the black zigzag symbol re-appeared on a white disc on the fin, and on the nose on each side of the Squadron badge. Phantoms sported the same basic markings but in the form of a broad arrowhead on the engine intakes with the roundel superimposed. The aircraft's 'last three' was painted in white on the fin. Replacement Jaguars reverted to the rectangular marking painted on the engine intakes on each side of a diagonally divided black and white shield which enclosed a red gauntlet.

The Squadron re-introduced the broad arrowhead zigzags on the sides of the forward fuselage of their Tornados, the aircraft also carrying the 'red gauntlet' shield on the fin with the unit code letter 'C' and an individual aircraft letter.

No 18 Squadron

Badge

Pegasus rampant — approved by HRH King Edward VIII in May 1936. The authorized badge was little changed from an unofficial one in use during the early 1930s, the Pegasus commemorating the unit's co-operation with the Cavalry Corps on the Somme during the First World War.

Motto

Animo et fide — 'With courage and faith'

History

No 18 Squadron's very varied career started at Northolt on 11 May 1915 when it formed from a nucleus provided by No 4 Reserve Squadron. After a spell in the training role, the Squadron went to France in November 1915 equipped with the Vickers FB 5 'Gunbus' pusher and intended for fighter-reconnaissance work. Re-equipped in April 1916 with FE2Bs, just in time for the disastrous Somme battle,

it expanded its activities to take in 'art obs', contact patrol and bombing, the latter becoming paramount in May 1917 when DH 4s were received. The 'Flaming Coffins' were replaced by the efficient DH 9A in October 1918, but they had little opportunity to show their worth before the Armistice. The Squadron moved into Germany as part of the occupation forces but returned to the United Kingdom in September 1919 and was disbanded at the end of the year.

Reformed on 20 October 1931 with Harts in the light bomber role, the Squadron received the improved Hind in April 1936, soldiering on with these biplanes until May 1939 when conversion to twin-engined Blenheim monoplane bombers commenced. No 18 Squadron went to France at the outbreak of war as part of the Air Component of the BEF and suffered heavy losses during May 1940 in desperate efforts to stem the German breakthrough. The remnants of the Squadron were withdrawn to the United Kingdom and, after re-grouping, started daylight bombing of shipping and targets in France and the Low Countries. It was on 19 August 1941, during one of these raids, that a Squadron Blenheim dropped a box containing an artificial leg over St Omer airfield. It was a spare for the legless fighter ace Wing Commander Douglas Bader, shot down ten days earlier.

In October, the bulk of the Squadron was detached to Malta for anti-shipping operations in the Mediterranean. The survivors were dispersed and it was virtually a new unit which reformed in the United Kingdom during March 1942 and resumed 2 Group bombing missions. Re-equipping with the Blenheim V (Bisley) in September, the Squadron moved to

A Valiant B 1 'jammer' of No 18 Squadron at a 'Battle of Britain' display, September 1962.

North Africa as part of the build-up after Operation 'Torch' and continued its hazardous daylight bombing activities. During just such an operation on 4 December 1942, the Commanding Officer, Wing Commander H.G. Malcolm, led the Squadron on an unescorted low-level attack on an enemy fighter airfield near Chouigui. The raid was a success, but during a hard-fought withdrawal the formation was shot down one by one, Malcolm's aircraft finally crashing in a mass of flames. It was the last of a series of dangerous missions led by this gallant officer, and resulted in the posthumous award of the Victoria Cross.

Converting to Bostons in March 1943, the Squadron had fought its way to central Italy by VE Day. In September 1945 came a move into Greece, and the Squadron disbanded there on 31 March 1946. For 15 days during September 1946, No 18 was a general reconnaissance unit flying Lancasters in Palestine, but its real re-birth was delayed until 15 March 1947 when 1300 (Met) Flight at Butterworth in Malaya was re-numbered No 18 Squadron. After flying Mosquito VIs for some eight months, the Squadron again disbanded, to be reformed once more on 8 December 1947 at Waterbeach, this time as a transport unit flying Dakotas. The Squadron took part in the Berlin Airlift but was disbanded in February 1950, just after the crisis was over.

On 1 August 1953, the Squadron reformed at Scampton with Canberra B 2s, and was one of the many Bomber Command units deployed to Cyprus for the Suez operation. It was disbanded on 1 February 1957 soon after its return to the United Kingdom but re-appeared, again in Bomber Command, when the Valiant element of No 199 Squadron was re-designated as No 18 Squadron. The unit flew the Valiant on electronic countermeasures duties until suitable equipment was installed in standard Vulcans and Victors, disbanding on 31 March 1963.

Less than a year later, on 27 January 1964, No 18 was reformed at Odiham with yet another role, the provision of tactical transport for the Army in the form of the Wessex medium-lift helicopter. On 1 January 1965, the unit moved to Germany and stayed there until disbanded in 1980, apart from a spell in the United Kingdom from 1968 to 1970.

Personnel began to assemble at Odiham in August 1981 to form the first RAF Chinook heavy-lift helicopter squadron. Conversion and work-up was completed on 25 February 1982 when No 18 Squadron was 'officially' reformed; in May a detachment was sent to the South Atlantic following the Argentinian invasion of the Falklands. Three of the four Chinooks were lost when *Atlantic Conveyor* was sunk, but the survivor performed prodigious service in support of the Army during the re-occupation of the islands. The

One of the Squadron's Wessex HC 2s drops off a platoon in a cornfield shortly before the unit temporarily disbanded in 1980 (RAF Germany PRB2975/36).

Squadron moved back to Germany on 3 May 1983 and is presently based at Gutersloh.

Standard

Granted by HRH Queen Elizabeth II and promulgated on 14 October 1959. Presented by HRH The Princess Margaret, Countess of Snowdon CI GCVO at Finningley on 14 June 1962.

Battle Honours

*Western Front 1915-1918
*Somme 1916
*Somme 1918
*Hindenburg Line
Lys
France & Low Counties
*Invasion Ports 1940
Fortress Europe 1940-1942
*Channel & North Sea 1940-1941
Egypt & Libya 1942
*North Africa 1942-1943
Mediterranean 1943
Sicily 1943
Salerno
South East Europe 1943-1944
*Italy 1943-1945
Gothic Line
South Atlantic 1982

*Denotes Honours emblazoned on Standard

Affiliation

Gloucester — under the Municipal Liaison Scheme, April 1939.

Aircraft insignia and markings

No unit markings were carried prior to re-designation as a DH 4 day bomber squadron in June 1917. These aircraft carried a white square aft of the fuselage roundel and an aircraft letter or number, this individual marking being repeated on the upper wing centre section of the flight leader's aircraft.

The silver-painted Harts carried the numerals '18' forward of the fuselage roundel and some had a 'Pegasus' badge on the fin. Hinds had similar markings, a few also carrying a version of the Squadron badge on the fin. It is probable that Blenheims also used the Squadron number until the Munich Crisis of September 1938, but it is not known whether the allocated code letters 'GU' were then painted on the aircraft. From September 1939, the code 'WV' was used until the unit went to the Mediterranean area where both Blenheims and Bostons only carried individual aircraft letters, as did the post-war Lancasters and Mosquitos.

Transport Command Dakotas carried no unit markings because the aircraft were pooled, but when the Squadron reformed in August 1953 their silver-painted Canberras carried a black 'speedbird' insignia on each side of the nose, and later wore a red 'Pegasus' badge on the tip tanks. When the unit moved to Upwood, the Station shield embellished the fin.

The Valiant B 1s were unmarked except for a red 'Pegasus' on a light blue disc painted on the fin, and the Wessex helicopters continued to display this emblem, the disc at first white changing to black during the general tone-down of the 1970s. Also in 1970

two-letter codes were introduced, 'B' denoting the Squadron as a suffix to the individual aircraft letter. Chinooks carry the same basic markings on the rear rotor mounting, the 'Pegasus' in blue on a red disc background and the code letters in black, repeated on the front of the forward rotor mounting.

No 19 Squadron

Badge

Between wings elevated and conjoined in base, a dolphin head downwards — approved by HRH King Edward VIII in May 1936. The general design of the badge had been in use unofficially for some time. The dolphin was used because the Squadron had been equipped with the Sopwith Dolphin in 1918, and it was reputed to be a very active creature.

Motto

Possunt quia posse videntur — 'They can because they think they can'

History

There are other squadrons which have always had the same role but few for as long as No 19. Formed

Left *Chinook HC 1 ZA675 'BB' off-loads a Land Rover during a demonstration. The No 18 Squadron 'Pegasus' badge is on the tail rotor 'fin'* (RAF Germany TN9497/9).

Right *Gauntlet 1 K4092 resplendent in No 19 Squadron checks and fin badge* (RAF Museum P12167).

at Castle Bromwich on 1 September 1915 from a No 5 Reserve Squadron nucleus, the unit spent nearly a year training crews on BE 2Cs and working up on RE 7s before going to France on 30 July 1916 equipped with BE 12 single-seater fighter scouts. Unsuitable though these aircraft were, the Squadron took part in the Somme battles in August and flew contact patrols until December 1916 when it re-equipped with the French Spad S V11. With this agile aircraft the pilots built up a respectable score being heavily involved in the battles of Arras, Messines Ridge and Ypres, ground strafing forward troops. During the latter set piece onslaught in January 1918 the Sopwith Dolphin was received, this aircraft also being used mainly for ground strafing, changing to bomber escort after the German spring offensive. The Squadron remained on the Continent after the Armistice until February 1919 when it was reduced to cadre and returned to the United Kingdom for disbandment at Ternhill on 31 December.

Reformed on 1 April 1923, initially as a Grebe-equipped fighter Flight attached to No 2 Flying Training School, Duxford, No 19 was brought up to Squadron strength on 1 June 1924 and became independent, remaining at Duxford throughout the inter-war years. Siskins replaced Grebes in March 1928, Bulldogs arrived in September 1931, Gauntlets in May 1935 and the superlative Spitfire in August 1938, the Squadron pioneering the latter two aircraft into service. Despite inevitable teething troubles, the Spitfires were on standby during the Munich Crisis and fully operational when war declared.

At first they remained in the United Kingdom for defensive patrols, the 'Phoney War' providing little activity, but all that changed in May 1940, starting with fierce battles over the approaches to the Dunkirk beaches, followed by the Battle of Britain. After a short spell with cannon-armed Spitfire Is, the Squadron received Mk IIAs in September 1940; in March 1941 it started using them for offensive sweeps over Northern France. In October, the unit re-equipped with Spitfire Vs, replaced by Mk IXs during August 1943 when day bomber escort was the main task. In February 1944, the Squadron converted to Mustangs for army close-support work. After D-Day, No 19 Squadron moved on to the Continent but returned in September to start long-range escort to Coastal Command's Strike Wings operating off Norway.

Mustangs were retained until March 1946 when Spitfire XVIs replaced them until Hornets became available in October. This long-range fighter was operated until the advent of jet-powered bombers, day fighter Meteors arriving in April 1951, and Hunters in October 1956. Eight years later, Lightning F 2s were received at Leconfield, the Squadron moving to RAF Germany on 29 June 1959 to become the Command's first supersonic unit. In 1968 the F 2A version of the Lightning, considered by many the best variant, reached No 19 and these aircraft remained at Gutersloh until December 1976. In the meantime, an element had begun training on the two-seater Phantom in July 1976 and moved into Wildenrath on 1 October, resulting in the disbandment of the Lightning contingent at Gutersloh at the end of the year. Alongside its sister unit, No 92, the Squadron has formed the dedicated all-weather fighter force of RAF Germany ever since, and still flies Phantoms from Wildenrath.

Standard

Granted by HRH George VI and promulgated on 27 March 1952. Presented by Air Chief Marshal Sir Donald Hardman GBE KCB DFC at Church Fenton on 11 July 1956.

Lightning F 2A XN731 *breaks away to reveal its silver underside, the 'dolphin' on the fin and No 19 Squadron checks on the nose* (RAF Germany 1475/18).

Phantom FGR 2 XV485 *in the current low-visibility markings at Waddington in 1986* (Military Aircraft Photographs).

A new Standard was presented by Air Marshal Sir Anthony Skingsley KCB MA at Wildenrath on 15 January 1988.

The old Standard was laid up in St Clement Danes on 26 June 1988.

Battle Honours
*Western Front 1916-1918
*Somme 1916
Arras
*Ypres 1917
Somme 1918
Lys
Amiens
Hindenburg Line
*Dunkirk
Home Defence 1940-1942
*Battle of Britain 1940
Channel & North Sea 1941-1942
Dieppe
*Fortress Europe 1942-1944
*Normandy 1944
*Arnhem
France & Germany 1944-1945

*Denotes Honours emblazoned on Standard

Affiliation
No 152 Squadron — linked as 19/152 Squadron from February 1949 to June 1954.

Aircraft insignia and markings
The BE 12s taken to France carried no unit markings, but soon after the Spads arrived a white square was painted on the fuselages aft of the roundels. For a short time during 1917, red, white and blue fuselage bands replaced the square, but then a dumb-bell became the official marking for No 19 Squadron on Spads (in black) and Dolphins (in white).

When the Squadron reformed in 1924, blue and white checks were adopted, painted on the fuselage sides and across the upper wing. This colourful marking was retained on silver-painted Snipes, Grebes, Bulldogs and Gauntlets. Aircraft belonging to COs and Flight Commanders often carried additional identification in the form of chequered fins and elevators or coloured fins. Bulldogs and Gauntlets also had a derivative of the Squadron badge on the fin.

Spitfires were uniquely marked with the Squadron number on the fin when they first entered service, aircraft of 'A' Flight in red, those of 'B' Flight in yellow. The numerals were painted out following the Munich Crisis of 1938 and the code letters 'WZ' were in use by March 1939, each aircraft also carrying a large individual letter. From September 1939, the unit code was 'QV', used throughout the war and afterwards until the arrival of the Meteor. Then the blue and white checks were re-adopted, miniature versions having already appeared on the fins of some Hornets. On Meteors, the markings were carried on each side of the fuselage roundel, on the outer side of the engine nacelles and on the wing tips. Individual aircraft letters were painted on the fins of Meteor F 8s and retained on Hunters, which also carried the unit marking on each side of the roundel despite the damage done to them by an engine oil vent.

The blue and white checks were moved to the nose of the Lightning which also carried on the fin the green 'dolphin' centrepiece of the unit badge enveloped by a pair of black and yellow wings. A similar scheme is used on the Phantom though both roundel and checks are on the sides of the engine intakes, the blue being lightened in 1977 to avoid confusion with No 43 squadron. With the introduction of low-visibility grey camouflage, the unit markings remain but considerably toned down, the 'dolphin' badge being in outline only, while aircraft code letters and serials are now in white.

No 20 Squadron

Badge

In front of the rising sun, an eagle, wings elevated and perched on a sword — approved by HRH King George VI in June 1937. The rising sun is intended to commemorate the unit's long association with the East. The eagle is perched on a 'Talwar' indicative of the Squadron's work with the Army in India.

Motto

Facta non verba — 'Deeds not words'

History

Formed on 1 September 1915 from No 7 Reserve Squadron at Netheravon and worked up on a variety of aircraft, No 20 Squadron took FE 2Bs to France

in January 1916 for fighter-reconnaissance duties. In June came re-equipment with the improved FE 2D and the Squadron soon devised the 'fighting circle' whereby the pilots flew a continuous orbit in formation while the gunners fired outwards, covering each other and enabling large numbers of attacking German scouts to be contained.

While on a fighting patrol on 7 January 1917, two FEs were attacked over Ploegsteert Wood by Albatros scouts. Lieutenant W.E. Gower, Flight Sergeant T. Mottershead's observer, shot one down, but almost immediately the FE burst into flames, hit by fire from the second Albatros. Mottershead managed to reach the Allied front line and force land, the aircraft falling to pieces on touch-down. Gower was thrown out, but Mottershead was trapped in the blazing wreckage He was extricated by Gower and nearby troops and, terribly burned, rushed to the nearest field hospital. For four days surgeons tried to save his life but to no avail, Mottershead dying on 12 January. He was posthumously awarded the Victoria Cross for saving his observer, the only Royal Flying Corps NCO to receive the decoration during the whole of the First World War.

In August 1917, the famous Bristol Fighter replaced the now outclassed FE, and the Squadron went from strength to strength, reaching a peak in May 1918 when 56 German aircraft were destroyed. No 20 Squadron remained on the Continent after the Armistice until May 1919 when the unit sailed for India. It arrived on 6 June and immediately moved up to the North-West Frontier to strengthen the meagre forces in the area. Now operating in the 'catch-all' army co-operation role, the Squadron spent the next 20 years in spasmodic action attempting to police the fierce tribesmen of the frontier region.

Wapitis were received in January 1932 and Audax general-purpose aircraft in December 1935, the latter remaining in use until December 1941, despite the arrival of some Lysanders in May 1939. Detachments were sent to southern India in February 1941 for coastal defence duty, a few Blenheims joining the Audax for this work during the year. In December, the Squadron was re-established as an army co-operation unit completely equipped with Lysanders. This did not last long, for in May 1942 the crews were used to form the nucleus of 151 OTU and a new No 20 Squadron was worked up for short-lived operations with the Chinese Army. By September, the Squadron was engaged on internal security with a detachment flying reconnaissance over the Japanese forward positions from Feni, moving to Imphal during November. Hurricane IIBs arrived for TAC/R work in January 1943, the Lysanders remaining until March on ASR duties. At that time the Squadron

Above *A fine shot of a No 20 Squadron Audax, identifiable by the broad red band forward of the roundel and the 'eagle' in the six-pointed star on the fin* (No 20 Squadron).

Left *Hunter FGA 9s of No 20 Squadron flying off Singapore in August 1965* (Far East Air Force).

was re-designated a fighter/ground attack unit with Hurricane IID 'tank busters' equipped with two 40 mm cannon underneath the wings.

The Squadron also carried out anti-malarial spraying until November 1944, when it converted to rocket-firing Hurricanes and entered the most successful operational period of the Second World War, being very active during the Irrawaddy River crossings of February 1945. Operations ceased in June and the Squadron converted to Spitfire VIIIs with which it went to Bangkok, Thailand, during September 1945, soon after the Japanese surrender. Back in India, No

20 Squadron received Tempest IIs in June 1946, but the general run-down of the RAF's strength caught up with the unit and it disbanded on 31 July 1947.

Engaged on anti-aircraft co-operation duties at Llanbedr in Wales, No 631 Squadron was renumbered No 20 Squadron on 11 February 1949, and for the next 2½ years the unit flew Spitfires, Oxfords, Beaufighters, Harvards, Vampires and Martinets on this mundane task, until disbanded again on 16 October 1951. The Squadron reformed at Jever, Germany, on 1 July 1952 with Vampire fighter-bombers, these being replaced by Sabres in October 1953 when

Tornado GR 1 of No 20 Squadron at Laarbruch in March 1985, with the 'eagle' emblem on the engine intake (Military Aircraft Photographs).

given a day fighter interceptor role. Hunter F 4s replaced the Sabres in November 1955, and the updated Mk 6s arrived during August 1957, No 20 remaining in Second TAF until disbanded on 30 December 1960.

It was not long out of action, however, for on 3 July 1961 No 20 Squadron reformed at Tengah, Singapore, again with Hunters, but in the ground attack role. For six months of 1962, the Squadron was in Thailand as part of a SEATO force intended to counter Communist incursions from Laos. Detachments were sent to Labuan, Borneo, during the Indonesian 'Confrontation' of 1962-64, and following the disbandment of No 28 Squadron in 1967, a token force was maintained at Kai Tak, Hong Kong. During 1969, four Pioneers, ex-No 209 Squadron, were added to the strength for forward air control work — surely a unique combination of aircraft types on a postwar operational squadron.

With Britain's steady withdrawal from the Far East well under way, No 20 Squadron disbanded on 13 February 1970, only to reform again on 1 December at Wildenrath equipped with Harriers. After seven years in Germany, a major reorganization of the Command's resources resulted in the Squadron's aircraft being transferred to Nos 3 and 4 Squadrons, the unit reforming at Bruggen on 1 March 1977 equipped with Jaguars.

Seven years later, on 30 June 1984, the Squadron became a Tornado GR 1 strike unit at Laarbruch, the Jaguar element disbanding at Bruggen the same day. the Squadron now forms part of the Laarbruch Wing alongside Nos 2, XV and 16 Squadrons, assigned to the Second Allied Tactical Air Force for operations in support of NATO's Central Region forces.

Standard

Granted by HRH King George VI and promulgated on 9 September 1943. Presented by HRH The Princess Margaret CI GCVO at Oldenberg on 13 July 1954.

A new Standard was presented by air Chief Marshal Sir Keith Williamson GCB AFC ADC at Bruggen on 26 November 1982.

The old Standard was laid up in St Clement Danes Church on 8 May 1983.

Battle Honours

Western Front 1916-1918
*Somme 1916
*Arras
*Ypres 1917
*Somme 1918
Lys
Hindenburg Line
Mahsud 1919-1920
Waziristan 1919-1925
North West Frontier 1930-1931
Mohmand 1933
North West Frontier 1935-1939
*North Burma 1943-1944
*Arakan 1943-1944
*Manipur 1944
*Burma 1944-1945

*Denotes Honours emblazoned on Standard

Mascots

Tortoise — named 'Elbert du Crosses', the Squadron mascot laid some claim to fame in the 1950s as the first supersonic tortoise. A new tortoise was acquired in 1980 but is no longer current.

Affiliation

Uedem — twinned in December 1984 with this town near Laarbruch.

Nickname

'Double Crossers' — a reference to the Roman numerals 'XX' which has been used on some of the Squadron aircraft, the nickname was in vogue at Bruggen during the early 1980s.

Aircraft insignia and markings

It is probable that the FE 2s which initially equipped the Squadron in France carried no unit markings, but the Bristol F2Bs used a single vertical white bar forward of the fuselage roundel. In India, the F2Bs carried large individual letters and, at one stage, the numerals '20' on the fin. Later, the aircraft had a coloured band denoting the Flight painted around the fuselage, a marking retained on Wapitis which also had chequered stripes across the upper mainplane centre sections and individual letters on a square panel aft of the fuselage roundel.

The Audax continued the coloured band theme and some aircraft also carried the eagle badge on the fin. After the Munich Crisis of 1938, the two-letter code 'PM' was allocated but probably not applied to aircraft, though the replacement 'HN' did appear on both Audax and Lysanders from September 1939 onwards. Hurricanes and Spitfires were unmarked apart from individual aircraft letters, but the 'HN' code was resurrected for Tempests.

The code 'TH' was used on aircraft flown at Llanbedr, but when the Squadron reformed in Germany a new marking, red and blue diamonds on a green background, was applied on each side of the roundel, this changing to red, white and green horizontal bars before the Vampires were withdrawn. Sabres and Hunters were similarly adorned, the Sabres also having the Squadron eagle on a white shield painted on the sides of the nose, and like the Hunters had aircraft letters on the fin.

In the Far East, the centrepiece of the badge was carried on a light blue disc on the nose, flanked by the 'fighter-style' red, white and green bars on a light blue background. This style of marking was retained on the Harrier, moved to the engine intakes of the Jaguar, and appeared on each side of the fuselage roundel on Tornados. Individual aircraft letters were carried on the fins of these aircraft, supplemented by the unit code 'C' on late service Jaguars, changed to 'G' on Tornados.

No 22 Squadron

Badge

On a Torteaux, a Maltese Cross throughout, overall a 'pi' fimbriated — approved by HRH King Edward VIII in May 1936. The Greek sign 'pi' denotes the Squadron's service in France with the 7th Wing, the pilots often taking off over the Wing HQ — hence 22 over 7, or 'pi'. The unit was in Malta when the badge was designed which accounts for the inclusion of the Cross.

Motto

Preux et audacieux — 'Valiant and Brave'

History

No 22 Squadron formed at Gosport on 1 September 1915 as an offshoot of No 13 Squadron, RFC, and used a variety of aircraft for work-up training prior to receipt of its first operational machines in February 1916. These were FE 2B two-seat pusher biplanes, twelve of which flew to France on 1 April to join the 14th Wing for reconnaissance duties. The sturdy FE served the Squadron well but was soon obsolescent, and it was with relief that the first Bristol F2Bs were received in July 1917. The Squadron moved into Germany with the Army of Occupation in May 1919 but was reduced to cadre at the end of August, and returned to the United Kingdom without its faithful Fighters for disbandment at Ford at the end of the year.

On 24 July 1923, the Squadron reformed — but in name only — as part of the Aeroplane Experimental Establishment (the forerunner of the A & AEE), Martlesham Heath. It had the task of testing prototypes, a large number of which passed through the unit's hands during the next ten years. In 1934 it was decided to dispense with RAF squadrons at the A & AEE, and on 1 May No 22 reformed at Donibristle with six Vildebeest torpedo bombers.

The Squadron moved to Malta during the Abyssinian crisis, arriving in October 1935 and remaining until August 1936. In March 1938, the unit moved into the brand-new airfield at Thorney Island, form-

Beauforts of No 22 Squadron being prepared for an anti-shipping strike early in the Second World War (RAF Museum P17207).

ing a Torpedo Bomber Wing with No 42 Squadron. At the beginning of the Second World War, the Vildebeests flew anti-submarine patrols over the North Sea and English Channel and continued to use these ancient craft until February 1940, despite the arrival of the first Beauforts during November 1939.

The Squadron was finally declared operational on Beauforts in April, but the aircraft had many teething troubles, and in August the unit started re-equipping with Marylands. In September, 'C' Flight became 432 (Maryland) Flight, but the rest of the Squadron remained on Beauforts and, cleared for torpedo strike work, the unit moved to North Coates. Detachments were frequent, and so were losses, the torpedo bomber role being extremely hazardous. Undoubtedly one of the most dangerous operations, and an outstanding example of cold courage, was the solo torpedo attack by Flying Officer K. Campbell's crew on the German battlecruiser *Gneisenau* on 6 April 1941. The only one of six Beaufort crews to find Brest in appalling weather, they managed to penetrate the awesome defences and damage the ship before being shot down over the harbour. It took months for the full story to emerge, but when it did Campbell was awarded a well-earned VC.

In March 1942, the Squadron started ferrying its aircraft to the Far East, finally reaching Ratmalana on 28 April after being held in the Middle East for a month. It was in Ceylon in anticipation of further forays into the area by the Japanese, but these did not materialize and the Squadron had to be content with convoy escorts and anti-submarine patrols. Re-equipped with Beaufighter Xs in June 1944, rocket attacks against targets in Burma became the Squadron's forte. With the sudden Japanese surrender, the

planned operations in Malaya were cancelled, and No 22 Squadron disbanded on 30 September 1945.

No 89 Squadron was renumbered No 22 at Seletar on 1 May 1946, and for 3½ months the unit flew Mosquito VI fighter-bombers before again disbanding. It was to be 10½ years before it reformed at Thorney Island on 15 February 1955, intended as the first Whirlwind helicopter search and rescue unit, but equipped with Sycamores. The first Whirlwind arrived in June, and, as the strength built up, a Headquarters Flight and independent Flights, each of two aircraft, were formed. The latter were detached to strategically placed airfields around the coast of the United Kingdom.

In August 1962, the improved turbine-powered Whirlwind HAR 10 reached the Squadron allowing much increased flexibility and load-carrying capacity. Both were enhanced by the Wessex HAR 2 which supplemented the Whirlwinds in May 1976 and replaced them in November 1981. Rescues made over the years, on land and from the sea, are legion, and the Squadron still keeps six aircraft and crews on round-the-clock standby. The headquarters is at Finningley, home of the RAF's SAR Wing, and detachments are maintained at Chivenor ('A' Flt), Leuchars ('B' Flt), Valley ('C' Flt), Manston ('E' Flt) and Coltishall ('F' Flt).

Standard

Granted by HRH King George VI and promulgated on 27 March 1952. Presented by Air Marshal Sir Ralph Sorley KCB OBE DSC DFC at St Mawgan on 20 October 1960.

A new Standard was presented by Air Marshal Sir David Evans KCB CBE, Air Officer Commanding-

Above *Demonstrating the standard rescue technique employed by the Squadron over many years — the Whirlwind HAR 2 XJ407.*

Below *Wessex HAR 2 XR504 demonstrating at Bodmin in July 1982 and displaying its bright over-all yellow paint scheme and the No 22 Squadron emblem on the tail rotor mounting.*

in-Chief, Strike Command, at Finningley on 15 March 1978.

The old Standard was laid up in St Mary the Virgin Church, Dover, Kent, on 1 February 1981.

Battle Honours
*Western Front 1916-1918
*Somme 1916
*Ypres 1917
Cambrai 1917
Somme 1918
Lys
Amiens
*Hindenburg Line
*Channel & North Sea 1939-1941
France & Low Countries 1940
Invasion Ports 1940
Biscay Ports 1940-1941
*Mediterranean 1942
*Eastern Waters 1942-1945
*Burma 1944-1945

*Denotes Honours emblazoned on Standard

Affiliation
No 29 Squadron — linked as 29/22 Squadron from February 1949 until reformed during February 1955.

Nickname
'Dinky Do's' — derivation unknown.

Memorial
Flanking the Roll of Honour in the Station Church of RAF North Coates are the badges of the Squadrons which flew on operations from the Station during the Second World War, including that of No 22 Squadron.

Aircraft insignia and markings
The Squadron's FE 2Bs did not carry any unit identification, but Bristol F2Bs were embellished with three bands around the fuselage, one on each side of the roundel and one just forward of the tailplane. By April 1918, these markings had been removed and aircraft carried a single code letter on the rear fuselage.

When reformed with Vildebeests, unit markings were in the form of a stripe down the fuselage and a chevron on the tail, but later Flight colours were added to wheel spats of Mk IV aircraft, and some carried a Maltese Cross. The code 'QD' was allotted during the summer of 1938 but not used. At the outbreak of the Second World War, the code was changed to 'OA' and this, together with an individual aircraft letter, was painted on both Vildebeests and Beauforts. When the Squadron left for the Far East, the unit code was deleted and did not reappear on Beauforts, Beaufighters or Mosquitos.

Whirlwind helicopters originally had a sea grey/white colour scheme without unit markings, but when the now familiar over-all yellow was introduced, the aircraft carried a stylized unit badge on the sliding cabin doors. This emblem consisted of a white Maltese Cross and black 'pi' on a dull red disc outlined in pale blue. On Whirlwind HAR 10s, a full Squadron badge was used until the 1980s when the stylized form returned. The first Wessex reverted to the full badge positioned on the fin, but this was soon replaced by the stylized version.

No 23 Squadron

Badge

An eagle preying on a falcon — approved by HRH King George VI in April 1937. Derived from an early unofficial Squadron emblem.

Motto

Semper aggressus — 'Always having attacked'

History

Formed at Fort Grange, Gosport, on 1 September 1915, No 23 Squadron was commanded by Captain L.A. Strange, already an experienced operational pilot. Inevitably, No 23 was equipped with the usual selection of training aircraft, some of which were used for air defence detachments at Sutton Farm in an attempt to combat German airship intrusions. In January 1916, the Squadron received the first of its FE 2Bs, and it was these aircraft which were taken to France in March to escort almost defenceless reconnaissance machines.

Tactics slowly evolved, and by the end of 1916 the 'Fees' were mainly engaged on offensive fighter reconnaissance patrols, these continuing when single-seater Spads were received in February 1917, though ground attack was already becoming an important secondary role. The Squadron converted to Dolphins during March 1918, operating them with great success for the rest of the war. Remaining on the Continent until March 1919, the Squadron was then

reduced to cadre, returning to the United Kingdom for disbandment at Waddington at the end of the year.

Reformed at Henlow on 1 July 1925 as a Snipe-equipped fighter squadron, the aircraft were replaced by Gamecocks in April 1926 and Bulldogs five years later. The Bulldogs were supplemented in October 1931 by experimental Hart fighters which were deemed successful, and in April 1933 the Squadron was completely re-equipped with these two-seaters, renamed Demons.

When the Abyssinian crisis erupted in September 1935, most of No 23's crews and aircraft were despatched to the Middle East to bolster other units sent to the area, but by May 1936 the Squadron was back up to strength. Conversion to Blenheim I fighters began in December 1938, and the Squadron was operational as a night fighter unit when war was declared. There was little night activity, however, and shipping protection became the main occupation until the Germans broke through into France during May 1940. The Squadron's first night action came on 18 June, but the Blenheim was not satisfactory in the role and 'intruding' over France was found more rewarding.

In March 1941, the Squadron received a new lease of life when Havocs arrived, the aircraft quickly proving their worth as intruders, and this remained the Squadron's role after converting to Mosquito IIs in July 1942. The Squadron went to Malta in December for operations over Sicily, Italy and Tunisia, a move to Sardinia a year later putting Southern France and Northern Italy in range of the excellent Mosquito. Equipped with Mk VIs, the Squadron continued its intruder work with 100 Group, Bomber Command, from June 1944, flying from East Anglian bases for the remainder of the war.

On 25 September 1945, No 23 Squadron disbanded, but reformed a year later as a Mosquito night fighter unit. In September 1951, the first Vampire NF 10s were received, completely replacing the Mosquito 36s during May 1952. The Vampires were troublesome, but conversion to the more effective Venom night fighter commenced in November 1953, replaced in turn by the 'all-weather' Javelin in April 1957. The Squadron worked their way through Javelin 4s, 7s and 9s before converting to Lightning F3s in September 1964. Up-dated Lightning 6s started arriving at Leuchars during May 1967 and were to remain there until disbandment on 31 October 1975.

Crews were already going through the Phantom OCU, however, and on 1 December the Squadron reformed at Coningsby, moving to Wattisham in February 1976 on joining the United Kingdom air defence organization. But for the Falklands War, No 23 would probably still be at Wattisham, but instead it was nominally disbanded on 30 March 1983 when

Gloster Gamecock J8092 *with an early version of the Squadron's markings and the emblem on the fin* (RAF Museum P3778).

its aircraft were handed over to No 29 Squadron, and reformed the same day from the Phantom detachment at Stanley Airport. In May 1986, the Squadron moved to the newly completed Mount Pleasant airport but was reformed at Leeming on 1 November 1988, the Falkland unit becoming 1435 Flight.

Standard

Granted by HRH King George VI and promulgated on 27 March 1952. Presented by Marshal of the Royal Air Force Sir John Slessor GCB DSO MC at Coltishall on 28 June 1957. Sir John had served with the Squadron as a Second Lieutenant in 1915.

A new Standard was presented by Air Marshal Sir Anthony Skingsley CB MA, Air Member for Personnel, at Mount Pleasant, Falkland Islands, on 2 February 1987.

Battle Honours

*Home defence 1916
Western Front 1916-1918
Somme 1916
Arras
*Ypres 1917
*Somme 1918
*Channel & North Sea 1939-1940
Fortress Europe 1940-1944
*North Africa 1943
Sicily 1943
*Italy 1943
*Anzio & Nettuno
*France & Germany 1944-1945
Ruhr 1944-1945

*Denotes Honours emblazoned on Standard

Affiliation

No 151 Squadron — linked as 23/151 Squadron from February 1949 to September 1951.

Nickname

'Eagle Squadron' — derived from the badge.

Aircraft insignia and markings

The Spad S 7s were the first Squadron aircraft to carry unit markings — a white triangle aft of the fuselage roundel — but on re-equipment with Dolphins in March 1918 a white circle was used. Individual aircraft letters were painted on both aircraft.

Soon after reforming in 1925, the official 'fighter-type' markings of alternate red and blue squares appeared on the aircraft, painted along the fuselage sides and across the upper mainplane of Gamecocks, Bulldogs and Demons — and probably Snipes too. The Gamecocks, Bulldogs and early Demons also carried a stylized 'eagle' emblem on the fin, but this was deleted from Turret Demons and, following the Munich Crisis, the aircraft were camouflaged, the unit code 'MS' painted in light blue forward of the fuselage roundel and an individual aircraft letter aft. Blenheim IFs also carried the 'MS' code, changed to 'YP' in November 1939. As befits nocturnal activities, the code letters were painted in dull red on Havocs and Mosquitos, and were retained after the war until 1951 when the alternate red/blue squares returned on the booms of Vampires and, later, Venoms.

Javelins were unusual in having the Squadron markings above the serial on the engine intakes. They

Above *Javelin FAW 9R XH890 of No 23 Squadron at Luqa in October 1964 complete with the massive refuelling probe carried by this variant.*

Right *Phantom FGR 2 XV489 of No 23 Squadron 'tanking' from a Hercules C 1K over the Falklands (No 23 Squadron).*

Below *Lightning F 6 XR763 with overwing ferry tanks in 1968. The 'Union Jack' was painted on the fin for an overseas 'goodwill' tour (Military Aircraft Photographs).*

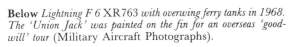

also carried the 'eagle' emblem on the fin at first without background, but on FAW 7s the eagle was on a white disc and the intake markings were white-edged. The FAW 9s were without the red-blue markings, but the 'eagle' was supplemented by an individual letter on the fin. Soon after Lightnings were received, the red/blue squares reappeared on each side of the roundel on the nose, and the fuselage spine and fin were painted white, providing a contrasting background for the colourful 'eagle' emblem. On Phantoms, the markings were reversed, a red eagle outlined in white being painted on the nose while the red/blue squares were across the upper fin between horizontal white stripes. When the overall 'low-visibility' camouflage was introduced, the unit markings were toned down considerably, the eagle reappearing in white-edged dull red on the fin. On reforming at Stanley in 1983 a miniature Falkland Islands badge, white on a blue background, was painted on the nose of the Phantoms, flanked by No 23 Squadron's red/blue squares.

One of the many pre-war communications aircraft used by No 24 Squadron — a Vega Gull carrying the unit number and, on the fin, the six-pointed star enclosing the 'black cock' emblem (RAF Museum P18037).

No 24 Squadron

Badge

A black cock — approved by HRH King George VI on June 1937 and presented to the Squadron by Air Chief Marshal Sir Hugh Dowding KCB CMG, Air Officer Commanding-in-Chief, Fighter Command, on 8 July 1937. Chosen because of its speed and strength on the wing, the cock is in fighting attitude to suggest the Squadron's ability to turn itself into a war unit at short notice despite a peacetime communications role.

Motto

In omnia parati — 'Prepared for all things'

History

No 24 Squadron must surely hold the record for the variety of aircraft types which have been on its strength over the years, though it started normally enough when formed at Hounslow on 21 September 1915. After a period of training using the usual motley collection of 'hand-me-downs', the Squadron received a full complement of DH 2 pusher biplane fighter scouts and went to France early in February 1916. After playing a prominent part in defeating German efforts to gain air supremacy during 1916, the Squadron found its aircraft outclassed and re-equipment with DH 5s in May 1917 was not a moment too soon. This aircraft found its niche in the low-level attack role, but was replaced by the more versatile SE 5A in December 1917, the Squadron remaining in the thick of the fighting on the Western Front until the end of the war. Following the Armistice, the Squadron remained in France until early 1919, the aircraft being handed over to No 1 Squadron on 22 January when the unit returned to the United Kingdom. Attached to 41 Training Depot Squadron, London Colney, it existed in cadre form for another year, finally disbanding on 1 February 1920.

Reformation came quickly, No 24 being resurrected as a communications and training squadron at Kenley on 1 April 1920. Charged with providing air transport for Heads of State, the Government and leaders of the three Services, the Squadron was equipped with an extraordinarily varied collection of aircraft during the next 20 years. Initially, ex-wartime types were used, including Bristol Fighters, DH 9As and Vimys, only the latter providing any protection for passengers against the elements. Avro 504s were used for maintaining flying practice for pilots employed at the Air Ministry, these aircraft being progressively replaced by DH Moths, Tomtits and Tiger Moths.

During the 1926 General Strike, the F2Bs and DH 9As flew seven scheduled routes carrying Government despatches around the country, these venerable aircraft being replaced by Fairey IIIF and Wapiti variants by the end of the decade. In February 1927, the Squadron moved to Northolt and in July 1933 to Hendon, its headquarters until 1946.

During the early 1930s, communication flights were carried out in current two-seaters, mainly DH Moth variants and Hawker Harts, but in March 1935 a DH 89A Rapide was received for VIP flights, supplemented by a DH 86B four-engined airliner in October 1937, the first time any real comfort was provided for No 24 Squadron's passengers. A plan to replace the remaining two-seaters on strength with 20 Miles Mentors was defeated by the outbreak of war in September 1939, while the consequent expansion of the Squadron's task resulted in the acquisition of an even more diverse collection of aircraft, many of them 'impressed' civil types. Regular flights were made between London and Paris using Rapides, and other aircraft were detached to French airfields for communications work on the Continent until the German breakthrough in May 1940. A communications network within the United Kingdom then became the unit's main occupation, but air ambulance work and aircraft delivery were also carried out.

In April 1942, regular overseas flights to Gibraltar using Hudsons were introduced, and later extended to Malta. In October 1942, the Squadron's light communications aircraft were taken over by the newly formed No 510 Squadron, and No 24 concentrated on route flying, the task increasing in 1943 with the arrival of Dakotas and the famous York 'Ascalon'. In June, however, the Dakota element was hived off to form No 512 Squadron, the parent unit retaining the Hudsons for its services to Africa, and a few Flamingos and Ansons for liaison work.

Dakotas returned in February 1944, and by the end of the year the Squadron was almost entirely equipped with this aircraft, becoming the short-range VIP transport unit in 1945. Royalty, Heads of State and whole Governments were returned to their newly liberated countries, and the British Royal family were taken on numerous visits. Late in 1945, an experimental all-weather freight service was started between Blackbushe and Prestwick, and on 25 February 1946 the Squadron headquarters moved to Bassingbourn where the unit absorbed 1359 (VIP) Flight and again concentrated on VIP work, both long and short range, using Dakotas, Yorks, Lancastrians and, later, Valettas.

No 24 became known as the 'Commonwealth Squadron' in April 1947, and like the rest of Transport Command was heavily engaged on the Berlin Airlift during 1948-49. After several moves, the Squadron settled at Lyneham during November 1950, its first Hastings arriving the following month. Yorks were finally withdrawn a year later when No 24 Squadron embarked on 17 years of Hastings operation,

Hastings C 2 WD494 in June 1965 with the No 24 Squadron badge boldly displayed on the fin.

Hercules C 1 of the Lyneham Transport Wing climbs away on yet another freight flight, flown by a No 24 Squadron crew.

the VIP role continuing for a time but the accent gradually changing to general transport work.

The Squadron joined the Colerne Wing in January 1967 and commenced conversion to Hercules a year later, returning to Lyneham the following month. Designated a tactical transport unit, No 24 took part in many special operations in many parts of the world, including the evacuation of refugees, support for garrisons such as Belize, and famine relief in Nepal, Ethiopia and the Sudan.

The airborne assault role was relinquished in November 1975, and a greater proportion of flights were then concentrated on scheduled routes, though tactical work remained prominent. During the Falklands campaign of 1982, the Squadron was heavily engaged in the UK-Ascension part of the supply route. Currently the unit is still at Lyneham as part of the four-squadron Transport Wing.

Standard

Granted by HRH King George VI and promulgated on 9 September 1943. Presented by Air Marshal Sir Charles Guest KBE CB CBE, Air Officer Commanding-in-Chief, Transport Command, at Abingdon on 4 March 1954. It was the first transport squadron to be so honoured.

A new Standard was presented by HRH The Princess Anne, Mrs Mark Phillips, GCVO at Lyneham on 15 September 1981. The Princess is Lyneham's Honorary Air Commodore.

Battle Honours

*Western Front 1916-1918
*Somme 1916
Somme 1918
*Amiens
*Hindenburg Line

*France & Low Countries 1939-1940
*Malta 1942
*North Africa 1942-1943
Italy 1943-1944
*Burma 1944-1945

*Denotes Honour emblazoned on Standard

Mascot

A black cockerel — named 'Major' after Major Lance Hawker VC, it was on Squadron strength in 1978 but has not been replaced.

Affiliation

Commonwealth — from 1947 to 1962, the Squadron was organized on a Commonwealth basis with many unit members and some commanding officers emanating from the RAAF, RCAF, RNZAF and SAAF.

Memorial

A Squadron Memorial Tapestry was made during the First World War. It now hangs in the CO's office at Lyneham.

Aircraft insignia and markings

Unit markings were not carried until the introduction of the DH 5, these aircraft having a single white band around the fuselage of the roundel. On SE 5As, this was moved forward of the cockpit until March 1918, when the Squadron adopted two vertical white stripes, one on each side of the roundel. An individual aircraft letter adorned the rear fuselage.

After the war, a few Squadron aircraft appeared with coloured stripes down the length of the fuselage, but during the late 1920s a red/blue/red chevron on the fin became the standard, though unofficial, marking. In the 1930s, the numerals '24' were added, painted on the fuselage sides forward of the roundel. Following the Munich Crisis of 1938, all unit markings were removed and the code letters 'ZK' were issued, but almost certainly not used until the 1940s, when they appeared on a few Proctors and early Dakotas.

After September 1939, the unit should have used code 'NQ' ('ZK' having been re-allocated to No 25 Squadron), but the error was not noticed until 1943 when the correct code came into general use on Dakotas and Wellingtons. After the war, 'NQ' continued to be painted on some Dakotas, but Yorks and Lancastrians only carried their W/T callsigns, across the nose cap.

Hastings were initially unmarked, but in the late 1950s a blue diamond with the numerals '24' superimposed in white appeared on the fin, replaced in the 1960s by a black 'cock'. When the aircraft were 'pooled' under the Colerne Wing, such markings were removed and replaced by a Station badge. Centralized servicing at Lyneham has ensured that Hercules are even more anonymous, only the 'last three' of the serial painted on the fin now identifying individual aircraft at any distance. Originally in white, even these markings were toned down during the early 1980s by being repainted in black.

No 25 Squadron

Badge

On a gauntlet a hawk rising affrontée — approved by HRH King Edward VIII in October 1936. Developed from an early unofficial badge which had been devised when the unit was based at Hawkinge.

Motto

Feriens tego — 'Striking I defend'

History

Formed at Montrose on 25 September 1915 from the personnel of 6 Reserve Squadron, for the first three months of its existence No 25 Squadron was used as a pool from which pilots were drawn as replacements for the Expeditionary Force in France. On 31 December, the Squadron started moving to Thetford, and, after completing work-up on FE 2B two-seater pusher fighters, took them over to France on 20 February 1916. Fighter reconnaissance patrols over the Western Front with FEs continued until June 1917, when DH 4 day bombers were received and the Squadron concentrated on long-range photo-reconnaissance and high-altitude bombing.

During the March 1918 German offensive, No 25 was thrown into the front-line battle, bombing and strafing troops and artillery, but the aircraft was not really suitable for this role and it was with understandable relief that the Squadron returned to its normal duties. A few DH 9As were received in October, but the DH 4s outlived them, going with the Squadron into Germany as part of the occupation forces in May 1919. Six months later, the unit was back in the United Kingdom, disbanding at Scopwick, Lincs, on 20 January 1920.

The next day, No 25 commenced reforming at Hawkinge as a fighter squadron. By late April it was at full strength and equipped with Snipes — as Britain's only home-based fighter unit! Not for long though, for at the end of 1922 the Squadron was sent to San Stephano, Constantinople, to reinforce the garrison during the Chanak crisis. The detachment was short, for No 25 was back at Hawkinge in November 1923 and destined to stay there until a few weeks before the outbreak of the Second World War.

In October 1924, Grebes were received and this highly manoeuvrable little biplane was soon in use for synchronized aerobatic displays, continued with Siskins from May 1929 and with the Fury following re-equipment with this delightful aircraft in February 1932. During November 1936, the Squadron was the recipient of the first operational Fury IIs, but was forced to relinquish them a year later when two-seater Demons arrived as replacements. In June 1938, a return to single-seater day fighters was made when Gladiators were received, but this was short-lived for it was only six months later that Blenheim IF fighters were on strength.

Intended for night defence, the Blenheim fighters were moved to Northolt in August 1939; the Squadron instituted nocturnal patrols following the outbreak of war, but spent most of the next year on convoy protection work. Beaufighters were received in October 1940, but conversion was slow and the Blenheims were not finally relinquished until January 1941. Whirlwinds and Havocs were on strength briefly, but it was the Mosquito II which replaced the Beaufighters, the first arriving on the Squadron during October 1942. Intruder work started in February 1943, and in addition to defensive night fighter

patrols, bomber escort was flown from mid-1943. The Mosquito IIs were supplemented by VIs in September, and replaced by NF XVIIs in December 1943. Further updating saw the Mosquito XXX in operation from December 1944, the last of the Mk VIs leaving in February 1945 when the unit was almost exclusively flying bomber support missions.

After the war, No 25 Squadron was retained as part of the United Kingdom night fighter force, Mosquito NF 36s being received in September 1946 and remaining until finally replaced by Vampire NF 10s in November 1951. This was very much an interim night fighter and was replaced by a mixture of Meteor NF 12s and NF 14s during the spring of 1954, these aircraft remaining until disbandment of the Squadron on 23 June 1958.

On 1 July 1958, No 153 Squadron at Waterbeach was renumbered No 25 and the same mix of Meteor night fighters was flown until all-weather Javelins arrived in March 1959. These remained until the unit again disbanded on 30 November 1962. A year later, on 1 October 1963, the Squadron reformed, this time at North Coates as the first operational Bloodhound surface-to-air guided missile unit, responsible for defence of V-Force bases and for the training of all personnel employed on the missile.

During April 1970, 'C' Flight moved to Laarbruch, and following establishment of the Squadron Headquarters at Bruggen, 'A' Flight reassembled on the same base while 'B' Flight went to Wildenrath. The whole Squadron was operational on 31 January 1971, but after ten years service in RAF Germany, the unit

Left *Fury II* K7270 *in all its glory —
No 25 Squadron's black fuselage stripes set
off perfectly by the 'hawk' in the fin 'spearhead'* (C.E. Sergeant).

Below left *Meteor NF 14* WS752 *displays the black-edged silver 'bars' current
in the 1950s. The 'hawk' badge is prominent on the fin.*

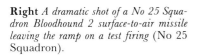

Right *A dramatic shot of a No 25 Squadron Bloodhound 2 surface-to-air missile
leaving the ramp on a test firing* (No 25
Squadron).

returned to the United Kingdom in March 1983 with
the HQ, 'B' and 'D' Flights at Wyton, 'A' Flight
detached to Barkston Heath and 'C' Flight to Wattisham — still with Bloodhound 2s.

Standard

Granted by HRH King George VI and promulgated
on 9 September 1943. Presented by Air Marshal Sir
Dermot Boyle KCVO KBE CB AFC at West Mall-
ing on 21 June 1954.

A new Standard was presented by Air Chief Marshal Sir Thomas Kennedy KCB AFC ADC, Air
Member for Personnel, at Wyton on 15 May 1984
in the presence of Marshal of the Royal Air Force Sir
William Dickson GCB KBE DSO AFC.

The old Standard was laid up in Ely Cathedral on
21 June 1984.

Battle Honours

Home Defence 1916
*Western Front 1916-1918
Somme 1916
Arras
*Ypres 1917
*Cambrai 1917
*Somme 1918
Lys
Hindenburg Line
Channel & North Sea 1939-1941
*Battle of Britain 1940
*Fortress Europe 1943-1944

*Home Defence 1940-1945
*France & Germany 1944-1945

*Denotes Battle Honours emblazoned on Standard

Aircraft insignia and markings

While fighter reconnaissance FEs were being operated, it appears that no unit markings were used, but
the DH 4s soon appeared with a white crescent
immediately behind the fuselage roundel and
individual aircraft letters further aft.

When reformed after the war, the Squadron's silver
Snipes were only distinguished by coloured fins, but
on return from Turkey and re-equipment with Grebes
two parallel black stripes painted across the top wings
and also along the fuselage sides became the
Squadron marking. The same scheme was used on
Siskins and Furies (on which the fuselage stripes
tapered to a point under the tailplane) and may have
adorned Gladiators until the Munich Crisis of 1938,
when the aircraft were camouflaged and the unit code
'RX' was introduced. In September 1939, the Blenheims were re-coded 'ZK', which was used on all subsequent Squadron aircraft until 1950. The parallel
black stripes had reappeared in miniature form on
the fins of Mosquito 36s in 1949, and this marking
was formalized on the Vampire as hollow black rectangles on each side of the boom roundels. With
Meteors, this was changed to a silver rectangle edged
top and bottom by black stripes, a marking moved
to the top of the fin on Javelins, which also carried
a unit badge superimposed on the rectangle. Later,

the badge became dominant, splitting a smaller rectangle into two parts above a large individual letter which was repeated on the sides of the nose. Bloodhound missiles are unmarked.

No 27 Squadron

Badge

An elephant — approved by HRH King Edward VIII in October 1936. The badge was based on an unofficial emblem first used in 1934 and commemorates the Squadron's first operational aircraft type — the Martinsyde G100 'Elephant' — and the unit's long sojourn in India.

Motto

Quam celerrime ad astra — 'With all speed to the Stars'

History

Formed on 5 November 1915 from a nucleus provided by No 24 Squadron, No 27 became the first squadron to be fully equipped with the Martinsyde G100 'Elephant'. Its nickname accurately described the aircraft which, although intended as a scout fighter, found its niche on reconnaissance and bombing operations behind enemy lines. The Squadron concentrated on these activities soon after arrival in France early in March 1916, and continued them after re-equipment with DH 4 day bombers during the autumn of 1917. The DH 4 was in use until after the Armistice, though replacement by DH 9s had started in September 1918. The Squadron remained in France until March 1919, when it reduced to cadre and returned to the United Kingdom, finally disbanding on 22 January 1920.

No 27 reformed in 1 April 1920 when No 99 Squadron was renumbered in India, the unit continuing to fly DH 9As and help 'police' the North-West Frontier. With good reason, RAF squadrons in India considered themselves the 'poor relations', and it was not until May 1930 that the worn-out 'Ninaks' were finally replaced by Wapiti general-purpose aircraft. These machines remained in service until October

Wapiti IIAs of No 27 Squadron on the North-West Frontier. The famous 'elephant' emblem is on the fin (via M.W. Payne).

1940 having been joined by Harts and Tiger Moths a year earlier when the Squadron became a Flying Training School at Risalpur.

On 21 October 1940, No 27 returned to operational status, and was equipped with Blenheim I fighters during November before moving to Malaya in February 1941. When the Japanese attacked in December, the Squadron was quickly decimated. Three surviving aircraft escaped to Sumatra but were soon destroyed, and when Allied forces on the island were overrun the unit was disbanded.

The Squadron reformed in India on 19 September 1942 with the first Beaufighters to reach the Far East, and after a three-month work up started ground attack operations in Burma on Christmas Day. Operational trials of the Mosquito II started in April 1943 and deliveries of the Mk VI followed in December, but before conversion was complete, rocket-firing Beaufighter Xs usurped them. In March 1944, the unit joined with No 47 Squadron to form an anti-shipping Strike Wing, but, with few targets available, transferred to ground attack work over Burma in November and proved highly effective, the aircraft being feared by the Japanese who dubbed it the 'Whispering Death'. With suitable targets again scarce, No 27 Squadron became an air-jungle rescue unit in April 1945. It was disbanded in Burma on 1 February 1946.

No 27 Squadron reformed on 24 November 1947 from a nucleus provided by No 46 Squadron, and flew Dakotas from Oakington until July 1948 when the unit went to Germany for the Berlin Airlift, operating as part of a Wing. The Squadron returned to Oakington in September, and from December 1949 concentrated on paratrooping and supply dropping, re-designated No 27 (Airborne Forces) Squadron during February 1950. The Squadron moved to Netheravon in July to be closer to the 'Paras' barracks, but was suddenly disbanded on 10 November 1950.

Two and a half years later, on 15 June 1953, the Squadron reformed at Scampton as a light bomber unit flying Canberra B 2s. It took part in the Suez campaign, Operation 'Muskateer', during October-November 1956 flying from Nicosia, Cyprus, to bomb Egyptian targets. Disbanded on 31 December 1957 at Waddington, still with Canberra B 2s, but reformed again at Scampton on 1 April 1961 with Vulcan B 2s, No 27 received 'Blue Steel' equipped aircraft in 1963. When 'Blue Steel' was withdrawn in December 1969, the Squadron continued as a conventional medium bomber unit until disbanded on 29 March 1972.

Eighteen months later, on 1 November 1973, the unit again reformed with Vulcans, but this time with the special SR 2 version for the maritime reconnaissance role. When satellites took over the surveillance task, the Squadron disbanded on 31 March 1982.

Officially reformed at Marham on 12 August 1983, though its Tornados had been in evidence on the Station for several months, the Squadron operated in the all-weather strike role. A successful deployment to the Middle East was followed by notable victories in the 1985 SAC Bombing & Navigation Competition, gained with the help of flight refuelling by Victors of No 57 Squadron. The Squadron remains at Marham as part of No 1 Group, Strike Command.

Standard

Granted by HRH King George VI and promulgated on 9 September 1953. Presented by Air Vice Marshal A.E. Borton CB CMG DSO AFC RAF (Retd) at Scampton on 7 January 1955. The AVM had been in command of the Squadron when it went to France in 1916. The Standard was temporarily laid up in the RAF College, Cranwell, from March 1972 to October 1974.

A new Standard was presented by Air Chief Marshal Sir David Evans GCB CBE CBIM at Scampton in June 1979.

The old Standard was laid up in Lincoln Cathedral.

Battle Honours

*Western Front 1916-1918
*Somme 1916
Arras
*Ypres 1917
*Cambrai 1917
Somme 1918
Lys
Amiens
Hindenburg Line
Mahsud 1920
Waziristan 1920-1925
Mohmand 1927
North West Frontier 1930-1931
Mohmand 1933
North West Frontier 1935-1939
*Malaya 1941-1942
*Arakan 1942-1944
*North Burma 1944
*Burma 1944-1945

*Denotes Honours emblazoned on Standard

Mascots

Two bears — named 'Elsie' and 'Rupert', they were with the unit in March 1944. 'Rupert' went to No 194 Squadron when No 27 left Agartala during October 1944.

Elephant — in June 1968, an elephant named 'Gosta' was adopted by the Squadron and Walt Disney Productions gave permission for the 'Dumbo' car-

toon character to be used as an unofficial marking. Whilst in Florida for the 1971 'Giant Voice' competition, the Squadron presented a plaque to Disney World making Pilot Officer 'Dumbo' an 'official' Squadron member.

Affiliation

No 27 (Chingford) Air Training Corps Squadron — from 19 May 1969.

Aircraft insignia and markings

Official unit markings were not carried by the Squadron's Martinsydes, though they provided an early example of the use of individual aircraft identification — large numerals painted on the sides of the engine cowlings. Most of the aircraft also had a small wooden shield on the forward fuselage on which was painted an 'elephant' symbol.

After the war, DH 9As featured code letters in white usually on a black square aft of the roundel, but sometimes on the engine cowling and occasionally on the top wing surfaces. Later aircraft appeared

with the numeral '27' painted in black on the fin, but by the late 1920s an emerald green 'elephant' profile was carried instead. On Wapitis, the aircraft letter was forward on the engine cowling, and there was a red band painted around the fuselage just forward of the tail unit, while the fin carried a green 'elephant' symbol on a white grenade-shaped shield. Following the 1938 Munich Crisis, the code letters 'MY' were allotted but probably not carried, and it was the replacement letters 'PT' used from September 1939 that were painted on Blenheims in Malaya.

Beaufighters and Mosquitos used individual aircraft letters but no unit markings, the jungle rescue version of the Beaufighter also carrying the SEAC identification stripes across wings, tailplane, fin and rudder. Unit markings were not used on No 27 Squadron Dakotas, and Canberras were at first only distinguishable by a red 'Speedbird' on the nose, but later by the Scampton stripe which ran the whole length of the fuselage.

Initially over-all white, the Vulcans only carried

a small Squadron badge on each side of the nose, but by the time the 'Blue Steel' stand-off weapon was in use the aircraft had acquired a green 'elephant' on the fin, and the badge was then immediately aft of the fuselage roundel. On camouflaged Vulcans the badge was deleted, but when the Squadron got its own specially modified aircraft, the 'elephant' symbol reappeared on the fin, painted on a white disc. With the arrival of the Tornado, colourful markings returned, No 27 Squadron sporting a yellow-outlined green arrowhead around the fuselage roundel while the fin carries a dull red stripe on which is superimposed a yellow disc enclosing the green 'elephant' motif. Numeral codes identify individual aircraft.

A Camel during April 1918 at Grossa, Italy, with the white square markings of No 28 Squadron on the fuselage (via Chaz Bowyer).

No 28 Squadron

Badge

In front of a demi-Pegasus, a fasces — approved by HRH King Edward VIII in October 1936. The demi-Pegasus represents the white horse on the downs near Yatesbury — the unit's first operational base — while the fasces commemorate service in Italy during the First World War.

Motto

Quicquid agas age — 'Whatever you may do, do'

History

No 28 Squadron was formed at Gosport on 7 November 1915 from a nucleus provided by No 22 Squadron, and spent its first 18 months as a training unit. Following a move to Yatesbury in July 1917, it re-equipped with Camels in September and took these fine aircraft to France the following month. The unit hardly had time to settle in before the BEF had to reinforce the crumbling Italian front, and No 28 was among the squadrons accompanying the troops. For the rest of the war, the Squadron flew offensive patrols over north-east Italy, remaining in the country until February 1919, and disbanding on 20 January 1920.

It was reformed on 1 April 1920 by renumbering No 114 Squadron at Ambala, India, and was equipped with Bristol Fighters, operating on the North-West Frontier as an army co-operation unit. Westland Wapitis were received as replacements during September 1931, followed by Audax in June 1936, but it was September 1941 before 'modern' equipment in the form of Lysanders was received. These were taken into Burma following the Japanese attack on Malaya, and carried out bombing and army co-operation work until the country was overrun.

Still with Lysanders, the Squadron regrouped at Lahore and co-operated in army exercises until December 1942 when Hurricane IIBs were received. TAC/R operations over Burma commenced in January 1943 and continued until the Japanese surrender. Although re-equipment with Spitfires commenced in July 1945, the last Hurricane did not leave until December. The following month, No 28 moved into Malaya as part of the permanent defence force.

The definitive Spitfire FR XVIII replaced earlier variants during February 1947, and these were taken to Hong Kong in May 1949 in response to the increasingly difficult situation posed by the civil war in China. Vampires arrived in February 1951, the Squadron moving from Kai Tak to Sek Kong the following month to operate in the primary fighter role. Three years later, the first Venoms were delivered, and in June 1957 the Squadron returned to Kai Tak. Hunter FGA 9s arrived in May 1962, combining the basic defence role with a ground attack capability. By the mid-60s it was clear that the Colony could not be defended against a determined attack, so the Squadron was disbanded on 15 December 1966.

The effective use of a helicopter during the Communist-inspired riots of 1967 convinced the Government that there was need for a rotary wing army support unit in the Colony, and on 1 April 1968 No 28 Squadron was reformed at Kai Tak from a

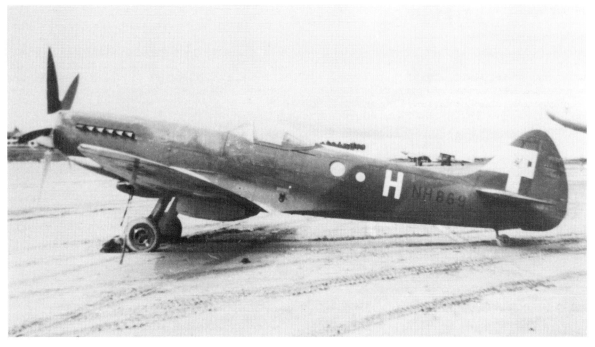

Spitfire FR XIV NH869 in August 1946 carrying the pre-war type 'spearhead' emblem on the SEAC band across the fin (Military Aircraft Photographs).

detachment of No 103 Squadron equipped with Whirlwind 10s. Replacement by Wessex 2s commenced during February 1972, this machine rapidly proving itself a willing workhorse, and following a move back to Sek Kong in June 1978 the Squadron extended its activities to include border and coastal patrols in an effort to stem the tide of illegal immigrants into the Colony.

Currently, the Squadron is still in Hong Kong and still equipped with Wessex. It will be withdrawn before the Colony is handed over to the Chinese authorities, but no date has been announced.

Standard

Granted by HRH King George VI and promulgated on 9 September 1943. Presented by Air Marshal F. J. Fressanges CB, Commander-in-Chief, Far East Air Force, at Sek Kong on 16 March 1955. The Standard was temporarily laid up in St Clement Danes Church on 30 April 1967, but withdrawn when the Squadron reformed a year later.

A new Standard was presented by His Excellency Sir Murray Maclehose, Governor of Hong Kong, at Kai Tak on 29 June 1977.

The old Standard was laid up in St John's Anglican Cathedral, Hong Kong, during September 1977, the first RAF Standard to rest in the Colony.

Battle Honours

*Italian Front & Adriatic 1917-1918
*Piave
*Vittorio Venito
Waziristan 1921-1925
North-West Frontier 1939
*Burma 1942
*Arakan 1943-1944
*Manipur 1944
*Burma 1944-1945

*Denotes Honours emblazoned on Standard

Aircraft insignia and markings

The official marking allotted to No 28 Squadron, RFC, was a white square aft of the fuselage roundel, and this was used in France and Italy, though often replaced by multiple white bands around the rear fuselage in the latter country. Individual aircraft letters were usually painted in white forward of the roundel, and after the Armistice these were embellished, senior pilots choosing their own highly coloured schemes.

In India the Bristol Fighters carried no unit markings, being confined to a single individual aircraft letter painted in black aft of the roundel, but the Wapiti replacements featured a black fuselage top decking and a black band immediately forward of the tail-plane. The Audax were similarly marked and also had a Squadron emblem painted on the fin within a white six-pointed star. Following the 1938 Munich Crisis, the Squadron code 'US' was allotted and carried forward of the roundel, the individual letter being moved aft. The black band was removed at this time, but most silver-painted Audax retained the Squadron emblem on the fin. In September 1939, the unit code was changed to 'BF' and slowly the aircraft were camouflaged, the codes on Lysanders being light grey in colour.

Hurricanes appeared in standard SEAC markings from mid-1943 (no red on the national markings) and reverted to a single aircraft letter aft of the roundel. White identification stripes were painted on wings, tailplanes, fins and rudders. Spitfires were similarly marked, though after the war a few aircraft also carried a Squadron emblem in a white arrowhead on the fin.

With the arrival of Vampires came more colourful markings. These consisted of dark blue bars outlined in yellow on each side of the boom roundel, the individual code letter appearing under the tailplane 'bullet'. The Venoms continued the basic Squadron markings but also had yellow tip tanks emblazoned with a blue 'lightning flash' and the code letter moved on to the rudders, later aircraft sporting blue rudders and yellow lettering.

Hunters retained the bar markings, but it was moved to the nose and flanked a white disc on which was painted the Squadron 'Pegasus'. The Whirlwinds carried a Squadron badge on the tail rotor pylon and a single white code letter on the aft fuselage sides, while on Wessex the markings reverted to a tail-mounted emblem, the 'Pegasus' in red on a blue background disc outlined in yellow. Individual aircraft identification letters are retained on the rear fuselage which also carry broad white bands.

Wessex HC 2 XT679 *supporting the local Hong Kong Police Force* (No 28 Squadron).

No 29 Squadron

Badge
An eagle in flight, preying on a buzzard — approved by HRH King George VI in April 1937. The badge symbolizes air combat and was developed from an unofficial emblem employed by the Squadron during the First World War.

Motto
Impiger et acer — 'Energetic and keen'

History
Formed at Gosport on 7 November 1915 from a nucleus provided by No 23 Squadron, No 29 moved to France in March 1916 with DH 2 fighters which were used at first to escort vulnerable reconnaissance aircraft over the lines, but gradually changed over to offensive patrol work. The little-known FE 8 pusher biplane was also used for a few months during the summer of 1916, but it was the arrival of the diminutive Nieuport Scout in March 1917 which really galvanized the Squadron, the destruction of German

Left *An early use of the famous red 'X's was on the Grebe IIs which equipped No 29 Squadron during the mid-1920s* (RAF Museum P16913).

Right *Phantom FGR 2* XV423 *on the Coningsby flight line with the 'eagle and buzzard' emblem on the nose and the 'X's on the fin* (RAF Coningsby).

reconnaissance balloons becoming a speciality. Like other fighter units, the Squadron also took part in ground attack operations during the third Battle of Ypres, though the Nieuport was not really suitable, the SE 5As which replaced them in April 1918 proving a much better ground strafer.

After the Armistice, No 29 Squadron moved into Germany with the Army of Occupation for a few months, but returned to the United Kingdom in August 1919 and disbanded on 31 December of the same year. The Squadron reformed at Duxford on 1 April 1923 equipped with Snipes at Flight strength, and a year later was still not up to full establishment. In January 1925, however, a full complement of Grebes was received and for the next ten years No 29 was part of the United Kingdom defence force, replacement Siskins arriving in March 1928 and Bulldogs in June 1932. In March 1935 came a radical change, the Squadron receiving two-seater Demons which were taken to Egypt in October as part of the build-up of the RAF in the Middle East during the Abyssinian crisis. A few Gordons were pressed into service to supplement the Demons on night patrols, but the crisis passed and the Squadron was back in the United Kingdom in September 1936. During December 1938, the Demons were replaced at long last, by Blenheim Is — the day of the multi-engined night fighter had arrived!

Following the outbreak of war, defensive shipping patrols were the Squadron's main occupation, but radar trials became increasingly important. Night fighter patrols became a priority from June 1940 when significant numbers of German bombers started penetrating the United Kingdom defences, and this role was accentuated with the arrival of the first

Beaufighters in November, though No 29 was not fully equipped until late February 1941. Night fighter Mosquitos were received in May 1943, and a year later the Squadron went on to the offensive, carrying out 'intruder' missions over the Continent.

After the war, No 29 Squadron became part of the much reduced peacetime United Kingdom night fighter force, updated Mosquitos surviving until replaced by Meteor NF 11s in August 1951, the unit being the first to fly them operationally. After seven years at Tangmere, the Squadron moved north to Acklington in January 1957, and during the following November received its first Javelins. The unit moved further north to Leuchars in July 1958, but in February 1963 was transferred to the Near East Air Force and was based in Cyprus.

The Rhodesian UDI problem resulted in a nine-month detachment to N'Dola, Zambia, but the Squadron was back at Akrotiri in September 1966, and the following May returned to the United Kingdom for re-equipment with Lightening F 3s at Wattisham. After seven years, the unit disbanded on 19 July 1974, but reformed on 31 December with Phantom FGR 2s and flew these aircraft for well over a decade. This included a spell in the Falklands from October 1982 until March 1983, when they exchanged identities with No 23 Squadron back at Wattisham.

In March 1987, the Squadron relinquished its Phantoms and started conversion to the Tornado F3 in April, being declared operational at Coningsby on 1 November 1987 as the first front-line unit with the aircraft.

Standard

Granted by HRH King George VI and promulgated

on 27 March 1952. Presented by Air Chief Marshal Sir Dermot Boyle KCVO KBE CB AFC at Tangmere on 18 July 1956.

A new standard was presented by HRH The Princess Margaret, Countess of Snowdon CI GCVO at Coningsby on 30 June 1987. Princess Margaret is Honorary Air Commodore, Coningsby.

Battle Honours

*Western Front 1916-1918
*Somme 1916
Arras
*Ypres 1917
*Somme 1918
Lys
*Channel & North Sea 1939-1940
*Battle of Britain 1940
*Home Defence 1940-1945
Fortress Europe 1943-1944
Normandy 1944
*France & Germany 1944-1945
Arnhem

*Denotes Honours emblazoned on Standard

Affiliation

No 22 Squadron — linked as No 29/22 Squadron from February 1949 to February 1955.

Aircraft insignia and markings

The DH 2s which the Squadron took to France were unmarked, but the silver-painted Nieuports received in the spring of 1917 were soon adorned with a red band around the fuselage immediately forward of the tailplane, and Flight colours were painted on wheel discs. When camouflage became the vogue in Decem-ber 1917, the markings changed, a white vertical stripe being painted on each side of the fuselage roundel. On the SE 5A, the aft fuselage band was re-introduced, but in white, aircraft codes being painted under the wings ('B' Flight) or on the engine cowl-ing ('A' Flight).

Between the wars, the Squadron carried various combinations of red 'X's along the fuselage sides and across the top mainplane until October 1936 when, newly equipped with Turret Demons, the 'X's were deleted and a representation of the badge painted on the fin within a red-outlined white 'spearhead' was substituted. Following the Munich Crisis, the Squa-dron code 'YB' was allotted and carried on Blenheim fighters until September 1939, when it was changed to 'RO'. After the war, Mosquitos also carried the Squadron badge on the fin, but with the introduc-tion of the Meteor the 'X' marking was re-introduced, this time on a red-outlined white rectan-gle on each side of the fuselage roundel, individual aircraft code letters being painted on the fin.

Javelins employed a similar, but single, rectangle on the fin, while on the Lightning the marking was moved to the nose, again on each side of the roun-del. The individual code letter appeared in black on the fin together with a representation of the Squa-dron badge. The Phantoms soon appeared with the familiar 'X's across the upper fin, while the cen-trepiece of the badge was superimposed on a large white shield on the nose.

With the introduction of 'low-visibility' light grey camouflage, the 'X's appeared in red on a white background across the fin RWR fairing and on each side of the miniature roundel on the engine intakes. Also on the fin was the 'shield' badge, and the rud-

Left *Just before being declared operational on 1 November 1987 with Tornado F 3s, No 29 Squadron put up this 'two-ship' formation for the benefit of the Press* (J.D.R. Rawlings).

Below right *A rather 'spidery' numeral on this Wapiti IIA at Mosul in 1930 serves to confirm the unit* (RAF Museum P17687).

Bottom right *Beverley C 1 XM111 of No 30 Squadron in April 1967 — an extraordinary sight in its dark and light earth camouflage.*

der carried the individual aircraft code letter in white. The similarly camouflaged Tornado F 3s have three red 'X's painted diagonally on the air intakes, while the eagles of the emblem, one in yellow, the other in red, are positioned on the fin above the serial together with a two-letter code, also in red.

No 30 Squadron

Badge
A date palm tree — approved by HRH King George VI in May 1938. The palm had been used as an unofficial marking on No 30 Squadron aircraft since the early 1920s, its incorporation in the authorized badge commemorating the unit's long service in the Middle East during the First World War and post-war years.

Motto
Ventre a terre — 'All out'

History
Officially formed at Ismailia, Egypt, on 24 March 1915, No 30 Squadron was the victim of confusion and circumstance and it did not become a homogenous unit until the end of the year. The nucleus was an RFC detachment of Flight strength raised at Farnborough in October 1914 and sent out to Egypt the following month for Suez Canal defence work. The aircraft, Maurice and Henri Farmans supplemented by the odd BE 2A, were quite unsuitable for the proposed role, and in practice carried out reconnaissance patrols during the unsuccessful Turkish attack on the Canal area. Expanded to Squadron strength in March 1915 by absorbing local forces, the unit sent a detachment to Basra to defend the oil pipeline from Abadan, supplemented by 'B' Flight in November and the remainder of the Squadron in December, when the HQ arrived from Egypt and all activities were concentrated in Mesopotamia. New detachments were then formed to operate along the Mesopotamian front on reconnaissance and artillery spotting, an additional task being the world's first air supply operation — the dropping of ammunition and food to the besieged defenders of Kut-el-Amara during April 1916.

Reconnaissance and bombing occupied the Squadron for the rest of the war, BE 2Cs not being completely replaced by RE 8s until February 1918. A very mixed collection of fighter scouts were also in use during 1917, but most had departed by the Armistice, the Squadron remaining in the Baghdad area until April 1919 when it was reduced to cadre.

On 1 February 1920, the Squadron was brought up to strength as a day bomber unit equipped with DH 9As and RE 8s. The last of the 'Harry Tates' left in January 1921, but the Squadron remained in Iraq for another 19½ years, receiving Wapitis in April 1929, Hardys six years later and Blenheim Is in January 1938 — the first in the Middle East.

A few days before the outbreak of war in September 1939, the Squadron took its Blenheims to Egypt, and, when the Italians joined on the side of Germany

Above *Harrier GR 3A XZ133 of No 1 Squadron at Chivenor in July 1984 in the drab camouflage typical of RAF strike aircraft. The unit markings stand out on the nose but the code '10' is hardly visible on the tail.*

Below *The alternative 'ET' — a Chinook of No 7 Squadron. The famous 'stars' badge is clearly visible on the rear rotor pylon.*

Top *The oldest operational aircraft in the RAF, No 8 Squadron's Shackleton AEW 2s, still retain the overall dark sea grey colour scheme, enlivened by 'fighter' style unit markings on each side of the fuselage roundel and the 'dagger' badge on the nose.*

Above *The sinister 'bat' marking on the fin reveals this Tornado GR 1 to be a No 9 Squadron aircraft. The unit's small chevron marking is on the nose.*

Left *The famous Lightnings have gone, but they live on in every air display visitor's memory. XS925 is seen here in the final colour scheme adopted by No 11 Squadron — the badge on the tail together with a two letter code.*

Above *This Buccaneer S 2B of No 12 Squadron carries the famous 'fox mask' on the engine intake and the two-letter unit code on the tail — the latter is not currently carried during the refurbishing programme. An unusual feature is the use of the inside of the air brakes to identify the aircraft by its 'last three'.*

Right *A visitor to the UK from RAF Germany — Tornado GR 1 ZD709 of No 20 Squadron, coded 'GJ' and with markings on both nose and engine intakes.*

Below *Tornado GR 1 of No 27 Squadron complete with nose chevron, red tail stripe and green 'elephant' emblem — one of the more colourful schemes.*

Above *Civilian executive jets are often shy about their ownership, and the RAF's BAe 125s seem to have caught the 'bug' — this CC 3 of No 32 Squadron doesn't even carry the unit badge, but looks very smart in its 'transport' colour scheme.*

Below *The 'Fighting Cock' on the tail of Phantom FG 1 XV571, together with the black/white checks, reveal the unit as No 43 Squadron. Chivenor, July 1984.*

during June 1940, the aircraft were fitted with gun trays under the fuselage and flew bomber escorts over the Western Desert. In November, the Squadron moved to Greece to operate in defence of Athens, though bomber sorties were also mounted. Officially re-designated a fighter squadron in March 1941, the unit moved to Crete in April and battled against hopeless odds until evacuated to Egypt in May. Re-equipped with Hurricanes which were used for the night defence of Alexandria until October 1941, the Squadron then returned to the Western Desert for coastal convoy patrols, and the much more exciting strafing of enemy motor transport.

In February 1942, the Squadron was withdrawn from the desert and embarked its Hurricanes in HMS *Indomitable*, arriving in Ceylon just in time to help defend Colombo from the Easter Sunday attack by Japanese carrier-borne aircraft. There was no follow-up, however and No 30 remained quietly on air defence duties until moved to the Burma front in February 1944 for ground attack and bomber escort duties. During May 1944 the Squadron re-equipped with Thunderbolts and resumed operations in October as a fighter-bomber unit. In May 1945, the Squadron was withdrawn for a rest and was still in India when the Japanese surrendered. Tempest IIs were received in June 1946, but the unit disbanded at Agra six months later on 1 December.

No 30 Squadron reformed at Oakington as a transport unit flying Dakotas on 24 November 1947. It was active during the Berlin Airlift before being re-equipped with Valettas in November 1950 on mov-

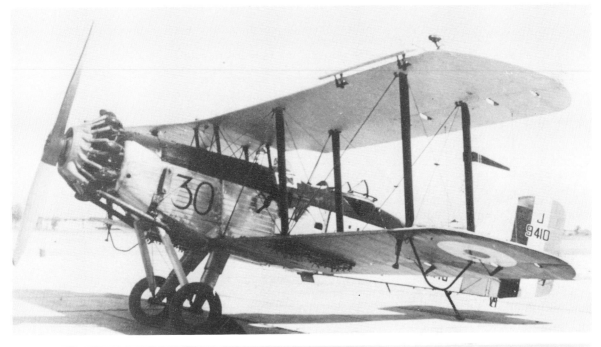

A Hercules C 1 of the Lyneham Transport Wing being flown by a No 30 Squadron crew.

ing to Abingdon. Beverleys were received in April 1957 when the Squadron was re-designated a tactical transport squadron, initially operating in the United Kingdom, but from November 1959 in Kenya. The strengthening of the forces in the Persian Gulf meant a move to Muharraq in September 1964, but three years later the Squadron again disbanded.

Reformed once more on 10 June 1968, No 30 was this time equipped with Hercules for the dual task of route flying and army tactical transport support at Fairford. With the concentration of the whole of the Hercules fleet at Lyneham, No 30 Squadron moved in during February 1971 and is still there as part of the Transport Wing. The Squadron was heavily engaged in Operation 'Corporate' in 1982 then provided Hercules 'tankers' for the Falkland 'Air Bridge' until the detachment at Stanley was re-designated 1312 Flight on 20 August 1983.

Standard

Granted by HRH King George VI and promulgated on 9 September 1943. Presented by Air Chief Marshal Sir James Robb KBE CB DSO DFC AFC at Dishforth on 1 July 1954.

A new Standard was presented by HRH The Princess Anne, Mrs Mark Phillips, GCVO at Lyneham on 18 May 1978. The Princess is Honorary Air Commodore, Lyneham.

The old Standard was laid up in St Michael & All Angels Parish Church, Lyneham, on 15 October 1978.

Battle Honours

*Egypt 1915
*Mesopotamia 1915-1918
Iraq 1919-1920
North West Persia 1920
Kurdistan 1922-1924
Iraq 1923-1925
Iraq 1928-1929
Kurdistan 1930-1931
Northern Kurdistan 1932
*Egypt & Libya 1940-1942
*Greece 1940-1941
*Mediterranean 1940-1941
*Ceylon April 1942
*Arakan 1944
*Burma 1944-1945

*Denotes Honours emblazoned on Standard

Aircraft insignia and markings

Like many Middle East-based units, it appears that no Squadron markings were carried during the First World War. In the early 1920s, the DH 9As sported orange stripes across the wing-tips and tailplane to assist location if force-landed, and some aircraft carried swastikas and stars on the fin. Later, a palm tree was painted on Flight-coloured fins and individual code letters were applied to the sides of the engine cowlings in Arabic-type script. Similar markings were used on Wapitis, the trunk of the palm tree dividing the figure '30'. Hardys also had a version of the now officially approved palm tree on the fin but it is believed that Blenheims were unmarked.

Hurricanes, Thunderbolts and Tempests in the Far East carried the unit code 'RS' and individual aircraft letters. The Thunderbolts also had the SEAC white stripes across wings, tailplane, fins and rudders, but were unusual in also featuring a version of the palm tree badge on the fin stripe. Surprisingly, when reformed with Dakotas in 1947, the Squadron code 'JN' was employed and this appeared on some Valettas before Transport Command decreed that unit markings should take the form of a coloured diamond on the fin. Introduced in the mid-50s, the diamond was red with '30' in white superimposed on it, and the same markings were used on Beverleys.

Most Valettas and Beverleys also carried the Squadron badge on the forward fuselage sides.

The Hercules are 'centralized' within the Lyneham Transport Wing and carry no unit markings.

No 31 Squadron

Badge

In front of a wreath of laurel, a mullet — approved by HRH King George VI in June 1937. The badge was based on an unofficial emblem, the mullet indicating the Star of India and the Squadron's claim to being the first military unit to fly in India.

Motto

In caelum indicum primus — First into Indian skies'

History

Formed at Farnborough on 11 October 1915 at Flight strength for service in India, 'A' Flight embarked at the end of November and arrived at Risulpur on 26 December, to be joined by two more Flights by the end of May 1916. Equipped with the ubiqituous BE 2C and few Henri Farmans, the Squadron spent the rest of the war co-operating with the Indian Army on the North-West Frontier — a daunting prospect in the flimsy BE.

Bristol Fighters arrived during September 1919, the last of the BE 2s staggering on until February 1920. The Squadron then settled down to a decade of army co-operation using the wonderful but steadily ageing 'Brisfit'. They escorted Victorias during the famous Kabul evacuation of 1928, but in February 1931 were finally replaced by Wapitis, which in turn soldiered on until 1939.

On 1 April 1939, the Squadron's role was officially changed from army co-operation to bomber transport, and the Indian Bomber Transport Flight was absorbed, forming one Flight, while the other two continued flying Wapitis until more Valentias were ferried to India from the Middle East during the summer. The obsolescent twin-engined biplanes performed prodigious feats on the North-West Frontier transporting troops and supplies around the area and bombing rebel villages with really impressive effect. In March 1941, army reinforcements were flown to Shaibah and in April DC 2s were received, these 'impressed' aircraft being put into immediate service flying supplies into beleaguered Habbaniya alongside the ancient Valentias.

Returning to India in May 1941, the Squadron continued conversion to the Douglas Transport and, following the Japanese attack on Burma, they flew a service between Rangoon and Calcutta. The first ex-civilian DC 3s were received in April 1942, and were later supplemented by Dakotas which were used for the rest of the war on supply drops and freight-carrying duties for the 14th Army in Burma.

After the Japanese surrender, the Squadron moved to Singapore and then to Java following an insurrection in the Dutch East Indies. It was while flying from Kemajoran that one of the Dakota crashed and the survivors were hacked to death in cold blood by

Canberra PR 7 WH775 of No 31 Squadron with the unit badge on the nose and illustrating the first use of the 'Star of India' on the fin.

Above *Jaguar GR 1 XX976 carrying a chaff dispenser, two underwing fuel tanks, two 1000-lb bombs and an ECM pod* (RAF Germany TN9594/15).

Left *A superb landing shot of Tornado GR 1 ZD707 of No 31 Squadron in 1984* (Military Aircraft Photographs).

Indonesian 'freedom-fighters' — a reminder that not all atrocities in the area were perpetrated by the Japanese.

Disbanded in Java on 30 September 1946, the Squadron re-appeared at Mauripur the next day when No 77 Squadron was re-numbered. Dakotas were still the unit's equipment, flown on general transport duties in India until again disbanded on 31 December 1947.

On 19 July 1948, the Metropolitan Communications Squadron at Hendon was re-designated No 31 Squadron and flew Ansons and Proctors, later replaced by Devons, on mundane liaison flights around the United Kingdom. The unit reverted to its former title on 1 March 1955, and No 31 Squadron reformed the same day at Laarbruch in Germany equipped with Canberras in the photo-reconnaissance role, and part of the Second Tactical Air Force.

After 16 successful years at Laarbruch, the Squadron was disbanded on 31 March 1971, and immediately reformed at Bruggen as a strike ground attack unit flying Phantoms. The first crews were already at Bruggen, but the aircraft did not arrive until June, and the Squadron was not operational until 7 October when an official reformation parade was held.

Jaguar replacements started arriving during December 1975, the Phantom element disbanding in June 1976 when the 'Jag' pilots were declared operational. Much the same drill, designed to maintain RAF Germany's front-line strength during re-equipment, was repeated nine years later, Tornado crews starting conversion in July 1984 and the Jaguar element standing down on 1 September. Currently, the Squadron forms part of the Bruggen interdictor/strike Wing alongside Nos 9, 14 and 17 Squadrons.

Standard

Granted by HRH King George VI and promulgated on 9 September 1943. Presented by Air Chief Marshal Sir Alec Coryton KCB KBE MVO DFC at Laarbruch on 13 September 1956. Sir Alec had served with the Squadron in the 1920s.

A new Standard was presented by Air Marshal Sir Leslie Mavor KCB AFC DL FRAeS at Bruggen on 14 November 1986.

The old Standard was laid up in St Clement Danes Church on 21 June 1987.

Battle Honours

*North West Frontier 1916-1918

Afghanistan 1919-1920
Mahoud 1919-1920
Wazaristan 1919-1925
North West Frontier 1939
*Iraq 1941
Agra 1941
*Egypt & Libya 1941-1942
*Burma 1941-1942
*North Burma 1943-1944
*Arakan 1943-1944
*Manipur 1944
*Burma 1944-1945

*Denotes Honours emblazoned on Standard

Aircraft insignia markings

No unit markings were carried on Squadron aircraft during the First World War, but some used letter/numeral individual identification during 1918-19. Bristol Fighters were similarly marked at first, using a single letter code aft of the roundel and Squadron number on the fin, but late in their careers a black band around the fuselage was substituted. Wapitis also featured a single band (probably Flight-coloured) together with an individual letter painted either on the rear or forward fuselage. Following the authorization of the unit badge, the 'mullet' emblem appeared on the fin.

Valentias were unmarked at first, except for individual code letters positioned aft of the fuselage roundel and repeated on the nose, but some aircraft latterly carried a name across the nose-cone. The Squadron was allocated the code 'ZA' after the Munich Crisis of 1938, and this was used on Valentias from April 1939, replaced by 'EE' in September. DC 2s and DC 3s were unmarked, and replacement Dakotas used only individual aircraft letters.

When reformed as a communications squadron, 'A' Flight used the code 'CB' and 'B' Flight 'VS', the Ansons also carrying the Transport Command diamond on the fin at one stage. Returning to operational flying, the Squadron painted the 'mullet' in yellow on a green disc on the fins of its Canberra PR 7s, and a Squadron badge on the nose. The same marking was retained on Phantoms, which also carried 'fighter-type' yellow and green chequered rectangles on each side of the badge on the nose. Jaguars featured the same markings, but on the sides of the engine intakes, and towards the end of their time on the Squadron the individual code letter on the fin was prefixed with 'D' to denote the Squadron. Tornados introduced a new scheme, the Squadron 'mullet' being displayed on the fin with the two-letter code, while a yellow and green arrowhead was painted around the nose roundel.

No 32 Squadron

Badge

A hunting-horn stringed — approved by HRH King George VI in December 1936. The horn indicated the unit's ability to hunt the enemy.

Motto

Adeste comites — 'Rally round, comrades'

History

No 32 Squadron was formed at Netheravon on 12 January 1916 from a nucleus provided by No 21 Squadron. After a short period of training, DH 2 fighter scouts were received in February and the Squadron took these single-seat pusher biplanes to France on 28 May. They were soon in the thick of battle with the Fokker 'Eindekker', the scourge of the Western Front at that time. During a patrol on 1 July, the first day of the 1916 Somme offensive, the CO, Major L.W.B. Rees, encountered a formation of eight Albatros scouts and immediately attacked them. Despite the odds he succeeded in scattering them, and, though wounded, forced two down out of control before his ammunition ran out. He was awarded the Victoria Cross for this gallant action.

For the battle of Arras in April 1917, No 32 turned to low-level strafing of troops and transport for which the DH 2 proved very effective, as did the more substantial-looking DH 5 which arrived during May and was operational in time to demonstrate its close support prowess during the exhausting Third Battle of Ypres. In January 1918, the formidable SE 5A re-equipped the Squadron, and No 32 played its full part in stemming the German spring offensive and during the subsequent Allied advance. Soon after the Armistice, the Squadron was reduced to cadre, personnel returning to the United Kingdom in March 1919 and the unit disbanding at the end of the year.

Reformed at Kenley on 1 April 1923 with Snipes initially at Flight strength, No 32 was upgraded to a full fighter squadron in June 1924. In December, the pugnacious Grebe re-equipped the Squadron, these giving way to Gamecocks in September 1926,

Andover CC 2 XS794 of 'A' Flight sports No 32 Squadron's 'hunting horn' emblem on the fin (J.D.R. Rawlings).

Siskins in April 1928 and Bulldogs in September 1930. Two years later, No 32 moved to Biggin Hill, the steady re-equipment programme continuing with the Gauntlet in July 1936 and the Hurricane I in October 1938, the aircraft with which the Squadron went to war the following September.

During the early months, No 32 remained in the south-east but deployed to France after the German breakthrough early in May 1940. Back in the United Kingdom in June, the Squadron was heavily engaged in the Battle of Britain before being withdrawn at the end of August. There was little further contact with the enemy until 1942 when the Squadron was back in the south-east flying escorts and sweeps followed by night intruder operations, before leaving for North Africa in November.

The long-serving Hurricanes were replaced by Spitfires during 1943 as the Squadron worked its way across North Africa, through Italy and, in September 1944, into Greece. During February 1945, No 32 transferred to Palestine and, still with Spitfires, moved to Cyprus in May 1948. Conversion to Vampires started in July 1948, these aircraft serving with the Squadron at various locations in the Middle East until January 1955 when Venoms completely replaced them.

After two years with the Venom, the fighter ground attack role of the Squadron was changed to light bomber, and Canberra B 2s were received in January 1957 by an element which worked up in the United Kingdom before deploying to Cyprus. The Squadron operated as part of the Near East Bomber Wing from Akrotiri for the next 12 years, receiving updated Canberra B 15 aircraft in July 1961.

The unit disbanded in Cyprus on 3 February 1969 but immediately reformed at Northolt from the Metropolitan Communications Squadron, and flew Bassets, Andovers and Sycamore helicopters. Whirlwinds were received in January 1970 and the HS 125 light jet transport in March 1971, resulting in the phasing out of Sycamores in August 1972 and Bassets in January 1976.

Today the Squadron operates three Flights, one with updated HS 125s crewed by both RAF and RN personnel, one with Andovers and the third with Gazelle helicopters, tasked with the transport of all VIPs below royal status as well as more ordinary mortals.

Standard

Granted by HRH King George VI and promulgated on 27 March 1952. Presented by Air Chief Marshal Sir James Robb KBE CB DSO DFC AFC at Akrotiri on 6 June 1957.

A new Standard was presented by Air Chief Marshal Sir Michael Knight KCB AFC ADC BA D.Litt FRAeS at Northolt on 6 June 1987.

The old Standard was laid up in the RAF Church, St Clement Danes, in November 1987.

Battle Honours

Western Front 1916-1918
*Somme 1916 & 1918
Arras
*Ypres
*Amiens
*France and Low Countries 1939-1940
*Battle of Britain
Home Defence 1940-1942
*Dieppe
*North Africa 1942-1943
Italy 1943
*South East Europe 1944-1945

*Denotes Honours emblazoned on Standard

Aircraft insignia and markings

Unit markings were not introduced until the DH 5 was in service with No 32 Squadron, these aircraft carrying a single white band around the fuselage aft of the roundel. Early SE 5As may also have carried this identification, but two white bars sloping inwards at the top positioned aft of the roundel were used during 1918.

Most of the 12 BAe 125s on the strength of 'B' Flight are without unit markings, but in January 1987 XX508 had the emblem on the fin.

None of the Gazelle HCC 4s of 'C' Flight carries unit markings, but they have a very attractive form of the 'transport' colour scheme (Military Aircraft Photographs).

The post-war Snipes carried a broad blue band down the length of the fuselage sides, white diagonal stripes being painted across the band. Similar markings were applied to Grebes, Gamecocks, Siskins and Bulldogs, most aircraft having the upper surface of the top mainplane adorned in the same fashion. Gauntlets used an abbreviated form on the rear fuselage but also carried on the fin the newly authorized badge on a white spearhead background.

Hurricanes arrived just after the Munich Crisis and were early recipients of a Squadron code, 'KT' being allotted to No 32. The code changed to 'GZ' on the outbreak of war and this remained in use in a rather haphazard fashion until the arrival of Vampires in 1949. These aircraft initially carried a Squadron badge and large individual letter on the nose, but reverted to the famous blue and white stripes on the FB 5 version, painted in bar form on each side of the roundel. Venoms were similarly adorned, but Canberras introduced markings on the fin in the form of a Squadron 'hunting-horn' emblem flanked by the 'candy bar' stripes. From mid-1958 onwards, most of the fin was used to display an enlarged version of the blue white Squadron colours.

Unit identification on the Northolt-based communications aircraft was much more restrained, confined to a small Squadron badge on Andovers and Gazelles and some of the 125s.

No 33 Squadron

Badge

A hart's head affrontée, couped at the neck — approved by HRH King Edward VIII in May 1936. The design of the badge was developed from an unofficial emblem produced in the early 1930s when the famous Hawker Hart day bomber was introduced into service by the Squadron.

Motto

Loyalty

History

No 33 Squadron was formed at Filton on 12 January 1916 from personnel left behind when No 12 Squadron went to France. After the usual work-up period, the Squadron took its BE 2 variants to Yorkshire during March and, split into three Flights, operated from landing grounds at Coal Aston, Bramham Moor and Beverley on Home Defence duty. The main task was the countering of enemy airship raids on North Midland towns and cities, but the Squadron was also involved in advanced training for pilots until June when No 57 Squadron took over the job. For the remainder of the First World War, No 33 operated from various fields in Yorkshire and Lincolnshire, FE 2B/D two-seat pusher biplanes being received in November 1916, Bristol F2Bs during the summer of 1918 and then single-seat night fighter Avro 504Ks, the latter remaining until disbandment on 13 June 1919. The Squadron had spent many hours on patrol and made several interceptions but could claim no success.

It was nearly ten years later that the No 33 Squadron reformed at Netheravon on 1 March 1929, this time as a day bomber unit. Briefly equipped with the ungainly Horsley, it quickly gained fame when the first in-service Harts were received in February 1930. This sleek two-seater biplane could outpace contemporary fighters and, together with the Fox already in service with No 12 Squadron, caused consternation in fighter circles.

The Squadron went to Egypt in October 1935 as part of the reinforcements sent to the Middle East during the Italian subjection of Abyssinia, and remained there after the crisis was over. On 1 March 1938, No 33 was re-designated a fighter squadron, having received Gladiators a month earlier, and was soon engaged on policing duties in Palestine where Arabs were already attacking Jewish settlements.

In May 1939, the Squadron returned to Egypt and was deployed in the Western Desert, active operations starting immediately Italy entered the war in June 1940. Conversion to Hurricanes was completed during September/October, and ground attack work continued until January 1941 when No 33 was sent to Greece for a chaotic stay of four months. Virtually reformed, the Squadron was operational again in June and started converting to Tomahawks. This plan was abandoned and the Hurricanes soldiered on until December 1943, despite the arrival of a few Spitfires the previous January.

In April 1944, the Squadron left Egypt for the United Kingdom and took part in the invasion of Europe flying Spitfire IXs. By the end of August 1944 the unit was in France engaged in ground attack work until December, when it returned to England to convert to Tempests. No 33 rejoined the Second TAF in February 1945 and flew fighter sweeps until the end of the war, when it moved into Germany. Spitfire XIVs were received in November 1945, but a year

Hart K4454 in trouble in the Middle East, but displaying the unusual location of the unit number on the fuselage and the 'Hart' symbol on the tail (via M.W. Payne).

later the Squadron again had Tempests, this time Centaurus-powered Mk IIs.

During July 1949, the Squadron was transferred to the Far East and flew ground attack missions against Communist guerillas in the Malayan jungle. The faithful Tempest was exchanged for the superlative Hornet during April/June 1951, and the unit continued operations until merged with its sister Squadron, No 45, on 31 March 1955.

No 33 Squadron reformed at Driffield on 15 October 1955 with Venom night fighters, but was short-lived, disbanding again on 3 June 1957. A few months later, on 30 September, No 264 Squadron was re-numbered No 33 at Leeming, and the Squadron flew Meteor NF 14s until converted to Javelins in July 1958. The unit remained part of the United Kingdom air defence force until disbanded on 17 November 1962.

The Squadron was reformed in Malaya on 1 March 1965 as a surface-to-air missile unit equipped with Bloodhounds. Nearly five years was spent at Butterworth on air defence duties until disbandment came again on 30 January 1970.

Eighteen months later No 33 rose again, as the first Puma helicopter squadron in the RAF, forming at Odiham on 14 June 1971. Intended for front-line troop and equipment transport in direct support of the Army, the Squadron has also been active in various trouble spots over the past 17 years, the air-transportable Puma having proved very successful in the rapid reaction role. No 33 Squadron is still based at Odiham as part of No 1 Group, Strike Command.

Standard

Granted by HRH King George VI and promulgated on 27 March 1952. Presented by Air Marshal Sir Philip Joubert de la Ferte KCG CMG DSO at Leeming on 24 April 1958.

A new Standard was presented by Air Chief Marshal Sir Denis Smallwood GBE KCB DSO DFC at Odiham on 19 May 1988.

Battle Honours

*Home Defence 1916-1918
Palestine 1936-1939
*Egypt & Libya 1940-1943
*Greece 1941
*El Alamein
*France & Germany 1944-1945
*Normandy 1944
*Walcheren
*Rhine

*Denotes Honours emblazoned on Standard

Affiliation

No 45 Squadron — linked as 45/33 Sqn from March 1955 to October 1955 whilst disbanded.

Memorial

Included on a Bomber Command memorial on the edge of Elsham Wolds airfield is a board detailing the activities of 'C' Flight, No 33 Squadron (based at Elsham Wolds during the First World War).

Aircraft insignia and markings

Squadron markings were not carried by Home Defence units in the First World War. On reforming as a day bomber unit, No 33's Horsleys had the numerals '33' painted on the fuselage forward of the roundels and some aircraft carried a black band aft. The '33' was continued on Harts, the numerals placed above the roundel and painted in Flight colours, those of 'B' Flight outlined in black. The 'hart' emblem appeared in black on the fin.

It is almost certain that, whilst in the Middle East for the Abyssinian crisis, no unit markings were carried, but soon after being re-designated a fighter unit, the Squadron badge was applied to the fins of Gladiators in the standard white 'spearhead' device. When code letters were allocated after the Munich Crisis, No 33 Squadron used 'SO' painted aft of the fuselage roundel with an individual letter forward. The 'spearhead' was removed when the Gladiators were camouflaged. It is likely that the Squadron used the allotted wartime code by mistake, for 'SO' was replaced by 'TN' in April 1939, and following the outbreak of war 'NW' was introduced on Gladiators and their replacement Hurricanes during the early desert and Greek campaigns.

From mid-1941 onwards, unit markings were deleted until the Squadron returned to the United Kingdom in 1944 when the code '5R' was introduced, remaining in use until about 1953. After experimenting with various coloured markings on the Hornets, the Squadron settled on pale blue rectangles edged top and bottom in dark blue and centred by a thin red stripe, painted on each side of the fuselage roundel. Individual aircraft letters were applied to the rear fuselage in white.

The same Squadron marking was used on Venom night fighters, repeated on the wing-tip tanks of later aircraft. The individual aircraft code appeared on the nose-wheel door, in red on 'A' Flight and blue on 'B' Flight aircraft. Meteor NF 14s were similarly marked, the code letter also being applied to the fin. The

Javelin FAW 9s of No 33 Squadron carried the 'Hart' emblem on the tail stripe, the colours of which were first used on the Hornet in Malaya (Military Aircraft Photographs).

Puma HC 1 XW214 of No 33 Squadron carried the 'Hart' emblem on the fuselage sides beneath the cockpit windows, seen here in October 1986.

introduction of Javelins forced a change, the Squadron colours being painted across the top of the fin and rudder just below the tailplane, while the aircraft code, pale blue outlined in the Flight colour, was placed between the roundel and engine intake. When Javelin FAW 9s replaced the 7s, a pale blue disc mounting a black hart's head was superimposed on the tail stripe and the individual letter was moved to the fin.

On Puma helicopters, the Squadron's 'hart' emblem flanked by blue/red bars is carried on the starboard cockpit door, and the unit code 'C' is painted in black on the tail boom together with the aircraft's individual letter.

No 38 Squadron

Badge

A heron volant — approved by HRH King George VI in February 1937 and presented by Air Chief Marshal Sir John Steel GCB KBE CMG, Air Officer Commanding-in-Chief, Bomber Command, in July 1937. The heron was chosen as the centrepiece because of its abundance in East Anglia where the Squadron was first formed, and because the bird had the reputation of fighting back when attacked.

Motto

Ante lucem — 'Before the dawn'

History

Originally formed at Thetford on 1 April 1916, a change in plan caused the unit to be re-designated 25 Reserve Squadron on 22 May. A new start was made on 14 July at Castle Bromwich where No 38 was raised as a Home Defence unit equipped with the standard BE 2C. In October 1916, the Squadron headquarters was established at Melton Mowbray, the three Flights operating from landing grounds at Stamford, Buckminster and Leadenham with BE 2 variants and a number of FE 2Bs. These aircraft were used to provide night flying training as well as to maintain an anti-Zeppelin standby.

At the end of May 1918, the FE 2Bs were taken to France and the Squadron was re-designated a night bomber unit, raids on enemy territory being made until August when No 38 was withdrawn for re-equipment with Handley Page 0/400s. This plan came to naught, however, and the Squadron resumed bombing raids with FE 2Bs in September 1918. After the Armistice, the Squadron remained on the Continent until February 1919, when its aircraft were handed over to No 102 Squadron and it returned to the United Kingdom to be disbanded at Hawkinge on 4 July the same year.

No 38 Squadron was reformed from a nucleus provided by 'B' flight, No 99 Squadron, on 16 September 1935. First equipped with Heyford night bombers, it became the only operational unit to receive the Fairey Hendon, these impressive monoplanes arriving at Mildenhall during November 1936. Two years later, Wellingtons replaced them at Marham and were used for anti-shipping sweeps from November 1939 until proper bombing raids commenced in May 1940. These continued until November when the Squadron was sent to Egypt for bombing attacks on targets in Libya and Italy. In January 1942, night torpedo bomber training started, and anti-shipping strikes commenced in March, the accent gradually changing to anti-submarine work during 1943.

In November 1944, the Squadron transferred to the Balkan Air Force and added supply-dropping to its repertoire, before concentrating on ASR work as the war ended. In July 1945, the Warwick ASR 1 started to supplement Wellington XIVs, and the Squadron moved to Malta where Lancaster ASR 3s were received during November 1946. Maritime reconnaissance was added to the basic ASR role when most of the unit went to Palestine for anti-immigrant patrols the following month.

The withdrawal from Palastine was made between March and May 1948, the Squadron receiving Lancaster GR 3s at Luqa, Malta. It continued to share an ASR standby with No 37 Squadron, one aircraft being maintained at readiness with an airborne lifeboat mounted until Shackleton MR 2s finally replaced the venerable Lancasters in February 1954. This dedicated maritime reconnaissance aircraft was used by No 38 Squadron for 13 years, during which time it took part in operations off Cyprus, Suez, Kuwait and Madagascar during the Beira Blockade of 1966-67. In September 1965 the Squadron moved from Luqa to Halfar, where it disbanded on 31 March 1967.

In July 1967, the Maritime Operational Training Unit (MOTU) at St Mawgan, which previously had a war role as No 220 Squadron flying Shackletons, assumed the task of raising a second 'shadow' squadron, No 38. When No 236 OCU reformed from MOTU on 1 July 1970, the new unit retained its war role as No 38 Squadron with Nimrod reconnaissance aircraft, and still maintains this commitment 18 years later.

Standard

Granted by HRH Queen Elizabeth II and promulgated on 30 July 1958. Presented by HRH The Duke of Gloucester at Luqa, Malta, on 14 February 1962.

The standard was laid up in St Clement Danes Church on 7 May 1967 following the disbandment of the Squadron.

Battle Honours

Home Defence 1917-1918
*Western Front 1918
*Channel & North Sea 1939
Fortress Europe 1940
*Norway 1940
*France & Low Countries 1940
*Invasion Ports 1940
Ruhr 1940
German Ports 1940
*Berlin 1940
Egypt & Libya 1940-1942
*Malta 1941
*Mediterranean 1941-1943

*Denotes Honours emblazoned on Standard

Aircraft insignia and markings

Squadron aircraft carried no distinguishing markings during the First World War, and neither did the Heyfords in use following reformation in 1935. The Hendons employed single letter individual codes in Flight colours.

Following the Munich Crisis, the code letters 'NH' were allotted and painted in white on the rear fuselage of Wellington Is, an individual aircraft letter appearing in front of the roundel. In September 1939, the code was changed to 'HD', and this was used until the Squadron joined No 201 Group in February 1942

Lancaster GR 3 TX269 was in service with No 38 Squadron coded 'RL-N' during the late 1940s for anti-submarine and ASR work from Malta (Military Aircraft Photographs).

Left *A Nimrod MR 2 XV250 lifts off St Mawgan's 31 Runway on 5 August 1987 at the start of its Air Day display in the hands of F/Lt Bill Mott of 236 OCU (38 'Shadow' Squadron).*

for anti-shipping work in the Mediterranean. For the remainder of the war, markings were confined to individual aircraft letters.

When Lancasters were received from the disbanded No 279 Squadron in 1946, their 'RL' code was retained for a time. Later, a Squadron badge was carried beneath the cockpit windows, and also featured on GR Lancasters and MR Shackletons, these aircraft having the aircraft individual letter painted on the rear fuselage. Following the introduction of dark slate grey camouflage in 1956, the Squadron number replaced the code letter, painted in red outlined in white on the rear fuselage, the individual letter being moved to the sides of the nose. In the 1960s, the 'heron' emblem from the badge was painted on the upper part of the fins within a white disc.

Nimrods carry no Squadron identity markings but have a St Mawgan station badge on both sides of the forward fuselage.

No 41 Squadron

Badge

A double-armed cross — approved by HRH King George VI in February 1937. The badge originated from the Squadron's First World War association with St Omer, the cross being part of the town's arms.

Motto

Seek and destroy

History

Originally formed in April 1916, but almost immediately re-designated 27 Reserve Squadron, No 41 had a fresh start at Gosport on 14 July and worked up on Vickers FB 5 and DH 2 pusher scouts, before re-equipping in September with the deceptively fragile-looking FE 8. These aircraft were taken to France in October 1916, but did not prove very successful fighters and were principally used for ground attack on forward troop positions.

In July 1917, the Squadron re-equipped with DH 5s, again more use as ground strafers than fighters, and in November the much more effective SE 5A was received. Fighter and escort missions now became the norm, though the Squadron retained its ground attack expertise and used it to great effect during the last desperate German offensive in March 1918. No 41 Squadron was reduced to cadre on the Continent in January 1919 before returning in skeleton form to the United Kingdom the following month in preparation for disbandment on 31 December.

A little over three years later, on 1 April 1923, No 41 reformed at Northolt as a Snipe-equipped fighter squadron, though it was a year before it reached two-Flight strength. In May 1924, Siskins replaced the Snipes, and in 1925 the Squadron at last reached full strength with three Flights. The up-dated Siskin IIIA was received in March 1927, but it was October 1931 before Bulldog IIAs arrived at Northolt.

A major change in tactics followed the introduction of two-seater Demon fighters in July 1934, these aircraft being taken out to Aden in October 1935. The hastily formed Demon Flight of No 8 Squadron was absorbed on arrival, and No 41 then engaged in helping to police the Protectorate while on standby during the Abyssinian crisis.

Returning to the United Kingdom in August 1936, the Squadron settled in at Catterick and in October 1937 reverted to its single-seater interceptor fighter role, 'temporarily' equipped with the delightful Fury II. In practice, it was to be a year before the first Spitfires reached the Squadron in January 1939, and when war was declared in September only one operational Flight could be placed at 'readiness', the remainder of the unit continuing to train. Fortunately, activity was slight and remained so until May 1940, when the Squadron flew cover for the Dunkirk evacuation, and spent further spells in the south during the Battle of Britain. Spitfire IIs were used for a few months, but soon after joining the Tangmere Wing in July 1941 for 'Rhubarbs', the Spitfire VB reached the unit.

Returning north for convoy patrols in August 1942, the Squadron's fortunes were at a low ebb until re-equipped with the Griffon-powered Spitfire XII. These aircraft were used to intercept low-level 'hit and run' fighter-bomber attacks on south coast towns during 1943, and were again in demand when the V1 flying bomb offensive began in June 1944. Sweeps and escort work followed, and soon after receiving the excellent Spitfire XIV during September, the Squadron joined the Second Tactical Air Force. In December, it moved to the Continent and flew sweeps over Germany for the rest of the war. On 11 July 1945, the Squadron moved forward into Germany as part of the occupation forces and was briefly equipped with Tempest Vs before being re-numbered No 26 Squadron at Wunsdorf on 1 April 1946.

On the same day, No 122 Squadron at Dalcross

Bulldog IIA K2184 — a superb shot showing No 41 Squadron's pre-war markings, including the gold crown above the 'Cross of Lorraine' (RAF Museum P19253).

Javelin FAW 8 XH982 in 1963 combines the red stripe and the emblem on the fin (Military Aircraft Photographs).

A Jaguar GR 1A of No 41 Squadron displays its recce pod under the fuselage and its attractive red and white markings on both engine intakes and tail, October 1987.

was re-numbered No 41, the unit taking its Spitfire F XXIs south soon afterwards. In August 1947, the Squadron was nominated as No 12 Group's instrument flying training unit and re-equipped with Oxfords and Harvards. Ten months later, good sense prevailed and No 41 was re-designated a fighter squadron and received twin-engined Hornets. A change to Meteors followed in January 1951 and Hunter F 5s in August 1955, the latter being flown until disbandment on 31 January 1958.

The following day No 141 Squadron, flying Javelin all-weather fighters from Coltishall, was renumbered No 41, and for the next six years the unit's hefty 'deltas' were a common sight over East Anglia. Disbandment came again on 6 December 1963, and it was almost two years, on 1 September 1965, before No 41 Squadron reformed, this time as a Bloodhound surface-to-air missile unit at West Raynham. Deployment changes brought disbandment yet again on 18 September 1970, but eighteen months later, on 1 April 1972, the Squadron reformed at Coningsby for fighter-reconnaissance/ground attack duties in No 38 Group, equipped with Phantoms.

In August 1976, an element of the Squadron was formed at Coltishall to work up on the Jaguar, being declared operational on 31 March 1977 when the Phantom element disbanded. The Squadron headquarters moved to Coltishall the following day and is still there, the only dedicated fighter-reconnaissance unit based in the United Kingdom. In 1988, the Squadron still flies Jaguars, but conversion to Tornados is believed imminent.

Standard

Granted by HRH King George VI and promulgated on 27 March 1952. Presented by Air Marshal Sir Theodore McEvoy KCB CBE at Biggin Hill on 14 July 1957. Sir Theodore served on the Squadron as a Flight Commander.

A new Standard was presented by Air Chief Marshal Sir Peter Harding KCB CBIM FRAeS, Air Officer Commanding-in-Chief, Strike Command, at Coltishall on 5 December 1985.

Battle Honours

*Western Front 1916-1918
*Somme 1916
Arras

*Cambrai 1917
Somme 1918
Lys
*Amiens
*Battle of Britain 1940
Home Defence 1940-1944
*Fortress Europe 1940-1944
*Dieppe
*France & Germany 1944-1945
Arnhem
Walcheren
*Denotes Honours emblazoned on Standard

Affiliation

No 253 Squadron — linked as 41/253 Sqn from February 1949 to April 1955 when 253 was reformed.

Aircraft insignia and markings

FE 8s carried no unit markings, but at one stage featured large identification numerals on each side of the gunner's cupola and across the centre section of the upper mainplane. DH 5s had a vertical white bar painted on each side of the fuselage roundel, and this unit identification was also used on SE 5As until March 1918 when it was changed to two bars aft of the roundel.

Soon after reforming in the 1920s, the Squadron's aircraft started appearing with a broad red stripe along the sides of the fuselage and across the span of the upper mainplane between the roundels. Versions of this basic Squadron marking were used on Siskins, Bulldogs, Demons and Furies, the Demons also carrying the Cross of Lorraine on the fin. Camouflaged Spitfires introduced the code letters 'PN', which had been allotted following the Munich Crisis of 1938. The code was changed to 'EB' in September 1939 and appeared on all the Spitfire variants used during the war.

In 1947, an attempt was made to re-introduce the pre-war red stripe, but this was frowned upon by 'higher authority' and the 'EB' code survived until the end of the Hornet era in January 1951. During 1950, however, a miniature version of the red stripe on either side of a white diamond enclosing the double-armed cross emblem had appeared on the fins of Hornets, and the red stripe was painted boldly on Meteors in the form of bars flanking the fuselage roundel. To make them stand out better, thin white strips were added to the top and bottom of the bars, and these were accentuated on the Squadron's Hunters, which had the marking on either side of a white outlined red cross on the nose. The same marking was used on Javelin fins, on the nose of Phantoms and the engine intakes of the current Jaguars. The Phantoms and Jaguars also carried the cross of Lorraine on the fin, outlined in white and surmounted by a gold crown and the Roman numerals 'XLI'.

No 42 Squadron

Badge

On a terrestrial globe, a figure of Perseus — approved by HRH King George VI in December 1938. Perseus was used as the centrepiece because of his legendary ability to achieve what he set out to do, and because the Squadron was equipped with Perseus-engined aircraft when the badge was being designed.

Motto

Fortiter in re — 'Bravely into action'

History

There is doubt over the actual formation date of No 42 Squadron, but no controversy over the use of a nucleus provided by No 19 Squadron, and that the unit was at Filton in April 1916 training for Western Front operations on corps-reconnaissance duties. Equipped with BE 2Cs, the Squadron arrived in France on 8 August to fly tactical recce and artillery spotting sorties. RE 8s replaced the old BEs during April 1917, and were taken to Italy in November to help stabilize the situation in the north of the country following Italian reverses on the Austrian front.

The Squadron was back in France in March 1918 just before the start of the German offensive on the 21st, and were thrown into battle as ground strafers, a most unsuitable role for the staid RE 8. Following the Armistice, the Squadron remained in France until February 1919 when it returned to the United Kingdom as a cadre and was disbanded at Netheravon on 26 June.

No 42 reformed on 14 December 1936 at Donibristle from 'B' Flight of No 22 Squadron. Equipped with the lumbering Vildebeest, the Squadron was one of only two torpedo strike units in the United Kingdom. A very nomadic existence followed until the Torpedo Bomber Wing settled on the brand new airfield at Thorney Island in March 1938, and remained there until moving to its war station of Bircham Newton on 12 August 1939.

North Sea patrols over coastal shipping lanes were the main occupation until re-equipped with Beauforts

No 42 Squadron entered the Second World War with biplanes — Vildebeeste torpedo bombers at Bircham Newton (RAF Bircham Newton).

in April 1940, the Squadron then enduring two years of intensive and extremely dangerous anti-shipping and mine-laying operations from United Kingdom bases. Leaving for the Far East in June 1942, the Squadron was delayed in the Middle East where its new Mk IIs were taken over by No 39 Squadron and the crews attached to No 47 Squadron for operations against Rommel's supply ships. Re-equipped with old Beaufort 1s, the Squadron aircrew finally arrived in Ceylon during December, but converted to Blenheim Vs in India during the following March for bombing operations over Burma.

Withdrawn in August, the Squadron was converted to Hurricanes in October and resumed operations as a ground attack unit in December. Intensive close-support work occupied the next 18 months, some of the time spent at Imphal completely surrounded by Japanese forces, and within a mile or two of their targets. The Squadron was disbanded on 30 June but

the 'number plate' was resurrected the following day by the re-designation of No 146 Squadron as No 42. Thunderbolts were flown for the remainder of the war, the Squadron being disbanded at Meiktala, Burma, on 30 December 1945.

The Squadron was reformed again on 1 October 1946 at Thorney Island by re-numbering No 254 Squadron, which was flying Beaufighters as part of the one remaining Strike Wing in Coastal Command. The intention was to re-equip with Brigand torpedo-fighters, but when this plan was cancelled the Wing was disbanded on 15 October 1947. No 42 Squadron was reformed, again in Coastal Command, at St Eval on 28 June 1952 using a nucleus provided by No 220 Squadron. Equipped with Shackleton maritime reconnaissance aircraft, the Squadron spent many hours on air-sea rescue standby, but also took part in 'colonial policing' in Aden, trooping, and the Beira Blockade, before converting to Nimrods in April 1971.

Mainstay of the Squadron for many years, a couple of Shackleton MR 2s over Trevose Head, North Cornwall.

Eleven years later the Squadron despatched two aircraft to the Ascension Islands within 24 hours of receiving the order to take part in the first phase of Operation 'Corporate', the recovery of the Falkland Islands from the Argentinians. Several operational sorties were flown deep into the South Atlantic in support of Royal Navy ships and submarines during April-May 1982 before Nimrod MR 2s from the Kinloss Wing took over the task.

No 42 Squadron still flies this fine maritime reconnaissance aircraft from St Mawgan, having received updated Nimrod MR 2s in 1983.

Standard
Granted by HRH Queen Elizabeth II and promulgated on 4 October 1961. Presented by Her Majesty at St Mawgan on 14 July 1966.

Battle Honours
*Western Front 1916-1918
*Italian Front & Adriatic 1917-1918
Somme 1916
Arras 1917
Ypres 1917
Lys
*Channel & North Sea 1939-1942
*Biscay 1940
*Baltic 1941
Fortress Europe 1941
Pacific 1943-1945
*Eastern Waters 1943
*Arakan 1943-1944
*Manipur 1944
Burma 1944-1945
South Atlantic 1982

*Denotes Honours emblazoned on Standard

Affiliations
No 141 Squadron — linked as No 141/42 Sqn from February 1949 until reformed in June 1952.

Borough of Bodmin, Cornwall — under the Municipal Liaison Scheme 1959.

Aircraft insignia and markings
On the Western Front, the BE 2s and RE 8s of No 42 Squadron carried a white square on the fuselage sides aft of the roundel. After reformation in 1936, the Vildebeests were initially identifiable only by wheel spat 'flashes', coloured according to Flight, but after the Munich Crisis the Squadron code 'QD' was allotted and probably carried. At the outbreak of war, the code changed to 'AW', painted on Vildebeests, Beauforts, Blenheims, Hurricanes and Thunderbolts. This was achieved on the latter by obliterating the 'NA' code of No 146 Squadron with black paint and replacing it with 'AW' in white.

When No 254 Squadron became No 42 in October 1946, the 'QM' codes of the former were retained, but Shackletons used the single Group/Squadron letter 'A' on the rear fuselage in grey with an individual code on the nose. In 1956, the unit code letter was replaced by the Squadron number, a red '42' outlined in white on the rear fuselage, the aircraft letter being retained on the nose.

In the early 1960s, the 'Perseus' emblem appeared in red on a white disc on the fins, but towards the end of the Shackleton's career, unit identification was deleted leaving just the aircraft individual letter on the nose and 'Royal Air Force' in white on the rear fuselage. Apart from special markings for particular occasions, the Nimrods have always been devoid of unit markings except for a St Mawgan Station badge.

Nimrod MR 2 XV242 *with Newquay, Cornwall, as a backdrop* (M. Turner).

No 43 Squadron

Badge

A black gamecock — approved by HRH King Edward VIII in July 1936. The official badge was developed from one produced in 1926 when the Squadron was equipped with the Gloster Gamecock.

Motto

Gloria finis — 'Glory is the end' (the motto of the Brook family, Sqn Ldr A.F. Brook being the Commanding Officer from July 1925 to January 1928).

History

Formed at Stirling as No 43 Squadron, RFC, on 15 April 1916 from a nucleus provided by 19 Reserve Squadron, the unit took nearly a year to reach the Western Front in France, by which time their 1½-Strutters were outclassed and really only suitable for reconnaissance work. However, they took part in one of the first strafing attacks, machine-gunning German troops concentrated on the Scarpe in May 1917.

Re-equipment with the formidable Camel was completed in September, and No 43 then began to establish an enviable reputation, two of its pilots, Captain J.L. Trollope on 24 March and Captain H.W.

Woollett on 12 April 1918, excelling by scoring six confirmed victories in a day. It became No 43 Squadron, RAF, on 1 April 1918, and in September was the first to become operational on the Sopwith Snipe. The Armistice meant a move into Germany for a few months, but No 43 Squadron was disbanded on 31 December 1919.

Reformed at Henlow during 1925, No 43 was again equipped with Snipes and became part of the United Kingdom fighter defences. Within a year, Gamecocks were received, followed by Siskins in June 1928 and the elegant Fury during May 1931. Well established at Tangmere by the 1930s, a healthy rivalry with No 1 Squadron developed and lasted for a decade during which No 43 gained an outstanding reputation for formation aerobatics at the annual Hendon displays.

Biplane days ended in February 1939 following complete re-equipment with Hurricanes, the first of which had arrived during November 1938. Moving north soon after the outbreak of war, the Squadron was back at Tangmere in time for the Battle of Britain. After two months of gruelling combat, No 43 was 'rested' back in the north and did not return south until June 1942 when it started 'sweeps' over France, and even tried night intruder work. Five months later, the Squadron went overseas, by sea to Gibraltar, before flying to North Africa. Early in 1943, Spitfire VCs replaced the trusty Hurricanes, and the unit played a leading part in the air battles over Sicily and Italy. Re-equipped with Spitfire IXs early in 1944, the Squadron moved into Austria at the end of the war and was subsequently disbanded in Italy on 16 May 1947.

Reformation came at Tangmere on 11 February 1949 by re-numbering No 266 Squadron, then flying Meteor 4s. The more potent Mk 8 arrived in September 1950, and in November the Squadron

A Fury biplane in close formation during the halcyon days of the 1930s. The distinctive arrangement of No 43 Squadron's checks is seen to advantage (RAF Museum P3808).

Phantom FG 1 XV572 *in the attractive markings employed by No 43 Squadron during the 1970s* (A.S. Thomas).

reluctantly moved north to Leuchars where the first Hunters to enter Squadron service were received in August 1954. Hunter 4s followed in March 1956, and Mk 6s in December of the same year, replaced in 1960 by the specialized ground attack version, the Hunter FGA 9. In June 1961, the Squadron went overseas again, first to Cyprus and then, in March 1963, to Aden where it formed an element of the Strike Wing and provided air support for the Army against various rebel factions until disbanded on 14 October 1967.

Re-born at Leuchars on 1 September 1969, No 43 Squadron was supplied with the first Phantom FG 1 all-weather fighters received by the RAF. Seventeen years later the Squadron still flies this aircraft as part of the United Kingdom air defence organization tasked with long-range interception of unidentified aircraft approaching the country from northern latitudes — a front-line job!

Standard

Granted by HRH King George VI and promulgated on 27 March 1952. Presented by HRH Elizabeth II at Leuchars on 4 June 1957, the first time that an RAF Squadron received its Standard from the hands of the reigning monarch.

The Standard was temporarily laid up in the RAF College, Cranwell, between November 1967 and September 1969 while the Squadron was disbanded.

Battle Honours

*Western Front 1917-1918
Arras
*Ypres 1917
Cambrai 1917
*Somme 1918
Lys
Amiens
*Dunkirk
*Battle of Britain 1940

Home Defence 1940-1942
Fortress Europe 1942
Dieppe
*North Africa 1942-1943
Sicily 1943
Salerno
Italy 1943-1945
*Anzio & Nettuno
Gustav Line
*France & Germany 1944

*Denotes Honours emblazoned on Standard

Mascot

A bantam cock — accepted by the Squadron at Tangmere in August 1949 and named 'Chequers', the cock was later joined by a number of hens, and replacement 'fighting cocks' were provided at intervals for several years.

Affiliations

City of Chichester — under the municipal liaison scheme of April 1939; despite lengthy absences from the area, the association was maintained after the war.

'China British' — following a contribution from British residents in Shanghai nominally sufficient to 'purchase' a squadron of fighter aircraft, No 43 was chosen by the Air Ministry in 1941 to be named the 'China British Squadron'. The unit objected on the grounds that they were already known as 'the Fighting Cocks', so the China connection was re-allocated to No 247 Squadron.

No 17 Squadron — linked as No 43/17 Sqn in March 1951 until 1955 when the scheme was dropped.

Nicknames

'The Fighting Cocks' — derived from the Squadron badge (and used for the Hunter formation team in the 1950s).

Phantom FG 1 XV572 on display at Fairford in July 1987. The miniaturized markings show up well against the light grey 'low-visibility' paint scheme (J. Bartholomew).

'Gamecocks' — an alternative to 'Fighting Cocks'.

'The Chicken Farmers' — derogatory name used by No 1 Squadron whilst both squadrons were at Tangmere.

'Mother Meyrick's Own' — after the notorious '43 Club' in pre-1939 Soho.

Aircraft insignia and markings

During the First World War, the Squadron was assigned a white triangle, painted on the fuselage sides aft of the roundel on 1½-strutters and Camels until March 1918, when it was replaced by two sloping white bars, one on each side of the roundel.

Markings were not carried after the war until black and white checks were introduced on silver painted Gamecocks in 1926. The chequers were painted across the span of the upper wing and on the fuselage sides. The same marking was used on all subsequent aircraft until the Munich Crisis of 1938, when camouflage was hastily introduced and the code letters 'NQ' were allocated to No 43. In September 1939, the Squadron code changed to 'FT', which was used throughout the war together with an individual aircraft letter.

Miniature black and white checks were painted across the fins of the Squadron's Spitfires during 1946-47, but when the unit reformed with Meteors, the code 'SW' was used. In 1951, code letters were dropped and the famous checks re-appeared on each side of the fuselage roundel on Meteor 8s, and subsequently on Hunters. A representation of a 'fighting cock', complete with boxing gloves, appeared on Hunter 4s, but when the checks were moved to the nose of the aircraft, the cockerel insignia became more like the Squadron badge and was superimposed on a white disc. When aircraft were 'pooled' in the Aden Strike Wing, No 43's checks were painted on one side of the roundel and No 208 Squadron's markings on the other — the cockerel was deleted.

Reformed with Phantoms, the Squadron painted the checks on the sides of the engine intakes on each side of the roundel, but it was two years before the 'fighting cock' re-appeared, this time on the fin. With the introduction of 'low-visibility' grey camouflage in the 1980s, the markings were toned down, the

checks being miniaturized and applied to the top of the fin, the cockerel losing its white background but remaining on the fin with the individual aircraft letter. In 1987, two-letter codes were introduced by adding the suffix 'A', to more easily distinguish the Squadron's aircraft from other Phantoms at Leuchars.

No 45 Squadron

Badge

A winged camel — approved by HRH King Edward VIII in October 1936. The badge commemorates the aircraft used for a major portion of the First World War and the Squadron's long association with the Middle East. It developed from an unofficial badge used during the early 1920s on aircraft on the Cairo-Baghdad air mail route.

Motto

Per ardua surgo — 'Through difficulties I arise'

History

Until recently, No 45 Squadron had spent virtually all its varied career overseas. Formed at Gosport on 1 March 1916, it moved to France in October after the usual working up period with its Sopwith 1½-strutters. Already outclassed as scouts, 'Strutter' casualties were heavy, but it was April 1917 before a few Nieuport 12s supplemented them, and July when relief came in the form of the agile Camel.

The Squadron was just getting established with

Two Hornets fly over the Singapore docks in the 1950s. The 'winged camel' markings can be seen on nose and tail — the style of code presentation is distinctive too! (M. Retallack).

Hunter FGA 9 of No 45 Squadron on detachment at Kinloss in February 1973 when the unit was acting as an 'OTU'.

their Camels when it was transferred in December to the Austro-Italian front to start six months of hectic operations. Escorts, offensive patrols and ground attack sorties were flown almost non-stop, but with the Italian front stabilized, the Squadron returned to France during September 1918 and flew with the independent Air Force as a long-range bomber escort unit. Re-equipment with special Snipes was intended, but only two had been received by the Armistice and the Squadron remained in France with Camels until February 1919. It was then reduced to cadre and returned to the United Kingdom for disbandment on 31 December that same year.

No 45 Squadron reformed in Egypt on 1 April 1921, initially using a few DH 9As on loan from No 47 Squadron. In November, a number of Vimys were received, replaced by Vernon bomber-transports in March 1922. These extraordinarily versatile, albeit lumbering, aircraft were taken to Hinaidi, Iraq, in April, and for the next five years played a very active part in the 'policing' of the area by transporting troops and supplies into the hinterland and then bombing rebel positions. During quieter periods they flew the Cairo-Baghdad air mail route and operated as air ambulances. During 1926 it was decided to reduce the forces in Iraq, and on 1 November the unit was cut to Flight strength before returning to Egypt and being absorbed by No 47 Squadron on 17 January 1927.

The Squadron reformed again on 25 April 1927 as a bomber unit with DH 9As, still in Egypt, though it was not long before a detachment was operational at Ramleh, Palestine, on 'policing' duties. General purpose Fairey IIIFs re-equipped the Squadron in September 1929 and remained in use for six years. The Abyssinian crisis caused considerable upheaval, 'D' Flight being formed with Harts in September 1935 and 'B' Flight going to Kenya the same month. In November, Vincents started to replace the IIIFs of 'A' and 'C' Flight, while those of 'B' Flight were exchanged for Gordons. Rationalization began in January 1936 when 'D' Flight joined No 6 Squadron, and continued in December when the 'B' Flight Gordons became No 223 Squadron. This left No 45 Squadron flying Vincents in Egypt and Palestine, but they did not stay long, Wellesleys arriving in November 1937.

Re-equipment with Blenheim in June 1939 heralded the end of the 'col pol' role, the Squadron moving into the Western Desert in August and starting border patrols when war was declared. All was quiet until 10 June 1940, when the Italians joined the German side and the Squadron started bombing raids which continued spasmodically for the next 18 months. Sent to Burma, the Squadron arrived in February 1942 just as British forces withdrew from the country and conditions became chaotic. Regrouping in India took some time, but the Squadron converted to Vengeance dive-bombers in December and finally resumed operations in June 1943. After six months, the unit was withdrawn for conversion to Mosquito fighter-bombers, and it was October 1944 before the Squadron was back in the front line. It was not a happy period, with frequent grounding resulting from problems with the Mosquitos' all-wood construction which proved unsuitable for tropical conditions.

After the Japanese surrender, the Squadron retired to India, nominally as an anti-shipping strike unit, but actually doing very little. In May 1946, the Squadron moved to Ceylon, and in November received Beaufighter Xs, this sturdy aircraft being used for ground attack on Communist insurgents during the early stages of Operation 'Firedog', flying from its detachment base of Kuala Lumpur. In June 1949, the whole Squadron moved to Malaya and operations intensified despite the conversion to Brigand light bombers which started in October. The Brigand suffered structural problems, but it was January 1952 before Hornets arrived to continue the job of flushing out guerrillas.

In May 1955, the Squadron re-equipped with Vampires prior to the delivery of Venoms in October. 'Firedog' operations continued, though the pressure slackened, and in November 1957 a 'new' No 45 Squadron, equipped with Canberra B 2 light bombers, flew out to Singapore and was engaged in the 'mopping-up' operations. 'Firedog' finally came to an end in 1960, but No 45 Squadron remained on Singapore Island for another ten years before disbandment came on 13 January 1970.

Re-birth at West Raynham on 1 August 1972 was something of a surprise, for it was as a Hunter ground attack unit tasked with the job of providing post-Tactical Weapon Unit training for pilots destined for Jaguar squadrons. Joined by No 58 Squadron in 1973, the unit performed valiantly until the Jaguar force was well established. Then it was disbanded on 4 June 1976.

Strong rumours that No 45 Squadron was to be a third Binbrook-based Lightning squadron proved incorrect, but on 1 December 1983 the Tornado Tactical Weapons Unit at Honington assumed the number as its 'shadow' designation. In the event of hostilities, the unit would join the front line as a fully-fledged Tornado squadron using the instructional staff of the TWCU as crews, and training as such is carried out during exercises.

Standard

Granted by HRH King George VI and promulgated on 9 September 1943. Presented by Air Marshal F.J. Fressanges CB, Commander-in-Chief, Far East Air Force, at Tengah on 9 February 1955. Laid up in 1976.

Battle Honours

*Western Front 1916-1917
Somme 1916
Ypres 1917
*Italian Front & Adriatic 1917-1918
Piave
*Independent Force & Germany 1918
Kurdistan 1922-1924
Iraq 1923-1925
*Egypt & Libya 1940-1942
*East Africa 1940
Syria 1941
*Burma 1942
*Arakan 1943-1944
*Burma 1944-1945

*Denotes Honours emblazoned on Standard

Affiliation

No 33 Squadron — linked as No 45/33 Sqn from April 1955 until October 1955.

Nickname

'Flying Camels' — derived from the Squadron badge.

A Tornado GR 1 of the Weapons Conversion Unit carrying 'shadow' No 45 Squadron markings on the nose and the TWCU badge on the tail (RAF Honington).

Aircraft insignia and markings

Some 1½-strutters had a white band around the fuselage aft of the roundel as a locally inspired identity marking, but the first official Squadron insignia was a white dumb-bell painted on the top and sides of the rear fuselage of the unit's Camels. Individual aircraft letters were also carried, sometimes applied with considerable artistic licence.

The markings on post-war Vimys were confined to a red individual letter on the nose. This was deleted on Vernons, but they featured the first use of the 'camel' symbol, in black on a pennant or shield on the nose. Most of the aircraft were also individually named. Many DH 9As had coloured fins on which was superimposed an individual number which was repeated on the top of the upper wing centre section.

When Fairey IIIFs re-equipped the Squadron, they were initially unmarked, but by the early 1930s had the 'camel' badge on the tail in a white disc flanked by a diagonal red-blue stripe. Vincents carried similar markings, but Wellesleys introduced the Squadron number and individual aircraft letter, painted in light grey on either side of the fuselage roundel. Later, the 'camel' badge reappeared on the fin within a white grenade.

After the Munich Crisis, the Squadron number was deleted and the code letters 'DD' were allocated, but it is not certain that they were carried. Blenheim replacements were apparently unmarked until September 1939, when the Squadron was allotted the new code 'OB', which appeared aft of the fuselage roundel until the unit moved to the Far East. Only individual code letters were used on Blenheim IVs, but, perhaps surprisingly, the 'OB' code re-appeared on the Vengeance, now painted forward of the SEAC-type fuselage roundels with an individual letter aft.

Similar markings were applied to Mosquitos, Beaufighters, Brigands and Hornets, the 'Flying Camel' badge being reinstated on the nose of some of the latter aircraft. Towards the end of the Hornet's time with the Squadron, the codes were removed and replaced by red rectangles on which was superimposed a version of the white dumb-bell. The same marking flanked the boom roundels on Vampires and Venoms, the latter also having red tip-tanks on which was painted a white arrow and a 'Flying Camel' badge. A large individual aircraft letter adorned the rudders. Canberras were in standard 'bomber' colours, but featured a blue camel with red wings in a white disc on the fin, while 38 Group Hunters carried a similar marking on the nose, flanked by white-edged blue bars on which were superimposed red diamonds — a very pleasing scheme.

The same markings reappeared on the nose of the TWCU Tornados when No 45 Squadron became its

'shadow' number, with the original badge of the unit, an upright sword and two diagonal arrows piercing a golden crown, on the fin together with the aircraft's 'last three' as an individual identification.

No 47 Squadron

Badge

In front of a fountain, a demoiselle crane's head erased — approved by HRH King George VI in November 1938. The original unofficial badge had been a sun rising over a pyramid, but service in Russia and the Sudan inspired the use of the crane (found in both countries) which, when navigating, flies high like a bomber. The fountain commemorates the amphibious role when seaplanes were flown off the Nile.

Motto

Nili nomen roboris omen — 'The name of the Nile is an omen of our strength'. (An earlier unofficial motto was *Sans peur* — 'Without fear'.

History

No 47 Squadron, RFC, was formed at Beverley, Yorkshire, on 1 March 1916, ostensibly for the defence of Hull and East Yorkshire against Zeppelin attack, though its first six months were spent training pilots to fly using BE 2s, BE 12s and FK 3s. It was mobilized as a 'service' squadron in August and left Devonport aboard the transport *Menominee* bound for Salonika on 6 September for duty with Allied forces fighting the Bulgarians in Northern Greece. In common with most squadrons in the area, it had a mixed complement of aircraft, mainly BE 2C for reconnaissance, and BE 12s and a few Bristol Scouts for fighting.

During 1917 the Scouts were replaced by DH 2s, and both FK 8s and SE 5As supplemented earlier aircraft, some of which remained in service until April 1918, when the Fighter Flight transferred to No 150 Squadron and No 47 concentrated on bombing and reconnaissance using DH 9As and FK 8s. The Squa-

dron remained in Greece after the Armistice and in April 1919 was sent to South Russia to help General Denikin's White Russian forces in their ill-fated attempt to contain the Bolshevik armies. Equipped with Camels and DH 9s, it was re-designated 'A' Squadron RAF Mission on 7 October 1919.

On 1 February 1920, No 206 Squadron at Helwan, Egypt, was re-numbered No 47 Squadron to operate DH 9 day bombers. These were replaced by Liberty-powered DH 9As during 1921 when a detachment was formed at Khartoum to co-operate with ground forces in the Sudan. The Squadron made the first flight from Egypt to Nigeria during 1925, and in October 1927 the main body joined the detachment in the Sudan where their first Fairey IIIFs were received in December. From February 1929 onwards, some of the IIIFs were fitted with floats and operated off the Nile, as were the replacement Gordons which arrived in January 1933. These remained in service when three of the Squadron's Flights were re-equipped with Vincents in July 1936, and were not finally withdrawn until June 1939 when Wellesleys were received. Some of the Vincents also soldiered on, and it was July 1940 before the Squadron had the luxury of operating just one type of aircraft.

The Second World War affected the Squadron little until the Italians joined in on 10 June 1940, an event which signalled a bombing campaign which lasted until they capitulated in East Africa in May 1941. After a spell in Ethiopia, the Squadron returned to Egypt in December and was soon engaged in general reconnaissance work off the coast. In September 1942, the unit was joined by a detachment from No 42 Squadron, and they were introduced to the Beaufort and the torpedo-bomber role. Build-up was slow, some Wellesleys being retained until March 1943. In June, the very effective Beaufighter TF X was received and successes mounted, the Squadron roaming all over the Eastern Mediterranean on 'Armed Rovers'.

During March 1944, the Squadron transferred to India to form part of a Strike Wing, receiving Mosquito VIs in October. These aircraft suffered severe structural problems caused by the humidity, and Beaufighters returned in November for ground attack work in Burma. The problems largely solved, Mosquitos were back on strength in February 1945, and for the next six months the Squadron flew low-level interdiction, concentrating on Japanese rail and river traffic. A short respite followed the Japanese surrender in August before a detachment was sent to Java in support of Allied forces trying to restore order in the country. The Squadron mounted ground attack sorties against dissident gangs until the situation was brought under control.

The Squadron disbanded on 21 March 1946, but not for long. On 1 September, No 644 Squadron, an airborne support unit flying Halifaxes in Palestine, was re-numbered No 47. A month later, the Squadron flew to the United Kingdom and occupied itself on exercises with airborne forces until becoming the first Hastings Squadron during September 1948. After a hasty conversion, the Squadron joined the Berlin Airlift in November, making over 3,000 sorties, mainly carrying coal, before being withdrawn in May 1949 to start flying standard Transport Command scheduled routes. In March 1956, the Squadron resumed its pioneering role, becoming the first operational unit to fly the lumbering Beverley heavy-lift transport, and to despatch tracked vehicles and bulldozers by parachute.

Disbanded again on 31 October 1967, the Squadron was back on transport duties within months when it re-formed at Fairford on 25 February 1968 equipped with Hercules. In September 1971, the short hop to Lyneham was made and the unit remains part of the Transport Wing. No 47 is one of the two Hercules squadrons trained on tactical support, and also has a Special Forces element which was used to good effect during Operation 'Corporate', the recapture of the Falkland Islands, when the unit carried out the majority of the extended-range air-drop missions.

Standard

Granted by HRH King George VI and promulgated on 9 September 1943. Presented by Marshal of the

Left *Hastings C 1 TG518 of No 47 Squadron in the markings employed during the 'Berlin Airlift' of 1949.*

Right *Hercules C 1P XV187 of the Lyneham Transport Wing taking off from St Mawgan in August 1987 flown by a No 47 Squadron crew.*

Right *Beverley C 1 XB287 lands at Luqa in January 1965. It carries No 47 Squadron's 'crane' emblem on the fin and the Abingdon badge on the nose.*

Royal Air Force Sir John Slessor GCB DSO MC DL at Abingdon on 25 March 1955. The Standard was temporarily laid up in the RAF College, Cranwell, from October 1967 until February 1968.

A new Standard was presented by HRH The Princess Anne, Mrs Mark Phillips, GCVO in a dual ceremony with No 70 Squadron at Lyneham on 3 May 1984. Princess Anne is Honorary Air Commodore of Lyneham.

The old Standard was laid up in St Michael & All Angels Church, Lyneham, on 14 April 1985.

Battle Honours

*Macedonia 1916-1918
*East Africa 1940-1941
*Egypt & Libya 1942
*Mediterranean 1942-1943
*Burma 1945
South Atlantic 1982

*Denotes Honours emblazoned on Standard

Mascot

A lioness — named 'Belinda', and on strength in May 1930.

Aircraft insignia and markings

It is almost certain that no unit markings were carried during the First World War, whilst in Russia or during the early years in Egypt. During the latter years of the DH 9A era, however, Flight letters were painted on the sides of the engine cowlings together with an individual aircraft number in Roman characters. Later, individual letters were used and some aircraft carried checks on the fin in Flight colours. At one stage, the aircraft were also individually named.

The IIIFs were unmarked at first, but by 1930 had the unofficial badge, a pyramid silhouetted by the rising sun over an eagle, painted on the fin. Gordons appeared with the Squadron number in black on the forward fuselage, and an aircraft letter on the fin, but the Vincents were unadorned until the outbreak of war despite the allocation of code letters 'EW' during the Munich Crisis of 1938. In September 1939, the official code letters were changed to 'KU' and these were carried on both Wellesleys and Vincents whilst in East Africa. From January 1942, when with 201 Group, the aircraft only carried individual letters, but surprisingly the 'KU' code reappeared on Mosquito VIs at the end of the war.

Halifaxes and Hastings were unmarked apart from individual letters, but Beverleys carried a Transport Command fin diamond in green with the figures '47' superimposed in white. Later, the diamond was replaced by the Squadron emblem.

Hercules aircraft are on the strength of the Lyneham Wing and carry no unit markings.

No 51 Squadron

Badge

A goose volant — approved by HRH King George VI in December 1937. It was chosen as a play on the word 'Anson', the type of aircraft in service with the Squadron at the time the badge was being designed, as 'Anser' is the Latin word for goose, and it was felt that a heavy wild fowl was appropriate for a bomber squadron.

Motto

Swift and Sure

History

Formed at Thetford, Norfolk, on 15 May 1916 as a Home Defence unit equipped with BE 2 and BE 12 aircraft, No 51 used a variety of landing grounds in East Anglia. The Squadron flew anti-Zeppelin patrols for the rest of the First World War, and also provided night flying training for newly qualified pilots. A number of FE 2B two-seater pusher biplanes were received in June, and it is likely that the type was used

for all operational flying; the BEs, and from January 1918 the Avro 504Ks, were employed on training. In the closing weeks of the war, a few Sopwith Camels were on strength, and in May 1919 these were taken to Sutton's Farm where the Squadron disbanded on 13 June the same year.

The Squadron reformed on 5 March 1937 when 'B' Flight of No 58 Squadron was re-designated No 51 at Driffield. Virginias and Ansons were flown until February 1938 when Whitleys were received, and on the first night of the Second World War, 3-4 September 1939, three Squadron aircraft were over Germany on the first leaflet 'raid'. Real bombing started during May 1940, and continued for the next two years, interrupted only by two paratroop operations, one in Italy, the other in France — and both successful!

From May until October 1942, the Squadron was attached to Coastal Command for anti-submarine patrols over the Bay of Biscay. On return to 4 Group, Bomber Command, the unit received Halifaxes and resumed bombing operations in January 1943, flying as a 'main force' squadron for the remainder of the European War. During May 1945, the Squadron transferred to Transport Command and converted to Stirlings the following month for troop and freight flights to India. These continued until the end of the year when conversion to Yorks commenced, the Squadron returning to the Far East routes in August 1946.

The start of Operation 'Plainfare' on 1 July 1948 ended an ordered existence, No 51 finding itself operating from Wunsdorf flying supplies into Berlin. The Russian blockade broken, the Squadron reformed at Bassingbourn in September 1949 and recommenced long-range route flying during January 1950. Not for long, however, for with transport strength reductions in full swing, No 51 Squadron was disbanded on 30 October 1950.

Comet 2R XK659 of No 51 Squadron, distinguishable by its oddly shaped fairings and square windows — and by the caricature of a goose on the fin.

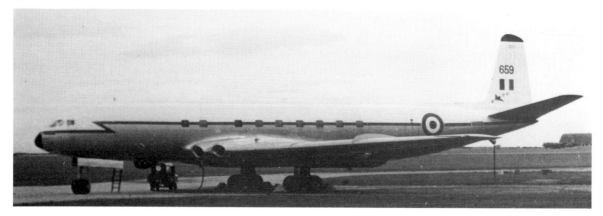

Canberra B 2 WJ640 in 1960 when No 51 Squadron was part of RAF Signals Command (Military Aircraft Photographs).

The Nimrod R 1 is a version unique to No 51 Squadron, but the unit confirms its ownership with its emblem, a goose (RAF Wyton (1 PRU) via No 51 Squadron).

The Squadron reformed on 21 August 1958 by redesignating No 192 Squadron, then at Watton operating as a Special Duties unit in Signals Command. Flying Comet 2Rs and various Canberras on surveillance duties, the Squadron transferred to Bomber Command on 13 March 1963 and moved to Wyton where it is still based. As Comet replacements, three Nimrod R 1s were brought on strength, the first being commissioned in May 1974 after a long gestation period. Following disposal of the Canberras during the late 1970s, the specially equipped Nimrods are solely responsible for carrying out the unit's tasking from 18 Group, Strike Command.

Standard
Granted by HRH Queen Elizabeth II and promulgated on 14 June 1967. Presented by Air Chief Marshal Sir William Kyle GCB CBE DSO DFC, Air Officer Commanding-in-Chief, Strike Command, at Wyton on 9 July 1968.

Battle Honours
*Home Defence 1916-1918
Channel & North Sea 1940-1943
*Norway 1940
*France & Low Countries 1940
*Fortress Europe 1940-1944
*Ruhr 1940-1945
German Ports 1940-1945
Invasion Ports 1940
Biscay Ports 1940-1944
Berlin 1940-1944
*Baltic 1940-1944
Biscay 1942
*Italy 1943
*France & Germany 1944-1945
Normandy 1944
Walcheren
Rhine
South Atlantic 1982

*Denotes Honours emblazoned on Standard

Affiliation
City of York — under the Municipal Liaison Scheme of April 1939.

Memorial
There is a memorial stone in the grounds of Selby Abbey.

Nickname
'York's Own' — an unofficial name used by the Press during the Second World War.

Aircraft insignia and markings
No official markings were authorized during the First World War but some aircraft carried a black 'crown' or 'coronet' on the sides of the rear fuselage. The Virginias and Ansons were unmarked except for

individual aircraft letters, but Whitleys followed the then current Bomber Command edict and carried the Squadron number forward of the fuselage roundel, and the individual letter aft.

During the 1938 Munich Crisis, the squadron number was removed and replaced by the code letters 'UT', changed to 'MH' following the declaration of war in September 1939. When 'C' Flight was formed, its aircraft used the code 'LK' until it was detached to form the nucleus of No 578 Squadron. The reformed 'C' Flight employed the unit code 'C6'.

On transfer to Transport Command, the code 'TB' was used on Stirlings and Yorks, later changing to 'MH' again. With Signals Command, a red 'goose' emblem was painted on the nose of Comets and the fins and wing-tip tanks of the Canberras, but was soon removed. It reappeared on the fins of the Comets, and has also graced the Nimrods at intervals, even following the introduction of the hemp camouflage scheme in 1982.

No 54 Squadron

Badge

Lion rampant semée de lys — approved by HRH King George VI. The badge combines features of the arms of France and Flanders, commemorating the Squadron's First World War battles on the Western Front.

Motto

Audax omnia perpeti — 'Boldness to endure anything'

History

No 54 Squadron was formed as a Home Defence unit on 15 May 1916 at Castle Bromwich, equipped with BE 2Cs, but a change of plan resulted in No 38 Squadron taking over the task and No 54 started training as a day fighter scout squadron, receiving Sopwith Pups in September. The Squadron moved to France in December, and was soon engaged in escorting bombers and attacking observation balloons, but had

to wait until April 1917 for the first successful air combat. Re-equipment with Camels in November 1917 heralded an additional role, that of ground attack, and it was this pugnacious little fighter which saw No 54 through the remainder of the war. In December 1918, the Camels were handed over to No 151 Squadron, and No 54 returned to the United Kingdom as a cadre, finally disbanding on 25 October 1919.

It was not reformed until 15 January 1930, initially with Siskins, the intended Bulldogs arriving in April. The Squadron settled down at Hornchurch, Gauntlets replacing the Bulldogs in September 1936. Gladiators were received in April 1937 and then, at last, Spitfires arrived in March 1939. Training on the new monoplanes was still in full swing when the Second World War was declared in September, but the Squadron was used for routine and largely uneventful patrolling of the Kent coast for the first eight months of the war.

In May-June 1940, air cover was provided over Dunkirk and the Squadron was heavily engaged during the Battle of Britain before being sent north for a rest. The next 18 months consisted of convoy patrols and training, but on 18 June 1942 the Squadron left Liverpool aboard *Stirling Castle* and arrived in Australia during August. In January 1943 it moved up to Darwin with Spitfire Vs and was soon in combat with the Japanese. The much improved Spitfire VIII was received in April 1944, but by this time the Japanese were in retreat and the Squadron found itself stuck in a backwater at Darwin. On 31 October 1945, the Squadron disbanded at Melbourne, most personnel having already embarked for the United Kingdom.

No 183 Squadron, flying Tempest IIs from Chilbolton, was re-numbered No 54 on 15 November 1945, and, after spending a short time training pilots destined for overseas squadrons, the unit converted to Vampire F 1s and joined the Odiham Wing. In

Meteor F 8 WL143 in typical No 54 Squadron markings of the mid-'fifties.

Above *Phantom FGR 2* XV482/K *at Kinloss on a cold December day in 1971. Well 'tanked-up', this No 54 Squadron aircraft also has the refuelling probe at the ready, unusual for a strike squadron.*

Right *A Jaguar GR 1A of No 54 Squadron in war configuration — a 1,200 litre centre line fuel tank, four 1000-lb bombs on tandem beam carriers, ALQ 101-10 jamming pod and Phinat chaff dispenser* (RAF Coltishall via No 54 Squadron).

April 1948, Vampire F 3s were received, and later in the year six of them made the first Atlantic crossing by jet aircraft. The Squadron remained on Vampires until April 1952 when Meteor 8s arrived, followed less than three years later by Hunter F 1s. This was the start of a long association with the Hunter which survived a role change to ground attack in March 1960 and a move from Fighter to Transport Command, the latter's 38 Group forming an Offensive Support Wing on 1 January 1962.

The Wing was frequently involved in overseas detachments, turning up at trouble spots all over the Middle East, an activity which continued under the control of Air Support Command from August 1967. On 1 September 1969, the Squadron disbanded, its aircraft and pilots forming the United Kingdom echelon of No 4 Squadron, a new No 54 forming at Coningsby with Phantom FGR 2s the same day to continue the 38 Group Offensive Support task.

Absorption by Strike Command in September 1972 had no effect on the task, nor did a change of aircraft to Jaguar in April 1974 and a take-over by No 1 Group in November 1983. Today, the Squadron still flies Jaguars as a ground attack/tactical reconnaissance unit of No 1 Group after 18 years at Coltishall.

Standard

Granted by HRH Queen Elizabeth II and promulgated on 15 October 1953. Presented by Major K.K. Horn MC RFC at Waterbeach on 24 May 1963. Major Horn was the Commanding Officer from August 1916 to December 1917.

A new Standard was presented by Air Chief Marshal Sir Peter Harding KCB CBIM FRAeS at Coltishall on 21 January 1988.

Battle Honours

Western Front 1916-1918
*Arras
*Ypres 1917
*Cambrai 1917
*Amiens
Home defence 1940-1942
France & Low Countries 1940
*Dunkirk
*Battle of Britain 1940
*Fortress Europe 1941
*Eastern Waters 1943-1945

*Denotes Honours emblazoned on Standard

Mascot

Lion — a toy lion named 'Pilot Officer Rochford' joined the Squadron in 1981.

Affiliation

Southend-on-Sea — No 54 Squadron was the first to fly from nearby Rochford aerodrome on fighter 'ops' during the Battle of Britain. The unit was affiliated with the town on 1 April 1971.

Nickname

'Black Knights' — the name used by the Hunter formation team flown by the Squadron in 1956.

Aircraft insignia and markings

Fighter units on the Western Front were allocated official markings soon after No 54 Squadron arrived, and the Pups were soon carrying a white horizontal bar along the upper longeron of the fuselage forward of the tailplane. On Camels this was changed to a white band forward of the roundels, and in March 1918 the marking became a white zigzag painted between the roundel and the tailplane.

When reformed in 1930, the Squadron marking was a yellow stripe painted across the upper mainplane between the roundels and along the rear fuselage sides. The Squadron requested, and received, permission to change the markings to a red band with oblique white bars across it, and this was introduced on Gauntlets from September 1936. The scheme was short-lived, however, for on Gladiators the fins were coloured to denote the Flight and status of the pilot, and also carried a white 'spearhead' enclosing the lion emblem.

Following the Munich Crisis, the code 'DL' was allotted but probably not used until Spitfires arrived in March 1939. In September, the code changed to 'KL', used until the Squadron went to Australia in June 1942. Then, surprisingly, the code reverted to the pre-war 'DL', usually painted in white forward of SEAC-type fuselage roundels.

On return to the United Kingdom, the Squadron adopted the 'HF' code formerly allotted to No 183 Squadron, and used it on Tempests and Vampire 1s, but not on Mk 3s which were unmarked apart from a Squadron badge on the nose until late 1948 when blue and yellow checks were added as flanking bars. Some aircraft also had blue tailplanes with a yellow stripe across them.

The checks were enlarged on Meteors and positioned on each side of the fuselage roundel, but returned to the nose on Hunters where they again flanked the unit badge; an individual letter graced the fin. Similar markings were applied to the nose of Phantoms, but on Jaguars the checks have been moved to the engine intakes and the lion badge

appears on the nose painted blue on a yellow shield, considerably toned down in recent years. The suffix 'G' was added to the aircraft letter in 1981 to indicate the Squadron.

No 55 Squadron

Badge

A cubit arm, the arm grasping a spear — approved by HRH King Edward VIII in May 1936. The badge was based on an unofficial emblem developed from remarks made by Wing Commander P.F.M. Fellowes, the Commander of 'Q' Force, while en route to Constantinople in 1920. He referred to No 55 Squadron as the 'spearpoint' of the force, and the aircraft as the 'haft of the spear'. An eagle was embodied in the emblem during 1923, but deleted in 1929.

Motto

Nil nos tremefacit — 'Nothing shakes us'. (Originally added to the unofficial emblem in 1921.)

History

No 55 Squadron, RFC, was formed at Castle Bromwich on 27 April 1916 from a nucleus provided by Nos 5 Reserve and 34 Squadrons. Initially it served as a training unit flying BEs, Avro 504s and FK 8s, but in January 1917 received DH 4 day bombers and mobilized for active service on the Western Front. The first to be equipped with this new aircraft, the Squadron went to France on 6 March and was soon heavily engaged in bombing and reconnaissance work, attacking enemy airfields and lines of communication.

In June 1918, the Squadron joined Trenchard's Independent Force for strategic bombing raids on German cities, continuing this activity until the Armistice. No 55 then undertook mail carrying until the unit returned to the United Kingdom in December, was reduced to cadre in January 1919 and a year later, on 22 January 1920, was disbanded.

On 1 February 1920, No 142 Squadron, at Suez with DH 9s, was re-numbered No 55. DH 9As

A Wapiti IIA of 'C' Flight, No 55 Squadron, awaits its crew 'somewhere in Mesopotamia' (via M.W. Payne).

started arriving in June and both types went aboard HMS *Ark Royal* in July for transport to Turkey as part of 'Q' Force, intended to give support to the Army in the defence of Constantinople and the Dardenelles against Turkish nationalists. After almost two months in Turkey, No 55 moved to Iraq and formed part of the Mesopotamian Wing engaged on 'policing' duties. For the next 19 years, the Squadron was in action intermittently against dissident tribesmen and foreign insurgents, the faithful 'Ninaks' being replaced by the equally reliable Wapiti in February 1930. Seven years later, the Vincent general-purpose aircraft took over and remained until the first Blenheims arrived in March 1939.

As war in Europe became inevitable, No 55 Squadron took its Blenheims to Egypt for shipping patrols over the Gulf of Suez, and when Italy entered the conflict on the German side in June 1940, bombing raids were made on targets in Libya. For a period in 1941, No 55 was the only day bomber squadron in the Western Desert, but transferred to anti-shipping sweeps in September until withdrawn in March 1942 for conversion to Baltimores. With these aircraft the Squadron resumed bombing, following the Eighth Army through Libya, Tunisia and into Italy. Bostons were received during October 1944, and a year later the Squadron moved into Greece where Mosquito fighter-bombers were received shortly before disbandment at Hassani on 1 November 1945.

It was nearly 15 years before the Squadron was again reformed, this time at Honington on 1 September 1960 equipped with Victors as part of Bomber Command's 'V' Force. In May 1965, it became a tanker squadron for in-flight refuelling using converted Victor K 1s, until K 2s became available in July 1975. These aircraft were the only tankers in RAF service during Operation 'Corporate' of 1982, and performed magnificently, No 55, alongside its sister squadron No 57, refuelling Hercules, Harriers, Nimrods and, for the epic 'Black Buck' bombing sorties, Vulcans, during the recapture of the Falkland Islands. The compulsory retirement of some Victors has resulted in the disbandment of No 57 Squadron, but an enlarged No 55 continues to fly Victor K 2s from Marham as part of an air-refuelling force which now includes Hercules, VC 10s and Tristars.

Standard

Granted by HRH King George VI and promulgated on 9 September 1943. Presented by HRH The Princess Marina, Duchess of Kent, at Honington on 20 July 1962.

Battle Honours

*Western Front 1917-1918
Arras
*Ypres 1917
*Independent Force & Germany 1918
Iraq 1920
Kurdistan 1922-1924
Iraq 1928-1929
Kurdistan 1930-1931
Northern Kurdistan 1932
*Egypt & Libya 1940-1943
*El Alamein
*El Hamma
North Africa 1943
*Sicily 1943
Salerno
Italy 1943-1945
Gustav Line
*Gothic Line
South Atlantic 1982

*Denotes Honours emblazoned on Standard

Affiliation

No 44 Squadron — linked as 44/55 Sqn whilst inactive from February 1949 to July 1957.

Aircraft insignia and markings

In France during the First World War, No 55 Squadron was allocated a white triangle painted aft of the fuselage roundel until March 1918 when, in company with all day bomber units on the Western Front, the markings were removed for security reasons. Only individual aircraft letters were retained, together with coloured wheel discs, the latter an unusual feature.

Whilst in Turkey it is doubtful whether any unit markings were employed, but in Iraq the CO's DH 9A carried the numerals '55' on the engine cowling and a white-edged black diagonal band around the rear fuselage. The other aircraft carried their Flight letter, 'A', 'B' or 'C', on the cowling with Roman

Above *Victor K 1 of No 55 Squadron refuelling a Lightning F 6 of No 74 Squadron in the '70s (MoD PRB 36231).*

Left *In pristine 'hemp' camouflage, Victor K 2 XH672 displays the current 'washed-out' national and squadron markings.*

numerals to indicate their pilot's status in the Flight. By the mid-1920s, a chequered band, black squares alternating with the Flight colour, was painted around the rear fuselage and repeated on the radiator shutters.

Wapiti replacements continued the Flight letter/numeral combination, but the latter was Arabic in style and the unofficial Squadron emblem was painted in black on the fin. Later, a single-letter identification was used, but Vincents were apparently unmarked except for the official badge on the fin, as were Blenheims despite the allocation of the unit code 'GM' during the Munich Crisis of 1938.

During the Second World War, the Squadron used individual aircraft letters only, variously positioned fore and aft of the fuselage roundel. On Baltimores, these letters were often in Flight colours edged in white, and a white 'flash' with the Flight colour superimposed as a vertical stripe was sometimes painted above the fuselage serial. Replacement Bostons employed red aircraft letters.

Markings on Victor B 1As were muted, the aircraft carrying pale anti-flash serial numbers and national markings while over-all white, but in normal colours when low-level camouflage was introduced. The 'spear' symbol appeared on the fin above the national markings, initially in the same pale blue with a pale red outline, but on camouflaged aircraft in standard 'roundel' blue edged in white. The same marking was retained on tanker aircraft, but superimposed on a white disc, and has survived the change from dark green/dark sea grey to the hemp/light aircraft grey camouflage now current.

Above *Victor K 2 XH671 of No 55 Squadron in the attractive 'hemp' colours adopted in the mid-80s. The blue unit emblem is prominent on the fin.*

Right *Resplendent in current 'Firebird' markings is Phantom FGR 2 XV474 of No 56 Squadron. The checks on the RWR fairing are much more prominent than the miniaturized unit markings on the nose.*

Below *Phantom FGR 2 XV499 of 228 OCU carrying 'shadow' 64 Squadron markings on the tail — in August 1986.*

Above *Tornado F 3 ZE201 of 229 OCU carrying the unit markings on the tail and the red/white chevron of 'shadow' 65 Squadron in August 1987.*

Below *A Canberra TT 18 of No 100 Squadron in camouflaged top surfaces now being replaced by 'hemp' and target black/yellow undersides. The blue/gold checks and the 'skull and crossbones' emblem adorn the tail.*

Bottom *BAe VC 10 K 3 ZA150 of No 101 Squadron at St Mawgan in August 1987. The unit badge can just be seen on the fin together with the code letter 'J'.*

Above *Phantom FG 1 XT872 showing off No 111 Squadron's markings against the aircraft's low-visibility grey colour scheme.*

Right *Hawk T 1A XX337 of No 2 TWU Chivenor carrying 'shadow' 151 Squadron markings on the attractive light grey overall scheme.*

Below *RAF Sea Kings in the standard SAR yellow are a common sight, but less well known are the sea-grey-painted ones used in the Falklands by No 78 Squadron. XZ599 was the reserve aircraft when this photograph was taken during September 1984, and was actually being flown by No 202 Squadron.*

Top XV863 *of No 208 Squadron in the current subdued markings employed by the Buccaneer force whilst the modification programme is in full swing. The unit chevron markings on the nose are joined by the 'winged eye' emblem on the tail which also carried the aircraft's 'last three', because the Spey engine exhaust smoke blackens the rear fuselage and obscures the full serial.*

Above *The familiar green/grey camouflage of No 360 Squadron's Canberras is rapidly being replaced by the 'hemp' scheme, here depicted by T 17A WH646 in May 1987. The colourful unit 'fighter' bars and tail-mounted 'trident' are retained on the updated aircraft.*

Below *Just visible through a forest of warning flags on the nose of this Tornado GR 1 is the 'lightning flash' of No 617 Squadron's unit markings repeated across the top of the fin.*

No 56 Squadron

Badge

A phoenix — approved by HRH King Edward VIII in July 1936. The badge, which employs a phoenix to underline the Squadron's ability to re-appear intact regardless of the odds, was based on an unofficial emblem used since 1928.

Motto

Quid si coelum ruat — 'What if Heaven falls?'

History

Always associated with the SE 5 in knowledgeable aviation circles, No 56 Squadron, RFC, was formed at Gosport on 9 June 1916 from a nucleus supplied by No 28 Squadron, specifically to bring the new fighter scout into service. After work-up on the usual odd collection of aircraft, the Squadron received its first SE 5 at London Colney on 13 March 1917. Less than a month later, the unit was fully equipped and in France. It operated on the Western Front for the remainder of the war, except for two weeks in June

1917 when it returned to the United Kingdom to bolster up Home Defence forces following the first of the Gotha bomber raids on London. Captain Albert Ball was a founder member, but he was killed on 7 May, the award of his VC being announced shortly afterwards. He was not the only famous pilot on the unit, for Lieutenant A.P.F. Rhys David was on the strength, and in August Captain J.T.B. McCudden took over 'B' Flight, arriving with seven confirmed victories. Six months later he left — with a score of 57!

Though mainly engaged on offensive fighter patrols and defensive escort work, the Squadron also took part in the ground strafing of troops and transport which became such a feature of the set piece battles of the First World War. The war ended with the Squadron still flying SE 5As, and claiming 427 German aircraft. The unit remained in France until February 1919, when it returned to the United Kingdom and was disbanded on 22 January 1920.

On 1 February 1920, No 80 Squadron, flying Snipes at Aboukir, Egypt, was re-numbered No 56, but it was to be a short-lived existence, for the unit was officially disbanded again on 23 September 1922, just before the Chanak crisis erupted in Turkey. The remnants of the Squadron were hastily formed into a Flight and transported to Turkey where the Snipes were attached to No 208 Squadron. The pilots, however, considered themselves to be No 56 Squadron personnel until the unit disbanded on 22 August 1923, despite official reformation of the Squadron at Hawkinge on 1 November 1922. To increase the confusion, the home-based Squadron was also equipped with Snipes! These were replaced by Grebes in September 1924 at Biggin Hill, and three years later Siskin IIIAs were received. During November 1927,

When camouflaged Hurricanes joined the Squadron in 1938, they were intially unmarked except for the unit badge in the standard white 'spearhead' on the fin.

the Squadron moved to North Weald where it remained until October 1939, receiving Bulldogs in October 1932, Gauntlets in May 1936, Gladiators in July 1937 and Hurricanes during May 1938.

With the declaration of war in September 1939, No 56 flew defensive patrols until the Dunkirk evacuation when they provided fighter cover. The Squadron remained in the south of England throughout the Battle of Britain and flew Hurricanes until the first service deliveries of the Typhoon were made in September 1941. Unfortunately, the aircraft had been rushed into service and a series of problems prevented the Squadron becoming operational again until May 1942. Sweeps, 'Rhubarbs' and bomber escorts followed, but the aircraft was a disappointment as a fighter and its true worth only became apparent when fighter-bomber operations started in November 1943.

Rather surprisingly, the Squadron was re-equipped with Spitfire IXs in April 1944, but in June conversion to Tempests commenced and, operational again in July, the unit concentrated on anti-'Diver' (V1 flying bomb) patrols until September when it moved to the Continent for armed recce over Germany. Following the German capitulation, the Squadron formed part of the occupation forces until 31 March 1946 when it was re-numbered No 16 Squadron. The following day, No 124 Squadron at Bentwaters was re-numbered No 56, and for the next 8 years variants of the Meteor were flown by the unit. In February 1954, the first Swifts were received, but proved a complete failure as interceptor fighters and there was much relief when replacement Hunters arrived in May 1955.

Lightning F 1s followed in January 1961, and the Squadron moved to Akrotiri, Cyprus, six years later with the Mk 3 variant of the aircraft. With the run-down of British forces in the Eastern Mediterranean, No 56 returned to the United Kingdom during January 1975 and the following year received Lightning F 6s at Wattisham. In March 1976, a Phantom 'element' was formed at Coningsby, and after work-up moved to Wattisham and took over from the Lightning element at the end of June. The Squadron still flies Phantom FGR 2s from Wattisham, though it will doubtless convert to Tornado F 3s in the not too distant future.

Standard

Granted by HRH King George VI and promulgated on 9 September 1943. Presented by HRH The Princess Marina, Duchess of Kent, at Waterbeach on 27 April 1956.

A new standard was presented by Air Chief Marshal Sir John Rogers KCB CBE CBIM FRAeS at Wattisham on 23 October 1986.

The old Standard was laid up in St Clement Danes Church on 18 January 1987.

Battle Honours

*Western Front 1917-1918
Arras
*Ypres 1917
Cambrai 1917
*Somme 1918
Amiens
Hindenburg Line
France & Low Countries 1940
*Dunkirk
*Battle of Britain 1940
Fortress Europe 1942-1944
Dieppe
*France & Germany 1944-1945
*Normandy 1944
Home Defence 1942-1945
*Arnhem

*Denotes Honours emblazoned on Standard

Affiliations

'Punjab' — officially named the 'Punjab' Squadron in April 1941 following a £50,000 gift from the Indian State, nominally sufficient to 'purchase' a squadron of aircraft.

No 87 Squadron — linked as 56/87 Sqn from February 1949 until December 1951.

Nickname

'Firebirds' — name given to the nine-strong Lightning F 1 formation team active from 1963 to 1965 inclusive.

Aircraft insignia and markings

The Squadron was allocated a white dumb-bell unit marking soon after arriving in France, but only used it briefly, for in June 1917 a letter/numeral code was in vogue, and by the end of the year an 18 in wide band was being painted around the rear fuselage. In March 1918, the marking changed to two thin white bars sloping inwards towards the top in the same aft position, with the individual aircraft letter positioned immediately to the rear of the roundel.

In Egypt, the Snipes carried a thin white band around the fuselage just aft of the roundel, but when reformed in the United Kingdom colourful markings were adopted, No 56 using a bold red and white chequerboard on the fuselage sided forward of the roundel and across the span of the upper mainplane top surfaces. In various forms, this marking was retained on Grebes, Siskins, Gauntlets and Gladiators, but camouflaged Hurricanes were confined to a 'phoenix' motif superimposed on a white 'spearhead' painted on the fin.

After the Munich Crisis, the code 'LR' was adopted. This changed to 'US' in September 1939,

Meteor F 4 VT339 of No 56 Squadron at Cranwell in 1950.

Red and white checks on the RWR fairing and on either side of the 'Phoenix' badge on the nose confirm this Phantom FGR 2 as belonging to the 'Firebirds'.

used on Hurricanes, Typhoons, Spitfires and Tempests. For a time, the Squadron's Meteors retained No 124's 'ON' code but reverted to 'US' in 1947 and to the pre-war red and white checks in 1950. This was carried in the form of bars on each side of the fuselage roundel on the Meteor and Swift, but on the Hunter's nose flanking the 'phoenix' badge. The latter aircraft also had chequerboard wing-tips.

Early Lightnings had the standard checks on the nose on either side of the roundel, with the 'phoenix' moved to the fin, but when the Squadron became Fighter Command's official formation aerobatic team the paint scheme became more flamboyant. It was toned down a little on the F 3 variant, which had chequerboard fin and rudder, a red fuselage spine and a large red and white arrowhead on the nose until standard 'fighter' markings were re-imposed by 'higher authority' in 1966. The Lightning F 6s were similarly marked, but with an enlarged red and yellow 'phoenix' on the fin, Phantoms retaining the same scheme until toned-down grey camouflage was introduced. Then the nose markings were miniaturized, and the 'phoenix' moved from the tail and superimposed on the nose checks. Further adornment appeared in the form of red and white checks on the top section of the fin and rudder, all these markings being easily removable in times of tension or conflict.

No 60 Squadron

Badge

A markhor's head affrontée — approved by HRH King George VI in December 1937. Chosen to commemorate many years of service in North-West India, the markhor being a mountain goat frequenting the Khyber Pass. The animal's head had also been used on an unofficial badge designed in 1923. (The horns of a markhor were presented to the Squadron in 1964.)

Motto

Per ardua ad aethera tendo — 'I strive through difficulties to the sky'

The pre-war black stripe of No 60 Squadron re-appeared in 1948 on Spitfire F 18s in Malaya during Operation 'Firedog'. Three were painted around the nose separated by white.

History

No 60 Squadron, RFC, was formed at Gosport on 30 April 1916 using personnel posted from other service and reserve squadrons on the base. Twenty-five days later, the Squadron went to France equipped with variants of the Morane Scout. Heavy losses were suffered during the Battle of the Somme, and in August the unit was re-equipped with Nieuport Scouts and soon acquired a first-class reputation. After a rocky start, Captain W.A. Bishop not only won his spurs on the tiny Nieuport 17C-1, but also the VC for his solo attack on a German aerodrome on 2 June 1917 when he destroyed three Albatros Scouts in the air and claimed several 'probables' on the ground, returning unhurt in a badly damaged aircraft.

In July 1917, SE 5s were received and these were flown on fighter and ground attack duties for the rest of the war. The Squadron remained in France after the Armistice until February 1919, when it returned to the United Kingdom and was disbanded on 22 January 1920.

A few weeks later, on 1 April, No 97 Squadron, stationed at Lahore in India with twin-engined DH 10 bombers, was re-numbered No 60 Squadron. A move to Risalpur heralded action on the North-West Frontier and this continued spasmodically for the next 20 years. The more flexible DH 9A was received in April 1923 and soldiered on until July 1930 when Wapiti general-purpose aircraft arrived. These vener-

able biplanes were only completely replaced by Blenheim Is a week or two before the start of the Second World War, the new aircraft being used for coastal patrol by detached Flights based strategically around the country.

In February 1941, the Squadron moved into Burma, and during July a single Flight of Brewster Buffalo fighters was added to the strength for escort and airfield defence duties. The Buffaloes were passed to No 67 Squadron in October, and when the Japanese attacked in December 1941, the Squadron was solely equipped with Blenheims, most of which were on detachment in Malaya. They bombed Japanese shipping and captured airfields but were hopelessly outnumbered and, decimated, the Squadron was declared non-operational, the remaining personnel returning to India where the unit was reformed with Blenheim IVs on 1 March 1942.

Bombing attacks on Japanese targets in Burma continued until May 1943 when the Squadron was withdrawn for conversion to Hurricane fighter-bombers. Initially employed as escorts to Dakota transports, strafing started in December and continued until May 1945 when, again non-operational, the Squadron was awaiting re-equipment with Thunderbolts. These arrived in July, but work-up was still in progress when the Japanese surrendered. This did not mean peace, however, for in October the Thunderbolts went to Java and were soon in action against

Javelin XH877 *of No 60 Squadron over Borneo during 1967. In addition to the black and white stripe, the 'markhor' had made an appearance* (Military Aircraft Photographs).

Indonesian rebel forces. Relieved by the Netherlands Air Force the following autumn, No 60 Squadron returned to Singapore on 21 November and in January 1947 Spitfire XVIIIs replaced the mighty Thunderbolt. With Spitfires, the Squadron operated in the fighter-bomber role against Communist guerrillas in Malaya, this work continuing after Vampires arrived in December 1950 and until subsequent replacement by Venoms during April 1955.

With the guerrilla threat removed at last, No 60 Squadron transferred to the all-weather fighter role in October 1959, when Meteor NF 14s arrived at Tengah. Replacement Javelin FAW 9s followed in July 1961, and it was these aircraft which saw service during the Indonesian 'confrontation' of the 1960s. The Squadron disbanded at Tengah on 30 April 1968, but was reformed at Wildenrath on 3 February 1969 when RAF Germany's Communications Squadron was re-designated. Equipped with Pembroke light transports, the Squadron flew both passengers and freight around the Continent, aeromedical flights to the UK, and even occasionally performed SAR work. Despite many rumours of imminent replacement over the years, it was not until 1987 that Andovers supplanted the venerable Pembrokes in Germany.

Standard

Granted by HRH King George VI and promulgated on 9 September 1943. Presented by Air Chief Marshal Sir John Baker GBE KCB MC DFC at Tengah on 6 May 1955. Sir John was at one time a Squadron member.

The Standard was temporarily laid up in the RAF College, Cranwell, from April 1968 to February 1969.

A new Standard was presented by Air Chief Marshal Sir David Lee GBE CB at Wildenrath on 18 May 1984.

The old Standard was laid up in St Clement Danes Church on 9 December 1984.

Battle Honours

*Western Front 1916-1918
*Somme 1916
Arras
Somme 1918
*Hindenburg Line
Waziristan 1920-1925
Mohmand 1927
North West Frontier 1930-1931
Mohmand 1933
North West Frontier 1935-1939
*Burma 1941-1942
*Malaya 1941-1942
*Arakan 1942-1944
North Burma 1944
*Manipur 1944
*Burma 1944-1945

*Denotes Honours emblazoned on Standard

Re-equipped with Andovers in 1987, the Squadron quickly added its 'markhor head' markings to the fin (Military Aircraft Photographs).

Aircraft insignia and markings

Moranes and Nieuports did not carry unit markings and were identified by a simple individual code number painted aft of the fuselage roundel. SE 5s were allotted a white disc positioned on the top and sides of the fuselage immediately aft of the roundel, changed in March 1918 to two parallel white bars just forward of the tailplane.

The post-war DH 10s and early DH 9As were unmarked, but later had an individual aircraft letter painted in white on a black square immediately aft of the fuselage roundel. Wapitis were similarly adorned and also carried the Kohat black stripe down the length of the fuselage and a stylized badge on the rudder. These markings were later changed to two black bands around the rear fuselage and a Squadron badge in a circle on the fin. Individual aircraft letters were painted in black on the forward fuselage of these aircraft.

After the Munich Crisis, the code 'AD' was allotted but probably not carried until the arrival of the first Blenheims. Following the declaration of war in September 1939, the code was changed to 'MU' and this was painted on Blenheims, Hurricanes and Thunderbolts in light grey on camouflaged aircraft and black on silver machines. Spitfires had black and white concentric bands around the nose, and on Vampires these colours were incorporated into the official 'fighter' markings, black rectangles on each side of the boom roundel having a white 'lightning flash' across them. Venoms were similarly marked, the Mk 4s having the boom markings edged in white, and black tip-tanks emblazoned with a white 'lightning flash'. The rudders of these aircraft were also painted black, the individual code being superimposed in white.

Meteor NF 14s retained the standard rectangular bar markings, the CO's aircraft also having black and white bands across the fin which also carried the 'markhor' badge, and these bands were used on the fins of Javelins, the bar markings having been dropped. The Pembrokes, painted in standard 'Transport' colours were initially unmarked, but in recent years have carried the 'markhor' badge on the fin above the national markings. The current Andovers are similarly marked.

No 63 Squadron

Badge

A dexter arm in bend couped below elbow grasping in the hand a battle axe — approved by HRH King George VI in December 1938. The badge symbolized the act of leading into battle, in keeping with the motto.

Motto

Pone nos ad hostem — 'Follow us to the enemy'

History

Formed at Stirling on 5 July 1916, No 63 Squadron, RFC, was intended as a DH 4 day bomber unit for the Western Front, but just before departure for France in June 1917 the destination was changed to Mesopotamia. The Squadron arrived at Basra on 13 August, but most of the personnel were ill and immediately put in hospital, so it was some time before the unit could take over the Tigris front from No 30 Squadron as intended.

Equipped with RE 8s for army co-operation, but also flying a few DH 4s, Bristol Scouts and Spads, the Squadron was allocated to the 1st Indian Army Corps. It proved invaluable during the advance up the Tigris, an expedition which resulted in the capture of 4,000 Turks at Khan Baghddi in March 1918 and culminated in the surrender of the whole Turkish Army at Sharqat. No 63 Squadron, now equipped solely with RE 8s, remained in Mesopotamia after the Armistice for over a year, finally disbanding at Baghdad on 29 February 1920.

Reformed at Andover on 15 February 1937 from a nucleus provided by 'B' Flight of No 12 Squadron, No 63 used No 12's Hinds until re-equipped with Audax whilst awaiting delivery of the first Battle light bombers to enter squadron service. The Battles arrived in May 1937 and the Squadron played a large part in solving the early problems in the aircraft for No 2 Group, Bomber Command, before being redesignated a training unit on 17 March 1939. An Anson Flight was added, and on 2 September the Squadron transferred to No 6 (Training) Group, merging with No 52 Squadron during April 1940 to form No 12 Operational Training Unit at Benson.

The Squadron reformed on 15 June 1942 when a detachment of No 239 Squadron was re-designated No 63 at Gatwick. Equipped with Mustangs for tactical reconnaissance, the Squadron was employed on Army exercises until January 1943 when operational flying started. During March 1944, Hurricanes were received, replaced by Spitfires in May, which were used to spot for naval guns during the invasion of Normandy the following month. More naval gun spotting in November during the bombardment of Walcheren, Holland, completed the Squadron's task, and its aircraft were passed to 41 OTU before disbandment on 30 January 1945.

No 63 was resurrected on 1 September 1946 when a fighter squadron, No 164, was re-designated at Middle Wallop. Flying Spitfire XVIs, No 63 Squadron moved to Thorney Island during December 1947 and had the doubtful distinction of being the last operational Spitfire unit in Fighter Command, Meteor replacements not arriving until April 1948. Variants of the Meteor were flown on day fighter duties until January 1957 when Hunter 6s were received, these being handed over to No 56 Squadron when No 63 disbanded at the end of October 1958.

In 1963, No 63 Squadron became the 'shadow' number for the Day Fighter Combat School, Binbrook, the unit flying Hunter F 6s until disbanded in January 1966. The aircraft and instructors then joined 229 OCU at Chivenor, the 'shadow' number being retained for one of the low-level air defence units formed by the OCU in times of tension or war. This scheme survived a move to Brawdy in August 1974 when the OCU became the Tactical Weapons Unit; re-equipment with Hawks came in 1979 and a return to Chivenor during August 1980.

Currently, No 63 Squadron remains the 'shadow' number for one of the two Chivenor-based training squadrons of No 2 Tactical Weapons Unit flying Hawk T 1As equipped with Sidewinder missile mountings as well as the normal gun pods and SNEB rocket racks.

Standard

Not granted.

Meteor F 4 VT219 of No 63 Squadron in 1950 soon after the introduction of black and yellow checks (RAF Museum P19027).

Hunter F 6A XE608 of the Tactical Weapons Unit in No 63 Squadron 'shadow' markings (RAF St Mawgan).

Hawk T 1A XX331 of 2 Tactical Weapons Unit, Chivenor, in No 63 Squadron 'shadow' markings and air defence colours (British Aerospace plc (Kingston) 8702587).

Battle Honours

Not determined (only applicable when Standard granted).

Affiliation

Wolverhampton — under the Municipal Liaison Scheme of April 1939.

Aircraft insignia and markings

No 63 Squadron's aircraft almost certainly remained unmarked during the First World War and it is doubtful whether the Hinds and Audax used briefly early in 1937 carried unit insignia. The Battles used the current scheme of a Squadron number forward of the roundels with an individual aircraft letter aft. During the Munich Crisis period, the code letters 'NE' were allotted and used until March 1939 when the Squadron became a non-operational training unit and the code changed to 'ON'. It is possible that the same code was retained after the unit joined No 6 (T) Group, but it was definitely abandoned when No 63 Squadron became part of 12 OTU.

Mustangs, Hurricanes and Spitfire VBs only carried individual aircraft codes, but when reformed as part of Fighter Command in September 1946, the unit retained the 'UB' code of No 164 on both Spitfires and early Meteors. In 1950, coloured 'fighter' markings were re-introduced and No 63 Squadron adopted a black and yellow check painted on each side of the roundels on Meteors and Hunters. The wing-tips were also chequered and individual aircraft letters were in yellow. At one stage, the CO's Hunter had the whole of the fin and tailplane chequered.

Day Fighter Combat School aircraft bore the No 63 Squadron badge on a white disc flanked by the black and yellow checks painted on the nose of its Hunters, and this format was retained on 229 OCU and TWU aircraft. When Hawks were received, the black and yellow checks returned to the rear fuselage where they appeared in bar form on each side of the roundel. When the low-visibility grey camouflage was introduced, the markings were miniaturized, but the aircraft's 'last three' remained on the fin.

No 64 Squadron

Badge

A scarabee — approved by HRH King Edward VIII in November 1936. The use of the Egyptian hieroglyphic indicates the Squadron's long association with the country.

Motto

Tenax propositi — 'Firm of purpose'

History

No 64 Squadron, RFC, was formed at Sedgeford on 1 August 1916 and spent the next ten months on instructional work using a selection of Henri Farman, Avro 504, FE 2B and Pup aircraft. In June 1917, DH 5s were received and work-up as a fighter squadron commenced, No 64 going to France in October. Almost immediately, the unit was thrown into the Battle of Cambrai and proved effective on ground strafing, despite heavy casualties. SE 5As replaced the obsolescent DH 5s in January 1918, and from March to September No 64 Squadron was in constant action, claiming 128 enemy aircraft in combat. Operations swung back to ground attack during the closing stages of the war, after which the Squadron remained in France until February 1919, when it returned to the United Kingdom and was disbanded at the end of the year.

On 1 March 1936, the unit reformed at Heliopolis from the Demon Flights of Nos 6 and 208 Squadrons as part of the steady strengthening of British forces in the area during the Abyssinian crisis. Its main role was defence of bombers being refuelled on forward landing grounds, but it was also intended that the Squadron's Demons would strafe enemy airfields. Fortunately, the war did not escalate and in August 1936 the Squadron embarked for the United Kingdom and work-up as an air defence unit.

During December 1938, the first Blenheim IFs were received and the Squadron became a night fighter unit, adding day patrols to its repertoire in October 1939. Re-equipping with Spitfires in April 1940 and changing its role to that of day fighter, the Squadron was soon operational, going into action over Dunkirk during the evacuation. No 64 remained in the south of England throughout the early part of the Battle of Britain, those hectic months being followed by the usual mixture of air defence, offensive sweeps and bomber escorts. The Squadron received the first operational Spitfire IXs in June 1942, but in the spring of 1943 reverted to obsolescent VBs for deck landing training aboard HMS *Argus*. The 'floating runway' plan fell through, but it was July 1944 before the Squadron was back on the front line with Spitfire IXs, replacing them in November with Mustangs for long-range escort of Bomber Command's daylight attacks on Germany.

The Mustangs were retained after the war, and were not finally relinquished until May 1946 when the Squadron became the first to receive the twin-engined Hornet. This superb aircraft was flown until April 1951, when Meteor conversion commenced. Day fighter Meteor 8s were replaced by night fighter versions in September 1956, followed two years later by 'all-weather' Javelins.

Numerous detachments to the Middle East followed, and in-flight refuelling became a Squadron speciality from 1960 onwards. It was put to good use

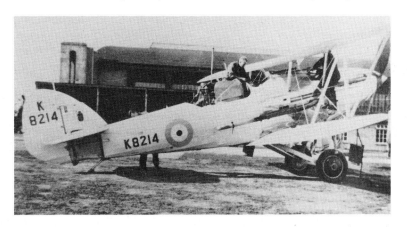

Turret Demon K8214 of No 64 Squadron in the late 1930s, complete with 'scarabee' on the fin (via B.C. Jones).

Meteor F 8 day fighters of No 64 Squadron in the mid-'fifties before camouflage was introduced. The red and blue diamonds are painted directly on to the silver finish (Sqn Ldr D. Hymans).

Phantom FGR 2 'CX' of 228 OCU in 'shadow' No 64 Squadron markings, including the 'scarabee' on the fin and red and blue diamonds on the engine intakes. Culdrose, July 1987.

in October 1963 when 12 aircraft were sent to India for a large-scale exercise, four of them continuing to Singapore in December to bolster No 60 Squadron during the 'confrontation' with Indonesia. During the following month, more Javelins were despatched eastwards and on 1 April 1965 the Tengah 'detachment' officially became No 64 Squadron. The Squadron operated alongside No 60 from Tengah and Labuan until the situation improved sufficiently to allow reductions in the force strength, No 64 Squadron disbanding in Singapore on 16 June 1967.

Reformation in July 1970 was a very low-key affair, for it was as the 'shadow' number for No 228 OCU, the Phantom training unit based at Coningsby. Activated as a front-line unit crewed by OCU staff in the event of tension or war, No 64 Squadron has a serious role as part of the UK air defence organization and would undoubtedly give a good account of itself. On 22 April 1987, the OCU moved to Leuchars and continued its 'shadow' role at the maintain Phantom force base.

Standard

Granted by HRH Queen Elizabeth II and promulgated on 30 July 1958. Presented by Marshal of the Royal Air Force Sir William Dickson GCB KBE DSO AFC at Duxford on 6 July 1960.

Standard laid up at St Clement Danes Church on 2 July 1967 ('shadow' units are not allowed to retain Standards).

Battle Honours

*Western Front 1917-1918
*Cambrai 1918
Amiens
*Hindenburg Line
Somme 1918
Lys
Channel & North Sea 1940
*Dunkirk
*Battle of Britain
Home Defence 1940
*Fortress Europe 1941-1944
*Normandy 1944
Arnhem
Walcheren
*France & Germany 1944-1945

*Denotes Honours emblazoned on Standard

Aircraft insignia and markings

DH 5s and SE 5As up to March 1918 carried a white triangle aft of the fuselage roundel as a unit marking, which then changed to a vertical white bar. It is doubtful whether the Demons carried markings whilst in the Middle East, but in the United Kingdom they appeared with red and blue diamonds painted between the roundels on the upper mainplane and along the fuselage sides.

Following the Munich Crisis, the unit code 'XQ' was allocated, but there is no evidence that it was carried. In September 1939 the Squadron's aircraft appeared with the code 'SH', and it remained in use into the post-war period, embellishing Blenheims, Spitfires, Mustangs and Hornets. On Meteors, the colourful pre-war markings were re-introduced in the standard bars on each side of the fuselage roundel, a large individual aircraft letter appearing on the fin.

When camouflage returned the diamonds were retained and a white arrowhead enclosing the 'scarabee' emblem was added to the fin on which the code letter appeared in yellow. This scheme was retained on night fighter variants of the Meteor, but the Javelin had the red and blue diamonds painted on the upper portion of the fin flanking the 'scarabee'.

When 228 OCU was designated No 64 (Shadow) Squadron, the 'operational' unit markings were applied to the fin of the Phantoms in a similar style to that adopted for the Javelin until May 1978 when the 'scarabee' was moved to the nose as the centrepiece of a blue-edged white spearhead. The red and blue diamonds were re-positioned on the engine intakes, one ahead of and two behind the roundel. This scheme did not last long, for with the introduction of the grey 'low-visibility' camouflage late in 1979, the markings were toned down and returned to the top of the fin, the diamonds now painted light blue and pink.

In preparation for the unit's move to Leuchars in April 1987, the 'scarabee' emblem was enlarged and moved to the centre of the fin, and a two-letter identification was adopted, the aircraft letter preceded by a 'C' to denote the unit.

No 65 Squadron

Badge

In front of fifteen swords in pile, the hilts in base, a lion passant — approved by HRH King George VI in December 1936. The number of swords refers to a famous combat during the First World War in which 15 enemy aircraft were destroyed. The lion was taken from the Arms of Dunkirk.

Motto

Vi et armis — 'By force of arms'

History

The nucleus of No 65 Squadron gathered at Norwich on 8 July 1916, but the unit officially formed at Wyton on 1 August as part of No 7 Training Wing. Maurice Farmans, Boxkites, Bristol Scouts, Sopwith Pups and DH 5s were flown, some of the latter going to Wye in the late spring of 1917 to work up for France. Following the fuss caused by the first daylight attack on the United Kingdom by Gotha bombers, the DH 5s were kept fully armed at Wye for *ad hoc* Home Defence duty, as were the Camels which started to arrive in July. After eight ineffective sorties the Squadron was relieved of the Home Defence task and, at full strength, arrived in France on 27 October 1917.

Standard line patrols occupied the unit until February 1918 when ground attack work started, continuing at intervals until August when escorting DH 9 bombers became the daily task. Back on ground attack in September, the Squadron occasionally undertook offensive fighter operations, and on such a mission just a week before the Armistice met 40 enemy aircraft. During the ensuing 'dogfight', nine of the enemy were destroyed and eight claimed as 'probable' for the loss of two aircraft and one pilot, the action commemorated by the badge. The Squadron remained in Belgium until February 1919 when it returned to the United Kingdom and formally disbanded at Yatesbury on 25 October 1919.

It was not reformed until 1 April 1934, when workup as a night fighter unit using Demons began at Hornchurch. A year later, in September 1935, many Squadron personnel were drafted to the Middle East as RAF strength in the area was increased in response to the tension over Abyssinia. By May 1936, No 65 was little more than a cadre, but then the situation started to improve and, back at full strength, the unit was re-designated as a day fighter squadron in July, Gauntlets replacing the Demons. A year later Gladiators were received, and in March 1939 Spitfires, the Squadron being operational on the latter when war was declared in September.

Patrols started immediately but without incident until May 1940, when air cover was provided for the withdrawal of the BEF from Dunkirk. More action came during the Battle of Britain when No 65 was in the forefront until sent north at the end of August. The usual spells of defensive standby interspersed with training followed, changed in January 1941 to night patrols and then to offensive sweeps over Northern France. Deck landing practice on HMS *Argus* was completed in January 1943, followed by bomber escort work while awaiting the Spitfire IXs which arrived in August.

At the end of 1943, the Squadron became the first RAF unit to receive Mustang IIIs, immediately transferring to the Second Tactical Air Force for fighter bomber operations. By the end of June 1944, No 65 was on the Continent providing close support for the Army, but in September returned to the United Kingdom and undertook long-range bomber escort for the remainder of the war.

In January 1946, the Mustangs were replaced by Spitfire XVIs, in turn supplanted by Hornets in August. This fine low-level fighter was declared obsolete by Fighter Command at the end of 1950, and Meteor 4s started to arrive, the last Hornet leaving in April 1951 when brand-new Meteor 8s were received. Meteors remained in service for six years, the Hunter 6, which had first reached the Squadron in December 1956, finally replacing them the following March. With its role of day interceptor fighter supplanted by a combination of missiles and long-range AI-equipped aircraft, the UK-based Hunter force was steadily reduced, No 65 Squadron disbanding on 31 March 1961.

Reformed in 1964 as a Bloodhound ground-to-air missile unit, the Squadron remained at Seletar, Singapore, for five uneventful years before again disbanding. It re-appeared in May 1971 as the 'shadow' number for 226 OCU, then flying Lightning F 1As. This reserve role, exercised annually in preparation for times of tension or war, continued until the Lightning OCU was disbanded in September 1974.

On 5 January 1987, No 65 Squadron was again resurrected to become the 'shadow' number for the Tornado F 3 element of 229 OCU at Coningsby, and was soon to be seen and heard at air displays around the country.

Standard

Granted by HRH Queen Elizabeth II and promulgated 16 October 1957. Presented by Marshal of the Royal Air Force Sir William Dickson GCB KBE DSO AFC on 6 July 1960. Laid up during 1969.

Battle Honours

*Western Front 1917-1918
*Cambrai 1917
*Somme 1918
*France & Low Countries 1940
Dunkirk

A Gauntlet in the red chevrons of No 65 Squadron soon after the unit assumed the day fighter role in July 1936 (RAF Museum P18033).

'Shadowing' for the first time — with Lightning F 1As of 226 OCU in the early 1970s (J. Bartholomew).

A Tornado F 3 ZE168 of 229 OCU with No 65 Squadron 'shadow' markings, the 'lion' and all 15 swords being flanked by the red chevrons first seen in the 1930s (RAF Lossiemouth).

*Battle of Britain 1940
Home Defence 1940-1942
*Fortress Europe 1941-1944
*Channel & North Sea 1942-1945
Dieppe
Normandy 1944
Arnhem
*France & Germany 1944-1945
Baltic 1945

*Denotes Honours emblazoned on Standard

Mascot

A mongrel dog—named 'Binder', the dog attached itself to Flying Officer 'Paddy' Finucane at Hornchurch and was adopted as Squadron mascot.

Affiliation

'East India' — officially named an 'East India' squadron following a £50,000 gift from the Indian State, nominally sufficient to 'purchase' a squadron of aircraft.

Aircraft insignia and markings

In France, the unit's Camels carried a white stripe down the length of the fuselage and on the top decking, changed in March 1918 to two vertical white bars, one on each side of the fuselage roundel. A large individual letter was painted in white immediately aft of the roundel.

When reformed in the 1930s, the Squadron adopted a red chevron as the basic marking, a series of them being painted along the sides of the fuselage and across the upper mainplane of Gauntlets and Gladiators, and probably also Demons. Following the introduction of camouflage after the Munich Crisis, the unit code letters 'FZ' were allotted and carried on Gladiators and Spitfires, replaced on the latter in September 1939 by 'YT', a marking also carried on Mustangs and Hornets. In 1947, the CO's Hornet, *PX252*, was painted with large red chevrons on the wings and fuselage — but 'authority' soon ordered its return to standard.

Four years later, however, Meteors appeared with chevrons painted in standard bar form on each side of the fuselage roundel. On camouflaged aircraft, the red chevrons were still applied directly on top of the basic colour scheme, the individual aircraft letter on the fin being changed from black to white. Hunters had the Squadron markings on the nose, a white disc carrying the badge, while the chevrons were applied on flanking white rectangles.

When 226 OCU transferred its 'shadow' number from No 145 to No 65 Squadron in 1971, the 'Hunter style' chevron markings were painted on either side of the fuselage roundel of the Lightnings, the Squadron badge appearing on a white disc on the fin. Tornado F 3s of 229 OCU also use the chevrons, but flanking the lion badge on the nose, initially in an 'arrowhead' form, but later 'fighter style' bars were standardized. The OCU's emblem, a flaming torch crossed by a sword, are carried on the fin. The handles of both sword and torch are brown, the blade is silver and the flame is orange.

No 70 Squadron

Badge

A demi-wing lion erased — approved by HRH King Edward VIII in October 1936. Developed from an unofficial winged lion badge probably derived from the Squadron's long dependence on the Napier Lion engine during the 1920s.

Motto

Usquam — 'Anywhere'

History

Formed at South Farnborough on 22 April 1916, No 70 was the first RFC Squadron to be equipped with the Sopwith 1½-strutter, famous as the first British fighter to be fitted with a gun synchronized to fire through the propeller arc. So desperate was the situation in France that the Squadron was sent across the Channel by Flights, 'A' Flight going on 21 May followed by the others at roughly monthly intervals. The Squadron was used for fighter patrols, reconnaissance and bombing, proving very successful in all three roles until the Germans perfected their scout 'Circus' formation. After a year of increasing losses, the Squadron was re-equipped with Camels in July 1917 and used them on both fighter patrols and ground attack for the rest of the war.

After the Armistice, No 70 Squadron moved into Germany with the Army of Occupation but returned to the United Kingdom in February 1919 and was disbanded on 22 January 1920. A mere nine days later it was resurrected when No 58 Squadron, a bomber unit at Heliopolis, Egypt, was re-numbered No 70 whilst in the throes of conversion from Handley Page 0/400 to Vickers Vimy aircraft.

The Squadron moved into Iraq in January 1922, and in November the first Vernon bomber/transports were delivered. The Cairo-Baghdad air mail route was the main task until it was taken over by Imperial Airways in 1927, but the Squadron also took part in operations against rebel tribesmen and insurgents on the Turkish frontier both as a bomber and transport unit.

The updated Victoria was received in August 1926, and the Squadron used it with effect during the famous evacuation of Kabul in 1928. The bomber/transport role was officially formalized in 1931, and the Victoria soldiered on until November 1935 when the slightly updated Valentia supplanted it. It was with these lumbering aircraft that the Squadron entered the Second World War. Not until September 1940 did the first Wellingtons arrive and the unit revert to the pure bomber role. Variants of the Wellingtons were used throughout the North African and most of the Italian campaigns, Liberators not finally replacing them until February 1945, by which time supply dropping to partisan forces was part of the Squadron's tasks.

At the end of 1945, the Squadron returned to the Canal Zone and was disbanded on 31 March 1946. On 15 April, No 178 Squadron at Fayid flying Lancasters was re-numbered No 70 and the Squadron continued its bomber role for another year, being disbanded again on 1 April 1947. Just over a year later, on 1 May 1948, No 215 Squadron, Kabrit, became No 70 and, equipped with Dakotas, the Squadron was engaged in transport duties around the middle East. In January 1950, the Squadron converted to Valettas, moving to Cyprus during December 1955 prior to re-equipment with Hastings. Used for both route flying and paratroop training, the Squadron's Hastings were prominent during the ill-fated Suez campaign, and also on many relief missions around the Middle East.

After 11 years with the Hastings, the Squadron took over No 215's Argosy aircraft in November 1967, though a VIP Hastings was retained until July 1968. Conversion to Hercules commenced in November 1970 flying alongside a few Argosys retained for VIP and passenger transport. After three more years in the Middle East, No 70 Squadron finally relinquished the Argosys and returned to the United Kingdom for the first time since 1920, joining the Lyneham Wing in January 1975.

Since then, the Squadron has carried out relief work and attended trouble spots all around the world. Very active during Operation 'Corporate', the recovery of the Falkland Islands, the unit had the distinction of making the longest Hercules flight to date when, on 18 June 1982, a crew flew from Ascension to East Falkland and back non-stop, making a night drop of Rapier spares, the air-refuelled sortie taking 28 hours 4 minutes.

Standard

Granted by HRH King George VI and promulgated on 9 September 1943. Presented by Air Vice Marshal Sir Hazelton Nicoll KBE CB at Fayid on 16 July

Hastings C 1A TG582 Hero carrying a 'Transport' diamond and 'LXX' on the fin, somewhere in the Middle East (Military Aircraft Photographs).

When operating as the NEAF transport unit in the 1970s, the Hercules of No 70 Squadron carried 'LXX' and the badge on the fin. XV182 is seen here at Salalah in 1972 (D. Lawrence).

Hero, an Argosy C 1 of No 70 Squadron, in Oman, 1975 (D. Lawrence).

1955. Sir Hazelton had been the Squadron Commanding Officer from 1926 to 1928.

A new Standard was presented by HRH The Princess Anne, Mrs Mark Phillips, GCVO at Lyneham on 3 May 1984 in a dual ceremony with No 47 Squadron. Princess Anne (now the Princess Royal) is the Honorary Air Commodore of Lyneham.

Battle Honours

*Western Front 1916-1918
*Somme 1916
Arras
*Ypres 1917
Somme 1918
Kurdistan 1922-1924
Iraq 1928-1929
Kurdistan 1930-1931
Southern Kurdistan 1932
North West Frontier 1937
Mediterranean 1940-1943
*Egypt & Libya 1940-1943
Greece 1940-1941
Syria 1941
*Iraq 1941
El Alamein
*North Africa 1942-1943
El Hamma
Sicily 1943
*Italy 1943-1945
Salerno
Anzio & Nettuno
Gustav Line
Gothic Line

*South East Europe 1944-1945
South Atlantic 1982

*Denotes Honours emblazoned on Standard

Aircraft insignia and markings

The Sopwith 1½-strutter probably remained devoid of unit markings, but the Squadron Camels carried a white zigzag aft of the fuselage roundel, changed in March 1918 to three white bands around the rear fuselage.

0/400s, Vimys, Vernons and Victorias were either unmarked or carried an individual code letter, usually aft of the fuselage roundel on Vernons and on the nose of the Victorias, which also carried the 'lion' badge. Valentias were initially similarly marked, but after the Munich Crisis of 1938 the unit code 'DU' was added, painted aft of the roundel with the individual code forward.

Following the declaration of war in September 1939, unit codes were changed, but it appears that No 70 Squadron ignored the instruction. Replacement Wellingtons were limited to individual letters, carried forward of the fuselage roundel, and this format was also used on Liberators and Lancasters.

It is doubtful whether any form of unit marking was employed on Dakotas, and Valettas only carried a small Squadron badge beneath the pilot's cockpit, a yellow cheat-line along the fuselage sides, and white propeller spinners. Hastings had the Transport Command-style diamond on the fin, black with the Roman numerals 'LXX' superimposed in white. Argosys and Hercules carried the Squadron badge in a white disc on the fin. When the Squadron joined the Lyneham Wing, the aircraft were 'pooled' and all distinctive markings were removed.

No 70 Squadron has a long tradition of individually naming its aircraft, starting in 1923 when Vernons carried such names as *Vagabond*, *Valkyrie* and *Venus*, and continuing into the post-Second World War era with Hastings, Argosys and Hercules all receiving similar recognition. Some of the aircraft names are listed below:

Hastings:

TG530	*Hanno*	TG557	*Hermes*	TG612	*Hadrian*
WD486	*Hero*	WD489	*Hannibal*	WD500	*Hibernia*

Argosy:

XN818	*Zeus*	XN847	*Horatius*	XP412	*Hannibal*
XP446	*Chevron*	XP450	*Hero*	XR107	*Jason*

Hercules:

XV192	*Horatius*	XV205	*Hyperion*	XV294	*Hephaestus*

No 72 Squadron

Badge

A swift volant — approved by HRH King George VI in February 1938, and intended to symbolize speed. An earlier unofficial emblem consisting of a quartered shield depicting a foaming tankard, a scroll of 'bumph', a heart pierced by an arrow and five aces, one of them a joker, was not submitted!

Motto

Swift

History

No 72 Squadron was formed at Netheravon on 2 July 1917 from a nucleus provided by the Central Flying School. After employment on advanced training work for four months, the Squadron mobilized for service in Mesopotamia, embarking on Christmas Day and

An unusual formation of Gladiator, Meteor NF 14 and Javelin FAW 4, all in No 72 Squadron markings (Military Aircraft Photographs).

finally re-grouping at Basra on 2 March 1918. Equipped with a variety of single-seater fighters, Spad S VIIs, Bristol M1Cs, Martinsyde G 100s and SE 5As, the Squadron operated in self-contained detached Flights, each allotted to separate army formations. Mostly employed on ground attack work, the Martinsydes also operated as bombers on occasion, sorties continuing until the Turks sued for peace. The Flights were re-united at Baghdad in November 1918 and the Squadron sailed for the United Kingdom in February 1919, disbanding on 22 September that same year.

The unit reformed at Tangmere on 22 February 1937 from 'B' Flight of No 1 Squadron, and collected its first Gladiators from Gloster's Brockworth factory the same day. Conversion to Spitfires came in April 1939, and from September air defence and convoy patrols were flown until June 1940 when the Squadron moved south to help cover the Dunkirk beaches. Returning south again at the end of August, No 72 was heavily involved with the enemy until the Battle of Britain petered out in October. More defensive patrolling followed before offensive sweeps over Northern France started in July 1941, but just over a year later, during September 1942, the Squadron prepared for overseas, going to Gibraltar in November for Operation 'Torch'.

Flying throughout the Tunisian campaign, the Squadron went to Malta in June 1943 with Spitfire IXs, and then followed the Eighth Army through Sicily and Italy and covered the landings in Southern France in July 1944, before returning to the Italian front. After the German surrender, the Squadron moved into Austria with the occupation forces, and was disbanded there on 30 December 1946.

No 72 Squadron reformed at Odiham as a day fighter unit on 1 February 1947 by the simple expedient of re-numbering No 130 Squadron, flying Vampires until converted to Meteor 8s during July 1952. These were exchanged for Meteor night fighters in

Belvedere HC 1 XG455 carrying the full No 72 Squadron marking on the tail rotor mounting — red-edged blue bars and the 'swift' emblem.

Wessex HC 2 XT675 in the very drab markings employed in recent years by No 72 Squadron. An outline badge and the unit's blue bars can be discerned on the tail rotor pylon.

February 1956, replaced in turn by Javelin all-weather fighters from April 1959. Just over two years later, on 30 June 1961, the Squadron disbanded.

Less than six months later, on 15 November, the Squadron reformed, but with a very different role. Now it was a 38 Group unit equipped with the troublesome twin-rotor Belvedere heavy-lift helicopter, used until Wessex 2s were received in August 1964. A very tractable medium-lift 'chopper', the Wessex has been detached widely at home and abroad for duties as diverse as Operation 'Bersatu Padu' in Malaya during June 1970, the clean-up of Cornish beaches after the *Torrey Canyon* tanker disaster of 1967, and SAR duties at Manston from September 1974. Much of its work, however, has been in Northern Ireland, first on detachment, but from November 1981 permanently based in the Province.

Today, the Squadron still flies from Aldergrove Airport on army support duties all over Ulster having flown the Wessex for the past 24 years — and with no end in sight!

Standard

Granted by HRH Queen Elizabeth II and promulgated on 26 October 1960. Presented by Air Marshal Sir Ronald Lees KCB CBE DFC at Odiham on 30 June 1966.

Battle Honours

*Mesopotamia 1918
Channel & North Sea 1939-1942

*Dunkirk
*Battle of Britain
*Fortress Europe 1941-1942
*North Africa 1942-1943
Mediterranean 1942-1943
*Sicily 1943
Italy 1943-1945
*Salerno
*Anzio & Nettuno

*Denotes Honours emblazoned on Standard

Affiliation

Basutoland — originally incorporated in the unit title as No 72 (Basutoland) Squadron during March 1941 in recognition of monies contributed by the people of that African colony to the war effort. The name was dropped from the Squadron title in 1952.

Aircraft insignia and markings

Like nearly all Middle East-based units during the First World War, no official Squadron markings were carried but at least one Bristol Monoplane Scout of 'C' Flight, probably the Flight Commander's aircraft, carried five white zigzags aft of the fuselage roundel.

At Church Fenton, the Gladiators had a broad blue stripe, edged with red, painted along the length of the fuselage and across the upper mainplane between the roundels. During the Munich Crisis, the aircraft were camouflaged and the unit code letters 'RN' were allotted and carried. When Spitfires arrived they were coded 'SD' and had the 'swift' emblem in a white 'spearhead' on the fin. The code reverted to 'RN' in September 1939 (which suggests it was originally used in error), a combination carried throughout the war and until disbandment in 1946.

When reformed early in the following year, the unit adopted 'FG' as a code on Vampire F 1s, but this was abandoned on the FB 5s received in 1950 in favour of a large individual code letter on the nose painted in Flight colours. Later in the same year, coloured markings were reinstated by Fighter Command, the red-edged blue bars of No 72 Squadron being painted on the nose on each side of the unit badge. On Meteors, the bars were repositioned fore and aft of the fuselage roundel, but moved back to the nose on Javelins. These aircraft also had a Squadron badge painted on a white disc superimposed on a blue arrowhead outlined in red.

Belvedere helicopters carried similar 'fighter-type' markings on the tail rotor pylon flanking a blue 'swift' emblem painted on a white disc. The same markings have been retained on the current Wessex, which from 1970 until 1982 carried a two-letter code, the prefix 'A' denoting the unit. Since 1982, only an individual aircraft letter has been used.

No 74 Squadron

Badge
A tiger's face — approved by HRH King George VI in February 1937. Developed from an unofficial emblem used by the Squadron during the First World War.

Motto
I fear no man — a motto first used during the First World War.

History
Formed at Northolt on 1 July 1917, No 74 Squadron spent its first six months as a training unit at London Colney using Avro 504s before commencing work-up as a fighter squadron equipped in March

1918 with SE 5As. The Squadron was in France by the end of the month and operations began on 12 April, almost exclusively on offensive fighter patrols until the closing stages when, in company with practically every other RAF unit in France, No 74 was thrown into the assault on German front-line troops, strafing 'everything that moved'! After a short spell with the Army of Occupation, No 74 Squadron returned to the United Kingdom in February 1919 and was disbanded on 3 July.

The manner of No 74 Squadron's rebirth was unusual. Detachments from Nos 3, 23, 32, 56, 65 and 601 Squadrons were sent to Malta aboard the troopship *Neuralia*, arriving at Hal Far on 11 September 1935, to provide air defence for the island using Demons. Then, on 14 November, the Air Ministry signalled that the unit had been No 74 Squadron since 3 September, the day the detachments embarked at Southampton! After ten months in Malta spent exercising, the Squadron returned to the United Kingdom and joined the newly-formed Fighter Command. It had to be rebuilt from scratch, but was up to strength by April 1937, when Gauntlets were received and No 74 became a day fighter squadron.

Conversion to Spitfires commenced in February 1939, and during the opening months of the Second World War the Squadron flew defensive patrols over south-east England. Late in May 1940, the unit joined in the air battles over Dunkirk before taking part in the Battle of Britain. This traumatic experience was followed by a rest in the north of England, but during January 1941 the Squadron commenced fighter sweeps over France before embarking for the Middle East in April 1942. After a spell without aircraft, during which the ground crew serviced USAAF Liberators, Hurricanes were received in Iran and taken to Egypt in May 1943 for

Gauntlet II K7862 shows off its 'tiger' stripes and, on the fin, the 'spearhead' and badge (via R.W. Elliott).

Above *Lightning F 3* XP705 *in the very distinctive colour scheme adopted by No 74 Squadron awaits its 'slot' time in the St Mawgan Air Display, September 1965.*

Right *Phantom F 4J(UK)* ZE357 *in the very attractive markings of the 'Tigers', July 1985* (RAF Lossiemouth).

shipping patrols. Reversion to Spitfires was completed in September, and during the following month the Squadron was active over the Aegean Sea, remaining in the Eastern Mediterranean area until it embarked for the United Kingdom in April 1944.

Arriving just in time for D-Day, No 74 Squadron used its fighter-bomber Spitfire IXs to good effect from British bases and subsequently from landing strips on the Continent as it continued its support of 21st Army Group during the advance through France, Belgium and into the Netherlands. After the German surrender, No 74 Squadron returned to the UK to convert to Meteors, and in October 1946 moved to its 'permanent' peacetime base at Horsham St Faith as part of No 12 Group, Fighter Command. It remained there for 13 years, receiving Hunters in March 1957.

The Squadron moved to Coltishall in 1959, and in June 1960 half the pilots started conversion to Lightnings, the unit becoming the first truly supersonic fighter squadron in the RAF when the second half completed the change-over from Hunters during November. After a move to Leuchars, the Squadron received Lightning F 3s in April 1964 and up-dated Mk 6s in November 1966, before transferring to the Far East in June 1967 to provide air defence for Singapore. Four years later, on 31 August 1971, the Squadron disbanded at Tengah as part of the general run-down of British forces in the area which had started in 1970.

Despite frequent rumours of imminent revival, it was nearly 13 years before No 74 was reformed at Wattisham on 31 July 1984 specifically to operate the F 4J (UK) variant of the Phantom. After crew training in the USA, the first deliveries of this ex-USN version of the aircraft were made in August, and the Squadron has now been fully integrated into the United Kingdom air defence organization for over three years.

Standard

Granted by HRH Queen Elizabeth II and promulgated on 14 October 1959. Presented by HRH The Princess Margaret, Countess of Snowdon CI GCVO at Leuchars on 3 June 1965.

Battle Honours

*Western Front 1918
*France & Low Countries 1940
*Dunkirk
*Battle of Britain 1940
*Fortress Europe 1940-1941, 1944
Home Defence 1940-1941
*Mediterranean 1943
*Normandy
*France & Germany 1944-1945
Walcheren
Rhine

*Denotes Honours emblazoned on Standard

Mascots

A tigress — the Bertram Mills Circus tigress 'Begum'

was adopted by the Squadron in 1957, but unfortunately she died early in 1958. The Sumatra tigress 'Roma', housed at Linton Zoo, was adopted during 1986.

Affiliation

'Trinidad' — in recognition of a £100,000 gift by the colony to purchase Spitfires, the Air Ministry decreed that the unit be known as No 74 (Trinidad) Squadron in March 1941. Despite the changed circumstances, and a lukewarm official attitude resulting in reversion to the previous standard Squadron title, contact was maintained during the immediate post-war period through the Trinidad & Tobago branch of the RAF Association.

Nickname

'The Tigers' — derived from the Squadron badge, this nickname was adopted for the Lightning formation team of 1961-62. The Squadron is a founder member of the international organization of units which have a tiger as their emblem, and assemble annually for a 'Tiger Meet'.

Aircraft insignia and markings

No 74 Squadron's SE 5As featured a white rectangle on each side and top of the rear fuselage. It is believed that Demons were unmarked, but Gauntlets carried a form of 'tiger skin' marking. This was on the rear fuselage sides and across the upper mainplane in yellow and black, the aircraft also carrying the 'tiger head' badge superimposed on the standard white 'spearhead' on the fin.

After the Munich Crisis of 1938, the aircraft were camouflaged and the code 'JH' allocated. This may have been used on Gauntlets, and it certainly was on Spitfires, being changed to 'ZP' on the outbreak of war in September 1939. On transfer to the Middle East, only aircraft letters were carried, but back in the United Kingdom in 1944 the code '4D' was introduced and used on both Spitfires and Meteors.

In 1951, colourful markings returned, yellow rectangles on each side of the fuselage roundel having black triangles painted on them. Hunters used the same marking on the nose flanking the Squadron badge, as did Lightnings, but with the badge moved to the fin on a white disc background. Lightning F 3s appeared with black fins, rudders and fuselage spine until 1966 when a tone-down was ordered. The black paint was then removed and the tail marking reduced in size, a scheme retained on F 6s.

The all-grey F 4J (UK) Phantoms currently in service also carry the 'tiger' badge on the tail, on a white disc in the centre of the black-painted fin, with the aircraft letter unusually on the rudder. The 'tiger head' also adorns the sides of the nose flanked by the black and yellow 'tiger skin' bars.

No 78 Squadron

Badge

A heraldic tiger rampant and double queued — approved by HRH King George VI in November 1939. The theme of the badge was based on the aircraft equipment of the time, the Whitley, which had Tiger engines and twin tails.

Motto

Nemo non paratus — 'Nobody unprepared'

History

Formed on 1 November 1916 with its headquarters at Hove, Sussex, No 78 Squadron controlled three Home Defence Flights of BE 2 aircraft dispersed along the south coast. Originally intended for anti-Zeppelin patrols, No 78 Squadron moved to landing grounds east of London and a HQ at Harrietsham when German bomber raids started. Re-equipped with Sopwith 1½-strutters in October 1917, the Squadron gradually replaced them with Camels during 1918, but despite achieving several interceptions was unable to claim any positive success with either aircraft. The first Snipes appeared at the time of the Armistice, but never fully equipped the Squadron which disbanded on 31 December 1919.

No 78 Squadron was reformed at Boscombe Down on 1 November 1936 using 'B' Flight of No 10 Squadron as a nucleus. Equipped with Heyford night bombers, the Squadron moved to Yorkshire in February 1937 and joined No 4 Group on its formation in April. Re-equipment with Whitleys commenced in July, and at the outbreak of war in September 1939 the unit became the Group Reserve Squadron responsible for the final training of newly-formed crews prior to posting to operational Whitley squadrons. This training role continued until July 1940 when the Squadron joined the 'active' list and started night bombing. Conversion to Halifaxes commenced in March 1942, the unit remaining a 'main force' No 4 Group Squadron for the remainder of the European war.

Above *In the Second World War, No 78 Squadron was a 'main force' bomber unit flying Halifax B IIIs during 1944* (Gp Capt J.E. Pelly-Fry DSO).

Right *The Squadron also flies Sea King HAR 3s. The unit emblem is just aft of the pilot's cockpit side windows* (D. Burrows).

In May 1945, No 78 Squadron transferred to Transport Command and, after re-equipment with Dakotas, went overseas to Egypt to become part of the Middle East Transport Wing. Route flying around the Mediterranean, North Africa and into Arabia, alternating with tactical transport for the Army, was the Squadron's day-to-day work, continued with Valettas from April 1950 until disbandment at Fayid on 30 September 1954.

The unit reformed on 24 April 1956 as a short-range transport Squadron based in Aden, initially with Pioneer STOL aircraft for Army support in the Protectorate. The larger Twin Pioneer supplemented the single-engined aircraft in October 1958 and completely replaced them the following August. Detachments ranged from Firq in Muscat to Sharjah in the Trucial Oman in support of the Sultan's armed forces, and it was felt necessary to provide the Squadron with offensive fire-power. Trials with a Bren gun mounted in the rear entrance, and Nord SS11 wire-guided missiles under the wings of the 'Twin Pin', were completed in 1962. The following year, the first missile was fired against rebel forces, believed to be the first

operational firing of a guided missile by the RAF — quite an achievement for a transport unit!

Still in Aden, the Squadron received Wessex 2 helicopters in June 1965 and moved to Sharjah during October 1967 for more permanent support work in the Trucial States. The Squadron disbanded in December 1971 when British forces withdrew from the area.

Fifteen years later, on 22 May 1986, No 78 Squadron was reformed at Mount Pleasant Airport in the Falkland Islands by absorbing No 1310 (Chinook) Flight and No 1564 (Sea King) Flight. Still operating as two Flights, the Squadron thus combines the heavy-lift capability of the Chinook with the dedicated SAR tasking of the Sea King HAR 3, the latter also having a maritime reconnaissance role.

Standard

Granted by HRH Queen Elizabeth II and promulgated on 11 July 1962. Presented by Lieutenant General Sir Charles Harrington KCB CBE DSO MC, Commander-in-Chief, British Forces Arabia Peninsula, at Khormaksar on 11 February 1965.

Chinook HC 1 ZA680 of No 78 Squadron on its dispersal at Mount Pleasant, Falkland Islands, in 1987. The unit emblem can be seen on the rear rotor pylon and on the forward fuselage (D. Burrows).

Battle Honours

*Home Defence 1916-1918
*Fortress Europe 1940-1944
*Ruhr 1940-1945
Invasion Ports 1940
Biscay Ports 1940-1943
*Berlin 1940-1941, 1943-1944
*Channel & North Sea 1942-1945
*Normandy 1944
Walcheren
*France & Germany 1944-1945
*Rhine

*Denotes Honours emblazoned on Standard

Affiliation

Preston — under the Municipal Liaison Scheme of April 1939.

Aircraft insignia and markings

Unit markings were not carried on the Squadron's aircraft during the First World War. Heyfords employed individual aircraft letters, but Whitleys were almost certainly the first type to use unit markings, initially the Squadron number on the fuselage forward of the roundel, changed to the letters 'YY' following the Munich Crisis of 1938. For security reasons, wartime codes were different, No 78 using 'EY' from September 1939 onwards, retaining the same marking on Halifaxes and, unusually, on the Dakotas flown in the Middle East.

By the time Valettas were in service, unit code letters had been dropped on MEAF transports and No 78 Squadron aircraft were only distinguishable by their red propeller spinners. Squadron markings were not carried in Aden until the arrival of the Wessex, when a large Squadron badge adorned the main cabin door and a white aircraft letter was painted aft of the fuselage roundel.

In the Falklands, a yellow 'tiger' on a black disc is painted just aft of the pilot's cockpit on both Sea Kings and Chinooks, and also appears on the tail rotor mounting of the latter, together with an aircraft letter. The grey-painted Sea Kings retain the unit marking 'S' formerly used by 1564 Flight, but no individual letter.

No 79 Squadron

Badge

A salamander salient — approved by HRH King George VI in March 1938. The salamander was adopted because it is renowned for always facing up to danger.

Motto

Nil nobis obstare potest — 'Nothing can stop us'

History

No 79 Squadron formed at Gosport on 1 August 1917 using personnel from the local training squadrons, and moved to Beaulieu a week later. The unit provided advanced training for new pilots until December when it was mobilized and worked up on the new Sopwith Dolphin. The Squadron crossed the Channel on 20 February 1918 and hardly had time to settle in before the start of the German spring offensive. The Dolphins were immediately thrown into the battle as a ground strafer with consequent heavy losses, but the role remained one of the unit's main occupations right up to the Armistice, though from May offensive patrols and bomber escorts were also flown. The Squadron moved into Germany with the Army of Occupation, but was disbanded at Bickendorf on 15 July 1919.

It was nearly 18 years later, on 22 March 1937, that 'B' Flight of No 32 Squadron became the nucleus of a reformed No 79 at Biggin Hill. Quickly brought up to strength with Gauntlets, the Squadron formed part of the defence forces for Greater London. Hurricanes were received in November 1938 and were fully operational when the Second World War started the following September. After scoring 11 Group's first confirmed 'kill' on 21 November, there was little further action until the unit was hurriedly sent to France following the German breakthrough during May 1940. In the ten days before returning to the United Kingdom, No 79 Squadron claimed 25 enemy aircraft, but France was lost and in August the unit was heavily engaged in the desperate Battle of Britain.

The final months of 1940 and the whole of 1941 were spent on dreary sector and convoy patrols, but in March 1942 the Squadron sailed for India. Arriving 3½ months later, new Hurricanes were collected and the Squadron flew defensive patrols until January 1943, then 'Rhubarbs', armed reconnaissance and bomber escorts were flown over Burma until July. In November, the Squadron concentrated on the escort of supply-dropping Dakotas, but in 1944 was almost exclusively engaged in army co-operation, attacking troop concentrations and supply lines. Con-

version to the hefty Thunderbolt started in May 1944, and operations recommenced in November on ground attack work, the Squadron becoming acknowledged experts in the fighter-bomber role during 1945.

No 79 Squadron disbanded at Meiktela, Burma, on 30 December 1945, but reformed on 15 November 1951 at Gutersloh, Germany, as a fighter reconnaissance unit flying Meteors. In June 1955, the Squadron re-equipped with the Swift FR 5, the only version of that ill-fated aircraft to become operational. It was flown until 1 January 1961 when the Squadron disbanded, personnel and aircraft being absorbed by a reborn No 4 Squadron.

The Squadron re-appeared in 1967 when it became the third 'shadow' squadron number allocated to 229 OCU, Chivenor. Operating Hunter FGA 9s and FR 10s for advanced fighter reconnaissance training, the 'shadow' unit was expected to supplement front-line

Right *A trainee pilot at 229 OCU, Chivenor, completes his checks before start-up of a Hunter FGA 9 in the 'shadow' markings of No 79 Squadron, August 1969.*

Below *The unit also flies a small number of Jet Provost T 4s for specialized training. XP547 is at a display at Fairford, July 1987 (J. Bartholomew).*

A current 'low-visibility' Hawk T 1A of No 1 Tactical Weapons Unit carrying the 'shadow' markings of No 79 Squadron (Military Aircraft Photographs).

squadrons during large-scale exercises, periods of tension and actual war. In September 1974, the OCU moved to Brawdy and became the Tactical Weapons Unit, No 79 (Shadow) Squadron concentrating on instructor, special and refresher courses flying Hunter T 7 and FGA 9s. Later, the four Jet Provosts on the TWU joined No 79, and the Squadron was also involved in the Hunter detachments maintained at Gibraltar during the mid-1970s.

On 31 July 1978, Brawdy became No 1 Tactical Weapons Unit and in 1984 No 79 finally relinquished its Hunters in favour of the Hawk, these aircraft later being equipped with Sidewinder missiles to improve their effectiveness in the day low-level interception 'shadow' role. Currently, the unit is still at Brawdy flying alongside No 234 (Shadow) Squadron.

Standard

Not granted.

Battle Honours

Not determined (only applicable when a Standard is granted).

Affiliations

'Madras Presidency' — the Squadron was authorized by the Air Ministry in March 1941 to include 'Madras Presidency' in its official title, to acknowledge the monetary gift of a nominal squadron of Spitfires from the Indian State. The affiliation was dropped soon after India became a Republic

No 264 Squadron — linked as No 264/79 Sqn from February 1949 until November 1951.

Aircraft insignia and markings

On arrival in France, the Squadron was allocated a white dumb-bell marking, painted on the Dolphins aft of the fuselage roundel. In March 1918, the marking was changed to a white square, and a large white identification letter was carried just forward of the tailplane.

Gauntlets carried a large red arrow, on which the fuselage roundel was superimposed, but after the Munich Crisis the unit code 'AL' was allocated and painted on camouflaged Hurricanes arriving during November 1938. The code was changed to 'NV' in September 1939 and used until the Squadron went to the Far East. The same code was resurrected late in 1943 and painted on both Hurricanes and Thunderbolts, but when reformed with Meteors, the Second Tactical Air Force allocated the single letter 'T' to No 79 Squadron. This was carried forward of the roundel with an individual letter aft. When colourful 'fighter type' markings were introduced in Germany during July 1954 the code letter was replaced by the pre-war red arrow painted on the sides of the rear fuselage directly on to the camouflage.

On Swifts, the markings were rationalized, becoming a forward-pointing red arrow painted on a white rectangle on each side of the fuselage roundel, a similar scheme being used on the Hunters of 229 OCU. At Brawdy, the TWU Hunters were 'pooled' and 'Shadow' markings gradually disappeared, only to be reinstated on Jet Provosts and Hawks, the markings on 'low-visibility' grey-camouflaged aircraft being considerably reduced in size and brightness.

No 84 Squadron

Badge

A scorpion — approved by HRH King George VI in December 1936. The original unofficial badge depicted an eagle perched on a pyramid, but the scorpion was chosen instead because it had been an emblem long carried on Squadron aircraft in the Middle East.

Motto

Scorpiones pungunt — 'Scorpions sting'

History

Formed at Beaulieu in January 1917, carried out training duties there until mobilized in August as a fighter squadron equipped with SE 5As. After a rapid work-up, the Squadron left for France on 23 September to escort bombers and fly offensive patrols over the Ypres sector of the Western Front.

During January 1918, the Squadron started flying special missions aimed at disrupting enemy wireless communications, interspersed with the strafing of German front-line troops, going over to ground attack almost exclusively in March. Later in the year, the unit gained a well-deserved reputation for an ability to destroy enemy observation balloons, a more dangerous occupation than might appear at first sight, the aircraft being vulnerable to ground fire during such attacks. It was during this period that Captain W.A. Beauchamp Proctor DSO MC DFC was awarded the Victoria Cross specifically for his tenacity and courage throughout two months of non-stop flying between 8 August and 8 October 1918, during which he was credited with the destruction of 22 aircraft and 16 balloons. Following the Armistice, No 84 moved into Germany with the Army of Occupation but returned to the United Kingdom in August 1919 to be disbanded on 30 January 1920.

No 84 Squadron was soon back on the Battle Order, however, being reformed at Baghdad on 13 August 1920 as a day bomber unit equipped with DH 9As. Moved to Shaibah in the south, the Squadron played a full part in the policing of Mesopotamia and Iraq for the next 20 years. Wapiti aircraft were received in July 1928, Vincents in January 1935 and Blenheims in February 1939, when the 'general-purpose' role of the unit was relinquished. The last Vincents left in June 1939, but the Blenheims remained at Shaibah until September 1940 when the Squadron transferred to Egypt and took part in Western Desert bombing operations against the

Wapiti IIA J9835 over Southern Iraq in 1931, the 'scorpion' badge already to the fore (RAF Museum P9658)

Italians. In November, the Squadron went to Greece but were forced to evacuate in April 1941 when the unit returned to Iraq to re-group before resuming Western Desert operations.

In January 1942 came a move to the Far East, to Sumatra in the Dutch East Indies, where all the aircraft were lost during the Japanese invasion. The surviving personnel were evacuated by sea and the Squadron was reorganized in India. New Blenheims were received in April, but relinquished in June when Vengeance dive-bombers were due. They did not become available until December 1942 and it was to be February 1944 before they were in action. The Vengeance was not a great success, however, and in July the Squadron was again withdrawn, this time to convert to Mosquitos. Technical problems, largely concerned with the aircraft's wooden construction, delayed conversion and the Vengeances were re-introduced in the autumn. In December 1944, plans changed again, the Vengeances were withdrawn and Mosquitos finally arrived in February 1945. When the Japanese surrendered in August, No 84 Squadron was still training, and their first action for well over a year was in Java, providing support for Allied forces trying to re-establish Dutch control of the East Indies!

The Squadron left Java in May 1946 and was soon settled in Singapore, receiving Beaufighters in November. These were used from the start of operations against Communist guerrillas in Malaya until the Squadron was moved to Iraq in October 1948. During February 1949, the unit re-equipped with Brigands and it was with these sturdy-looking light bombers that No 84 Squadron returned to Singapore and Operation 'Firedog' in April 1950. Flying in support of ground forces hunting the guerrillas in the Malayan jungle, the Squadron found the aircraft effective but troublesome, a succession of accidents forcing its grounding in January 1953.

The following month, No 84 Squadron was disbanded at Tengah but reformed the same day at Fayid, Egypt, by re-numbering No 204 Squadron, currently flying Valettas. These were used for general transport in the area, moving to Nicosia, Cyprus, when the Canal Zone was evacuated in March 1956. Newly gained expertise in paratroop dropping was used the following November during the ill-fated Suez operation, after which the Squadron transferred to Khormaksar to supplement the Aden Communications Flight. Army support during operations in the Protectorate was the main role, one Flight converting to Beverley tactical transports in June 1958 specifically for this task.

This commodious aircraft proved so successful that the whole Squadron was re-equipped in August 1960 when the Valettas were taken over by a newly-formed No 233 Squadron. Seven years later, the Beverleys

were replaced by Andovers and the unit moved to Sharjah for operations in the Persian Gulf area, but, with the withdrawal of British forces from the area, the Squadron was disbanded at Muharraq on 31 October 1971.

No 84 Squadron reformed at Akrotiri, Cyprus, on 17 January 1972 by re-numbering No 1563 (SAR) Flight and absorbing the No 230 Squadron detachment then on the island to provide support for the United Nations force. The Squadron operated two separate Flights for these very different tasks, both flying Whirlwind 10s until supplemented by Wessex 2 helicopters in March 1982. 'B' Flight at Nicosia re-equipped with ex-FAA Wessex 5s in 1984, followed by the rest of the Squadron at Akrotiri during 1985.

Today, the task remains the same, but these helicopters are dual-role, available for supplying the small UN control posts maintained in the Kyrenia mountain range and virtually inaccessible by other means, as well as for rescue work. No 84 Squadron was first into Beirut during the 1983 Lebanese crisis which resulted in the evacuation of the peace-keeping force from the city, and remains an essential element in this volatile part of the world.

Standard
Granted by HRH King George VI and promulgated on 9 September 1943. Presented by Air Chief Marshal Sir Francis Fogarty KCB KBE DFC AFC, Air Member for Personnel, at Abu Suier on 5 January 1956. Sir Francis was a former Commanding Officer.

A new Standard was presented by Air Chief Marshal Sir Keith Williamson GCB AFC ADC, Air Officer Commanding-in-Chief, Strike Command, at Akrotiri on 23 October 1980.

The old Standard was laid up in the Church of the Blessed Virgin and Child, Brockenhurst, Hants, on 19 July 1981.

Battle Honours
*Western Front 1917-1918
Cambrai 1917
*Somme 1918
Amiens
*Hindenburg Line
Iraq 1920
Iraq 1923-1925
Iraq 1928-1929
*Egypt & Libya 1940-1942
*Greece 1940-1941
*Iraq 1941
Habbaniya
Syria 1941
*Malaya 1942
*North Burma 1944
Manipur 1944

*Denotes Honours emblazoned on Standard

Whirlwind HAR 10 XK970 at Akrotiri in April 1975 carrying UN markings and the famous 'scorpion' (R. Clare).

Wessex HU 5C XS485 in October 1985 after the 'hearts' playing card emblem had been applied to the tail rotor mounting (A.S. Thomas).

Aircraft insignia and markings

The SE 5As first carried a white horizontal stripe along the fuselage sides and on the top decking aft of the roundel. From March 1918 onwards, they carried two white bars painted one on each side of the fuselage roundel and sloping inwards at the top.

In Mesopotamia, the first DH 9As on strength were only identifiable by their aircraft letter, but gradually Flight symbols were introduced in the form of playing cards, 'aces' for 'A' Flight, 'swastikas' for 'B' Flight and coloured triangles for 'C' Flight. Flight motifs were also painted on Wapitis, which additionally carried the 'scorpion' on the fin and used coloured wheel centres to denote the Flight.

By the time camouflaged Blenheims were on strength, the Squadron had been allocated the post-Munich Crisis code letters 'UR', but it is doubtful whether they were painted on the aircraft. The 'war' code 'VA', authorized in September 1939, certainly was used until the Squadron was made non-operational in January 1942. When reformed in India, only aircraft letters were used until right at the end of the war when Mosquitos started appearing with 'PY' painted on the rear fuselage. It is unlikely

that the replacement Beaufighters carried codes, and Brigands reverted to the pre-war 'playing card' symbols, displayed on the fins in a white square, a Squadron badge appearing on the nose.

Some Valettas also used the 'playing card' emblem, but most were pretty nondescript in a standard 'Transport Command' paint scheme, only the black-painted propeller spinners revealing the unit's identity. Beverleys were more colourful, employing the 'card' symbol on the fins and a large 'scorpion' emblem on the nose, these markings being retained when the aircraft were camouflaged. Replacement Andovers only carried the Squadron badge, on a white disc at the top of the fin, but the famous 'playing card' soon reappeared on the all-yellow 'Rescue' Whirlwinds of 'A' Flight, while camouflaged UNICYF machines carried the letters 'UN' in white on a light blue fuselage band in addition to a United Nations badge. Wessex 2s were similarly marked, depending on their dedicated role, but the Wessex 5 replacements are all camouflaged and carry the fuselage roundel on a narrow light blue band, the 'scorpion' on the nose and the 'card' symbol on the tail rotor mounting.

No 85 Squadron

Badge

On an ogress a hexagon voided — approved by HRH King George VI in January 1943, and presented by Air Vice Marshal H.W.L. Saunders CBE MC DFC MM, Air Officer Commanding No 11 Group, on 5 May 1943. The hexagon commemorates the Squadron marking first used during the First World War on SE 5As, possibly derived from the shape of the font in St Omer Church. The ogress alludes to the nocturnal activities of the Squadron.

Motto

Noctu diuque venamur — 'We hunt by day and night'

History

Formed at Upavon on 1 August 1917, No 85 Squadron moved to Norwich a few days later and was employed as a training unit until November, when it mobilized at Hounslow as a fighter squadron. Equipped with SE 5As, the Squadron left for France in May 1918 commanded by Major W.A. 'Billy' Bishop VC. He was soon transferred to the 'Home Establishment' because he refused to limit his flying, and in June the Squadron welcomed another great leader, Major 'Mick' Mannock DSO MC. On 26 July, he was over the trenches accompanied by a newcomer to the Squadron when he spotted and shot down a German two-seater, his 62nd victim. For some unexplained reason he then broke his own rule and followed the blazing aircraft down, and at 200 feet he was hit by an infantryman's bullet and he too crashed in flames. So ended the career of probably the greatest First World War fighter leader on either side, the posthumous award of the Victoria Cross being little compensation for such a loss.

Offensive patrols and ground attack remained the Squadron's main roles for the remainder of the war. It returned to the United Kingdom in February 1919 and was unceremoniously disbanded on 3 July the same year.

It was to be 19 years before No 85 Squadron reformed at Debden on 1 June 1938 from a nucleus provided by 'A' Flight of No 87 Squadron. Equipped with Gladiators until Hurricanes were received in September, the Squadron was worked up on the new monoplanes by June 1939 when they were allotted to the Air Component of the proposed British Expeditionary Force. Mobilized in August, the Squadron moved over to France on 9 September to spend a winter of interminable bad weather and standbys.

Apart from the official code letters, unit markings were banned during the war, but this No 85 Squadron Hurricane in France boldly carried the 'hexagon' (RAF Museum P19138).

Meteor NF 14 WS775 *carries the black and red checks of No 85 Squadron and, of course, the 'hexagon'* (Gloster Aircraft Co).

During the ten days of the Battle of France, the Squadron flew almost non-stop, and found itself back in the United Kingdom on 23 May 1940 with just four aircraft. Re-equipped, it resumed operations in June just in time for the early stages of the Battle of Britain. Moving to Yorkshire in September, the unit began night patrols in October for which Defiants were received during January 1941. These were quickly replaced by Havocs, flown alongside Hurricanes until July when the single-seaters finally left.

Airborne Interception (AI) radar training was now the main preoccupation, stepped up when Mosquitos arrived in August 1942. The first night success came on 16-17 May 1943 when four Fw 190 fighter-bombers were destroyed. In May 1944, the Squadron joined 100 Group, Bomber Command, and went over to the offensive, escorting heavy bombers and 'intruding' on enemy airfields. Over the D-Day period, the Squadron reverted temporarily to air defence, and then became involved in the V1 flying bomb 'war' before returning to 100 Group in September.

After the war, No 85 Squadron transferred back to Fighter Command, flying Mosquito night fighters until Meteor NF 11s replaced them in July 1951. Despite the arrival of the updated NF 14 in April 1954, the Meteor was rapidly becoming obsolete and the Squadron disbanded on 31 October 1958, only to be reborn a month later when No 89 Squadron was re-numbered. Flying variants of the Javelin all-weather fighter, the Squadron flew from various East Anglian bases until 31 March 1963 when it again disbanded.

The following day, the Fighter Command Target Facilities Squadron at West Raynham was re-designated No 85, the unit moving to Binbrook later in the month to provide interception training using Meteors and Canberras. The size of the Squadron gradually increased as more Canberras were added to the strength and, after moving back to West Raynham, the unit split into two, Nos 85 and 100 Squadrons. The task remained the same, continued by No 85 until 19 December 1975 when it was disbanded, to reform the same day on the same station as a Bloodhound-equipped ground-to-air missile unit. The Headquarters, 'A' Flight and 'D' Flight remain at West Raynham, the former controlling dispersed sites at North Coates ('B' Flight) and Bawdsey ('C' Flight). An 'E' Flight formed at Wattisham on 21 October 1981, became 'C' Flight No 25 Squadron in May 1983.

Standard

Granted by HRH Queen Elizabeth II and promulgated on 11 July 1962. Presented by Air Marshal Sir Douglas Morris KCB CBE DSO DFC, Air Officer Commanding-in-Chief, Fighter Command, at Binbrook on 4 June 1965.

Battle Honours

*Western Front 1917-1918
*France & Low Countries 1939-1940
*Battle of Britain 1940
*Home Defence 1940-1944
*Fortress Europe 1943
*Normandy 1944
*France & Germany 1944-1945

*Denotes Honours emblazoned on Standard

A demonstration 'round' — a Bloodhound 2 SAM on display in No 85 Squadron markings.

Affiliation

No 145 Squadron — linked as No 85/145 Squadron from February 1949 to March 1952.

Aircraft insignia and markings

During the First World War, a white hexagon was used as the unit marking, painted aft of the fuselage roundel. When the Squadron reformed with Gladiators in 1938, it was not allocated any unit colours because the decision had already been taken to use code letters on camouflaged aircraft then leaving the factories in increasing numbers. No 85 Squadron's peacetime code was 'NO', carried on Hurricanes after the Munich Crisis forward of the roundel with an individual letter aft. The unit code changed to 'VY' in September 1939 and was used on Hurricanes, Defiants, Havocs and Mosquitos. Many Hurricanes also carried the 'Hexagon' emblem, either on the fin or on the fuselage sides beneath the cockpit canopy, even on 'soot black' night fighters, an unusual, but not unique, contravention of security regulations.

In 1950, Fighter Command re-introduced coloured markings, No 85 being allocated red and black checks. These were carried as bars on each side of the fuselage roundels on Mosquito NF 36s and Meteors, the 'hexagon' being painted on the fin within a white ring. On Javelins, the red and black checks were moved to the upper portion of the fin, with a white 'hexagon' superimposed on them, but when re-equipped with Meteors and Canberras, the checks again flanked the roundel while the 'hexagon' remained on the fin.

Operational Bloodhounds do not carry markings, but the 'hexagon' has survived the missile age by being applied to display 'rounds'.

No 92 Squadron

Badge

A cobra entwining a sprig of maple — approved by HRH King George VI in January 1942. The cobra commemorates the Squadron's affiliation with eastern India, while the maple leaf signifies its association with Canadian units during the First World War.

Motto

Aut pugna aut morere 'Either fight or die'

History

The Squadron formed at London Colney on 1 September 1917, but was soon transferred to Chattis Hill as a training unit flying Avro 504s and Pups. In January 1918, it was mobilized as a fighter squadron and received its first SE 5As the following month. Work-up was slow and departure for France delayed until 1 July, but once on the Western Front No 92 gave a good account of itself on both offensive patrolling and ground strafing. After the Armistice, the Squadron moved into Belgium, and then into Germany the following June before disbanding at Eil on 7 August 1919.

Twenty years later, on 10 October 1939, No 92 Squadron reformed at Tangmere from a nucleus provided by No 601 Squadron. Intended as a night fighter unit, Blenheim IFs were provided and work-up began, but in March 1940 came re-designation as a day fighter squadron and Spitfire 1s arrived. The Squadron's first operation was flown on 10 May 1940, the day the Germans invaded the Low Countries, and it was soon in action over Dunkirk and again in the latter stages of the Battle of Britain. By January 1941, No 92 was providing cover for bombers raiding France, escorting convoys and going on fighter sweeps, all activities maintained until the Squadron was withdrawn in December to prepare for overseas. The Squadron left for Egypt aboard HMS *Ormonde* on 12 February 1942 and after 'kicking its heels' awaiting aircraft, operations over the Western Desert

A 'Blue Diamond' at Farnborough in the final paint scheme, in which the Hunter F 6s had the No 92 Squadron checks and badge on the nose.

started in August and moved into Tunisia and Italy. During July 1944, the Squadron underwent fighter-bomber training and then concentrated on army close support operations until the end of the war. Still with Spitfires, the unit moved into Austria in September 1946 and was disbanded at Zeltweg on 30 December.

A month later, No 91 Squadron was re-numbered No 92 at Acklington. The Squadron was now equipped with Meteor 3s, replaced in May 1948 by Mk 4s and in October 1950 by the Mk 8. A year earlier, No 92 had moved to Linton-on-Ouse, a delightful Station which was to be home for the next 7½ years, during which time Canadair-built Sabre 4s were received in February 1954, Hunter 4s in April 1956 and the superb Hunter F 6 during the following February. A series of moves found the Squadron at Leconfield in May 1961 where it was selected to form the RAF's official formation aerobatic team of the time, soon named the 'Blue Diamonds'.

In April 1963, the Squadron re-equipped with Lightning F 2s and took them to Germany in December 1965. The modified Mk 2A version, generally accepted as the best Lightning of all, was received in 1968 and, based at Gutersloh alongside No 19, the wing provided RAF Germany's interceptor force for the next ten years.

On 1 January 1977, No 92 Squadron (Designate) formed at Wildenrath to work up on Phantoms while the Lightnings at Gutersloh maintained the front-line strength of the unit. On 1 April, the Phantoms took over the Squadron's NATO commitments and the Lightning element disbanded.

No 92 remains at Wildenrath still flying Phantom FGR 2s, but will doubtless receive Tornado F 3s in due course.

Standard

Granted by HRH Queen Elizabeth II and promulgated on 20 November 1963. Presented by Air Chief Marshal Sir James Robb GCB KBE DSO DFC AFC, RAF (Retd) at Leconfield on 3 September 1965. As Captain J.M. Robb and senior Flight Commander, Sir James had drawn the Squadron's first blood on 22 July 1918.

Battle Honours

*Western Front 1918
Somme 1918
Hindenburg Line
Amiens
Home Defence 1940-1941
France & Low Countries 1940
*Battle of Britain 1940
*Fortress Europe 1940-1941
Egypt & Libya 1942-1943
*El Alamein
*El Hamma
Mediterranean 1943
*Sicily 1943
Italy 1943-1945
*Anzio & Nettuno
Gustav Line
*Gothic Line
*Denotes Honours emblazoned on Standard

Affiliations

'East India' — known officially from 1940 as No 92 (East India) Squadron in recognition of monetary gifts from the area which nominally purchased a complete Spitfire squadron. The name was dropped after Indian independence.

The best of the bunch — a Lightning F 2A in the dark green and silver paint scheme, miniaturized Squadron checks but a bold badge on the tail.

Phantom FGR 2 'X' of No 92 Squadron fires its 20 mm Vulcan gun during an Armament Practice Camp on Cyprus (RAF Germany TN9602/36).

Heinsberg — officially affiliated to the German town of Heinsberg in July 1977.

Nicknames

'Blue Diamonds' — given to the 16 Hunter formation team produced by the Squadron during 1961-62. The name 'Falcons' had been used for the team briefly in May 1961.

'The Cobras' — used locally in Germany and derived from the Squadron badge.

Aircraft insignia and markings

It is believed that a white dumb-bell was painted on the rear fuselage of SE 5As whilst in the United Kingdom and retained in France until March 1918 when the official marking became three vertical white bars, aft of the roundel.

When reformed in 1939, the Squadron incorrectly painted the 'peacetime' code 'GR' on its Blenheims, but this was changed to 'QJ' on Spitfires, a code used throughout the remainder of the war and until disbandment in 1946. The No 91 Squadron code 'DL' was retained when No 92 Squadron took over the aircraft, the Meteors also having red-painted engine intake rims. In 1950, the letters were changed to '8L', a code used until coloured markings were re-introduced.

No 92 Squadron adopted red and yellow checks painted in the form of bars on each side of the fuselage roundel and repeated in miniature on the nose of the aircraft, flanking the unit badge. Sabres also used the rear fuselage markings, and at one stage also had nose intakes in the red and yellow check, but Hunters had the main marking moved to the nose where the checks flanked the Squadron badge, the latter painted on a white disc.

When No 92 became the official formation aerobatic team as the 'Blue Diamonds' in 1961, the Hunters were painted over-all royal blue except for white wing-tips and a fuselage 'flash'. Replacement Lightnings were given royal blue fins and rudders, the fin carrying the Squadron badge on a large white disc. A red and yellow striped 'arrowhead' was painted around the nose roundel.

The Phantoms also carried red and yellow checks, but on each side of roundels painted on the engine intakes. The Squadron badge was retained in a white disc on the fin, the brown 'cobra' emblem flanked by red maple leaves. With the general introduction of 'low-visibility' grey camouflage, the unit markings have been toned down. The checks have been moved from the engine intakes to the RWR mounting on top of the fin, and the white disc background to the badge has been deleted.

No 100 Squadron

Badge

In front of the two human bones in saltire, a skull — approved by HRH King George VI in November 1937, and presented by Air Vice Marshal A. Tedder on 15 March 1938. The badge was the official version of a motif used by the Squadron on the Western Front in 1917. During the 1920s, a bulldog head had formed the basis for an unofficial badge.

Motto

Sarang tebuan jangan dijolok — 'Never stir up a hornet's nest'

History

The first RFC squadron specifically intended for night bombing, No 100 was formed from Home Defence Wing personnel at Hingham, Norfolk, on 23 February 1917, and crossed to France on 21 March. Twelve specially-equipped FE 2B two-seater pusher biplanes were collected at St André Aux Bois, and operations started in April, raids being concentrated on aerodromes, railway stations and rail junctions. In October, No 100 Squadron, together with No 55 and Naval 'A' Squadrons, formed the nucleus of the strategic bombing force which later became known as the Independent Force. During August/September 1918, the Squadron converted to the twin-engined Handley-Page 0/400, and undertook long-range bombing raids on major German towns. After the war, the Squadron spent nearly a year in France before returning to the United Kingdom in September 1919 as a cadre.

On 31 January 1920, No 100 Squadron absorbed the cadres of Nos 117 and 141 Squadrons at Baldonnel, Ireland, and, equipped with Bristol Fighters, became an army co-operation unit supporting the security forces in action against Sinn Fein in the Dublin area. When the Irish Free State was born, the Squadron returned to the UK and in March 1922 became a day bomber unit equipped with Avro 504Ks, DH 9As and Vickers Vimy aircraft, in practice functioning as an advanced training unit. The Squadron took up its designated role when Fairey Fawns arrived in May 1924, these ungainly aircraft being superseded by the rather more successful Horsleys in September 1926.

Four years later, still flying Horsleys, No 100 Squadron commenced torpedo-bomber training and was declared operational in this demanding role in March 1931. During November 1932, replacement Vildebeests started to arrive, the last Horsley departing in April 1933 when the unit was officially re-designated

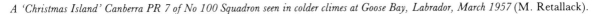

A 'Christmas Island' Canberra PR 7 of No 100 Squadron seen in colder climes at Goose Bay, Labrador, March 1957 (M. Retallack).

a torpedo-bomber squadron. Upgrading of the forces defending Singapore resulted in the despatch of No 100 Squadron to the Far East in December 1933 to join No 36 Squadron, but the planned re-equipment with Beauforts had not materialized by the time the Japanese attacked in December 1941. Both units had to face the might of Nippon with ancient and very obsolete Vildebeests in which they gallantly attacked landing ships and troop concentrations. The Squadrons were both decimated, the survivors being formed into a 'new' No 36 Squadron in February 1942.

No 100 Squadron was reformed at Waltham, Lincs, on 15 December 1942 in No 1 Group, Bomber Command, equipped with Lancasters, and commenced operations over Germany in March 1943. The rest of the European War was spent as a 'main force' unit, the Squadron being retained and converted to Lincolns in May 1946. These were detached to Malaya in June 1950 for bombing attacks on Communist guerrilla camps, and to Kenya in January 1954 during the Mau Mau uprising. On return from the latter excursion in March, the Squadron started conversion to Canberras, using them for trials work for the Bomber Command Development Unit and for photo-reconnaissance during nuclear weapons trials from Christmas Island.

Variants of the Canberra were flown until the unit disbanded on 1 September 1959, the Squadron reforming on 1 May 1962 as part of the V-Force equipped with Victor B 2 aircraft. Six years later came the withdrawal of the 'Blue Steel' stand-off weapon, resulting in a cut in the size of Strike Command, and No 100 Squadron was disbanded on 30 September 1968.

The Squadron was reformed yet again on 1 February 1972 following the splitting of the unwieldy target facilities unit, No 85 Squadron. No 100 concentrated on 'flag' training for fighter aircraft on armament practice camps, and the provision of 'silent' targets for radar installations. The unit moved from West Raynham to Marham on 5 January 1976, absorbing the flying personnel of Nos 85 and 98 Squadrons and their high-level radar calibration tasking at the same time. On 5 January 1982, No 100 moved to Wyton and took on yet another job, the drogue and flare target towing previously carried out by the disbanded No 7 Squadron for army and naval anti-aircraft gunnery practices. Currently, the Squadron is still at Wyton flying a mixture of Canberra B 2, PR 7, E 15 and TT 18 variants.

Standard

Granted by HRH King George VI and promulgated on 9 September 1943. Presented by Air Marshal Sir George Mills KCB DFC, Air Officer Commanding-in-Chief, Bomber Command, at Wittering on 21 October 1955.

A new Standard was presented by Marshal of the Royal Air Force Sir Michael Beetham GCB CBE DFC AFC at Wyton on 14 December 1984.

The old Standard, which had been temporarily laid up at St George with St Paul Church, Stamford, from 1959-62 and 1968-72, was finally laid in the same church on 20 October 1985.

Victor B 2 XM717 in anti-flash white and 'washed-out' markings including the 'skull and cross bones' on the fin (Military Aircraft Photographs).

After years of camouflage (as illustrated), No 100 Squadron Canberras are now appearing with 'hemp' upper surfaces but the blue and gold checks and badge remain on the fin (A.S. Thomas).

Battle Honours

Western Front 1917-1918
*Ypres 1917
*Somme 1918
*Independent Force & Germany 1918
*Malaya 1941-1942
*Fortress Europe 1943-1944
Biscay Ports 1943-1945
*Ruhr 1943-1945
*Berlin 1943-1945
German Ports 1943-1945
Baltic 1943-1945
France & Germany 1944-1945
*Normandy 1944
Walcheren
*Denotes Honours emblazoned on Standard

Affiliation

Stamford — a close association was formed under the municipal liaison scheme, the Squadron enjoying the Freedom of the Borough as part of the Wittering Wing. Since 1955, the Squadron's aircraft have carried a form of the Borough coat of arms.

Memorial

A memorial stone, with the badge of No 100 Squadron and the inscription '100 Squadron Royal Air Force, Waltham, Grimsby December 1942 — April 1945 Honour the Brave', is located in a lay-by on the western side of the A16 road by-passing Holton-le-Clay. Dedicated on 7 November 1978, it was created by members of Bravo 3 Post Fulstow, Royal Observer Corps.

Aircraft insignia and markings

Night bomber squadrons were not allocated unit markings during the First World War, so neither the FE 2Bs or 0/400s carried any official identification colours, symbols or codes. it is unlikely that Bristol Fighters used in Ireland carried unit markings either, but probable that individual numbers to identify particular aircraft were used on DH 9As. The Fawns definitely carried individual numbers, changed to the Squadron number just before the unit re-equipped with Horsleys. These aircraft had '100' painted forward of the roundel with an individual aircraft letter aft, while in the Far East Vildebeests carried an unofficial 'skull and crossbones' emblem on the fin for a time, but were later only distinguishable by individual aircraft numbers and serials.

Following the Munich Crisis of 1938, the official code letters 'RA' were allocated and apparently painted on Vildebeests; the code was changed to 'NK' in September 1939. When the Squadron reformed in Bomber Command, the code 'HW' was allotted and used on Lancasters, and subsequently Lincolns, until July 1951 when Squadron identification was reduced to the colour of propeller spinners, green on No 100 Squadron's aircraft. The following March, enlarged fuselage serials were introduced, usually aft of the roundel. A small Squadron badge was usually positioned beneath the cockpit side windows.

Wittering-based Canberras adopted gold and blue checked fins to denote the Station's association with the Borough of Stamford, No 100 Squadron superimposing a unit badge on a green disc, but detached aircraft at Wyton and Christmas Island usually featured a red fin with a white 'skull and crossbones' on the green disc. Victors retained this badge on the fin, toned down to a pale blue or red disc with a white emblem on aircraft painted in anti-flash schemes.

The blue and gold checks reappeared on the fins of target facility Canberras with the Squadron badge in a green disc superimposed on them. Some of the aircraft have also carried the Stamford coat of arms on the front fuselage, but this has been deleted since the Squadron has been based at Wyton. Two-letter codes were introduced in November 1981, the Squadron identification prefix being 'C'.

No 101 Squadron

Badge
Issuant from the battlements of a tower, a demi lion rampant guardant — approved by HRH King George VI in February 1938. The battlements symbolize the Squadron's pioneering role in the development of power-operated gun turrets, while the lion indicates the unit's fighting power and spirit. An earlier unofficial badge showed an eagle carrying a bomb intertwined with the Squadron number '101'.

Motto
Mens agitat molem — 'Mind over matter'

History
No 101 Squadron was formed at South Farnborough on 12 July 1917 as a night bomber unit. Two weeks later, the Squadron was in France equipped with the FE 2 two-seater pusher biplane which was to see it through the First World War. Night raids on communications, ammunition and aerodromes in Northern France and Belgium were the Squadron's main occupation, though strafing attacks on troops and special patrols aimed at drowning the noise of tanks positioning for battle, were also carried out. The Squadron remained on the Continent until reduced to cadre in March 1919 when it returned to the United Kingdom and was disbanded on the last day of the year.

Reformed at Bircham Newton on 21 March 1928, No 101 Squadron flew the DH 9As it took over from No 39 Squadron for nearly a year while awaiting delivery of the sprightly twin-engined Sidestrand day bomber, the first of which arrived in March 1929. In January 1935, the Overstrand, a development fitted with a power-operated nose turret, started to replace the Sidestrand and was used until Blenheims were received in June 1938.

Following the outbreak of war, the Squadron was used for training until July 1940 when the first bombing raid was made on Germany. Most early attacks, however, were on barge concentrations in the Channel ports, followed by a sustained attempt to close the Straits of Dover to enemy shipping. During April and May 1941, the Squadron converted to Wellington medium bombers and joined Bomber Command's night assault on Germany and Italy. Lancasters were received during October 1942, and in the following August the Squadron gained an additional role, their aircraft being fitted with 'Airborne Cigar', a device for jamming the R/T frequencies being used to control enemy night fighters. This work continued for the rest of the European war, after which No 101 was

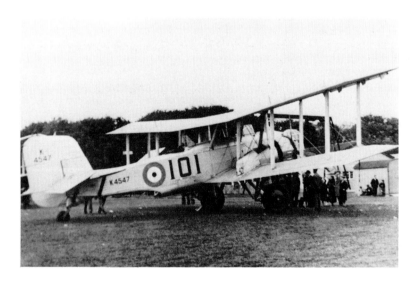

Overstrand K4547 at a display in the 1930s, possibly at Leuchars (RAF Leuchars via A.S. Thomas).

XM612 *during one of the Vulcan's always impressive displays. The Squadron emblem enclosed by the numerals '101' can just be discerned on the fin together with the Waddington Station badge.*

retained in Bomber Command, receiving Lincolns in August 1946 and Canberras in May 1951.

The Squadron pioneered the introduction of the jet-powered Canberra B 2 bomber into service and was also the first recipient of the improved Mk 6 variant, four of which were detached to the Far East in 1955 to take part in the offensive against communist insurgents in Malaya. A year later, the Squadron was operating from Malta bombing targets in Egypt, but was disbanded on 1 February 1957 soon after returning to Binbrook.

This was only a temporary situation, however, for the unit was earmarked for Vulcans and reformed at Finningley on 15 October in preparation for the first deliveries of the big delta during January 1958. The Squadron played a major role in the development of flight refuelling, achieving several notable long-range non-stop flights before re-equipment with Vulcan 2s started in January 1968. As part of the Waddington Wing, the Squadron took a full part in Bomber Command's deterrent role, and, right at the end of the Vulcan's career, the recovery of the Falkland Islands. The Squadron disbanded on 4 August 1982.

Less than two years later, on 1 May 1984, the Squadron reformed at Brize Norton to operate VC 10 tankers, receiving its first aircraft on 27 September 1985. It has since become a major component in the air defence organization of the United Kingdom, and has convincingly demonstrated the aircraft's flexibility during a number of long-range strategic air-refuelling operations.

Standard

Granted by HRH King George VI and promulgated on 27 March 1952. Presented by HRH The Princess Margaret, Countess of Snowdon, CI GCVO at Finningley on 14 June 1962. The Standard was temporarily laid up in the College Chapel, Cranwell,

from September 1982 until May 1984.

A new Standard was presented by Air Chief Marshal Sir Peter Harding KCB CBIM FRAeS on 24 June 1988 at Brize Norton.

Battle Honours

*Western Front 1917-1918
*Ypres 1917
*Somme 1918
Lys
Hindenburg Line
*Fortress Europe 1940-1944
*Invasion Ports 1940
*Ruhr 1940-1945
*Berlin 1941
Channel & North Sea 1941-1944
Biscay Ports 1941-1944
German Ports 1941-1945
Baltic 1942-1945
Berlin 1943-1944
France & Germany 1944-1945
*Normandy 1944
Walcheren
South Atlantic 1982

*Denotes Honours emblazoned on Standard

Mascot

A toy lion — named 'Clarrie'.

Memorials

During 1974, the Squadron 'adopted' a memorial to the crew of Wellington 1C *R1703* which crashed in Belgium on 31 August 1941. The memorial was built by the people of Boxbergheide in 1970 to replace a simple cross.

On 16 July 1978, at Ludford Magna, Market Rasen, Lincs, a memorial stone was dedicated to the personnel of the Squadron killed or missing while fly-

VC 10 K 3 ZA150 in the sunshine and standard 'hemp' colours at St Mawgan, August 1987. The No 101 Squadron badge is on the fin.

ing from the airfield during 1943-1946. The Roll of Honour is in the Lady Chapel of the village church.

Aircraft insignia and markings

Night bombers did not carry unit markings during the First World War, and DH 9As in service in 1928 were equally nondescript. Soon after the Sidestrands arrived, however, they were adorned with the Squadron number, painted forward of the fuselage roundel, red on 'A' Flight and yellow on 'B' Flight machines. Individual letters were carried on the nose, all markings being thinly outlined in black.

The scheme was retained on Overstrands, and possibly on Blenheims, though not for long because after the Munich Crisis of 1938 unit code letters 'LU' were allocated to the Squadron. These were painted on Blenheims aft of the roundel, an individual letter positioned forward. In September 1939, the code changed to 'SR', used on Blenheims, Wellington, Lancasters and Lincolns. In 1951, such codes were deleted and the few remaining Lincolns on the Squadron were then only distinguishable by their propeller spinners which were quartered black and white.

Binbrook Canberras were recognizable by a 'lightning flash' on the sides of the nose, those of No 101 Squadron being black and white in sections. From March 1952, much enlarged fuselage serials were introduced but the 'lightning flash' was retained, and a stylized Squadron badge appeared on the fin in a black disc. Canberra B 6s used during the Suez campaign had black and yellow bands painted around the rear fuselage as additional identification.

All-white Vulcans initially carried a Squadron badge at the top of the fin, but this was moved to the sides of the nose when the Waddington Wing started carrying the City of Lincoln coat of arms, a Crusader's shield. When centralized servicing was introduced in 1963, all Squadron markings were removed and it was not until 1975 that the policy was reversed and units again had their own aircraft. No 101 Squadron then introduced a version of its number painted in red on the fin, with the unit badge set inside the 'O', these markings being retained until disbandment.

The Squadron adopted similar markings for their VC 10 tankers, and additionally featured a large individual letter painted in white on the fins of hemp-coloured aircraft.

No 111 Squadron

Badge

In front of two swords in saltire, a cross potent quadrat, charged with three seaxes fesswise in pale —

approved by HRH King Edward VIII in October 1936. The cross commemorates First World War operations in Palestine, the seaxes signify its Essex base, and the swords signify London, the unit being part of the capital's defence force when the badge was designed.

Motto

Adstantes — 'Standing by (them)'

History

No 111 Squadron was formed at Deir-el-Belah, Palestine, on 1 August 1917 as the first dedicated fighter squadron in the area. Its task was twofold: to restrict the activities of enemy reconnaissance aircraft and to combat the increasing number of German fighters appearing on the Suez front. Initially equipped with such fighter aeroplanes as were available in Egypt, Bristol Scouts, Bristol M 1C monoplanes, DH 2s and Vickers FB 19s, the Squadron received Bristol F 2B Fighters in September and SE 5As in October. It was the latter types which did most of the work, joined by Nieuports in January 1918. The Bristol Fighters were handed over to No 1 Squadron, Australian Flying Corps, in February, and by the end of the month No 111 had one Flight of Nieuports and two of SE 5As. From July until the cessation of hostilities on 30 October 1918, the Squadron was completely equipped with SE 5s and concentrated on ground attack, harrying the Turkish troops so much that retreat turned into rout. After the Armistice, the Squadron withdrew into Egypt and was re-equipped with 'Brisfits' in February 1919. A year later, on 1 February 1920, the unit was renumbered No 14 Squadron.

No 111 Squadron was reformed at Flight strength on 1 October 1923 at Duxford equipped with Grebes. A second Flight was formed with Snipes on 1 April 1924 and a third received Siskins in June. This unsatisfactory state of affairs was not resolved until January 1925, when the Squadron was finally completely equipped with Siskin IIIs. Bulldogs were received in January 1931, replaced by Gauntlets during May 1936, and in January 1938 No 111 became the RAF's first Hurricane squadron.

Operational when the Second World War started in September 1939, No 111 Squadron was sent north to cope with enemy incursions over Northumberland, returning south in May 1940 to help stem the rapid German advance through northern France. After a brief spell operating from advanced landing grounds in France, the Squadron provided cover for troops on the Dunkirk beaches, and then took part in the early stages of the Battle of Britain.

The Squadron converted to Spitfires in April 1941, and during July started fighter sweeps over France in addition to unpopular bomber escorts. In November 1942, the unit embarked for Gibraltar for Operation 'Torch', the invasion of North Africa. After supporting the 1st Army through Algeria and Tunisia, the Squadron moved to Malta in June 1943 to cover the invasion of Sicily. Subsequently it moved into Italy

The special over-all glossy black used by the Squadron's Hunter F 6s when performing as the famous 'Black Arrows' (Military Aircraft Photographs).

The Squadron's Lightning T 5 XS450 'landing on' during the early 1970s and illustrating the colourful markings developed for the aircraft and retained on the Phantom.

and Corsica, from where the Allied landings in southern France were covered during July 1944. In October No 111 returned to Italy and operated in the fighter-bomber role for the remainder of the war. Following the German surrender, the Squadron went into Austria as part of the Occupation forces, but was disbanded, still with Spitfire IXs, at Treviso, Italy, on 12 May 1947.

No 111 Squadron reformed on 2 December 1953 at North Weald equipped with Meteor 8s. In June 1955, Hunter 4s were received, followed by Mk 6s in November 1956. The unit was nominated as the official RAF formation aerobatic team for 1957 and, starting with five Hunters, the Squadron worked up the numbers and surprised everyone with a nine-aircraft routine at the SBAC Show. The following year, with the help of No 56 Squadron, the 'Black Arrows' staggered the crowds at Farnborough by appearing with 22 Hunters and proceeding to loop, and even roll, in tight formation. This established 'Treble One' as the formation experts and gained the Squadron world-wide fame, which was consolidated by two more years of innovative nine-plane routines which set a standard others have striven hard to match.

In April 1961, the Squadron converted to Lightnings, flying variants of the aircraft for the next 13 years. On 1 July 1974 an element of the Squadron began conversion to Phantoms at Coningsby and took over the 'number plate' on 1 October, the day after the Lightning element at Wattisham had disbanded. The Squadron still flies Phantoms, unusual only in having changed from the FGR 2 version to ex-Royal Navy FG 1 when the latter became available in 1972. For the past 12 years, the Squadron has been responsible, alongside No 43, for the northern sector of the United Kingdom Air Defence Region, operating a Quick Reaction Alert (QRA) posture from Leuchars in Scotland.

Standard

Granted by HRH King George VI and promulgated on 27 March 1952. Presented by Air Chief Marshal Sir Harry Broadhurst KCB KBE DSO DFC AFC, Air Officer Commanding-in-Chief, Bomber Command, at North Weald on 30 April 1957.

A new Standard was presented by Air Chief Marshal Sir Patrick Hine KCB CBIM FRAeS at Leuchars on 2 August 1987.

Battle Honours

*Palestine 1917-1918
Megiddo
*Home Defence 1940-1942
France & Low Countries 1940
*Dunkirk
*Battle of Britain 1940
*Fortress Europe 1941-1942
Dieppe
*North Africa 1942-1943
Sicily 1943
*Italy 1943-1945
Salerno
Anzio & Nettuno
Gustav Line
*France & Germany 1944

*Denotes Honours emblazoned on Standard

Affiliation

No 66 Squadron — linked as No 66/111 Squadron from February 1949 until December 1953 when No 111 reformed.

Nicknames

'Treble One' — derived from the Squadron number.

'Tremblers' — derivation unknown, but probably first used by a rival squadron.

'Black Arrows' — name of No 111 Squadron formation aerobatic team, 1956-60.

Aircraft insignia and markings

No official unit markings were carried during the First World War, but individual aircraft were identified by fuselage paint schemes similar to those used on the Western Front. Soon after reforming in 1923, the Squadron's Grebes, Snipes and Siskins started appearing with a black stripe down the fuselage sides and across the top mainplane between the roundels. This was adopted as the official unit marking and used on Bulldogs and Gauntlets, the latter also carrying a Squadron badge on the fin.

Unusually for fighter squadrons, the Hurricanes had the numerals '111' painted in various colours on the sides of the fuselage and also continued to carry the badge on the fin. Following the Munich Crisis of 1938, the code letters 'TM' replaced the numerals and an individual aircraft letter was introduced. In September 1939, the code was changed to 'JU', used until the end of the Spitfire era in May 1947.

When reformed with Meteors in 1953, the pre-war black marking was adopted, applied in the form of yellow-edged rectangles on each side of the fuselage roundel. The same scheme was retained on Hunters, these also having a yellow-edged black letter on the dorsal fin and a Squadron badge on the forward fuselage beneath the cockpit canopy. When the Squadron became the RAF's official aerobatic team in 1957 various exotic paint schemes were tried before the simple, but extremely effective, over-all gloss black was adopted. Unit markings were confined to a small Squadron badge on the nose flanked by miniature gold rectangles.

In 1958, the roundels were outlined in white and a small individual aircraft letter was painted in red above swept-back national fin 'flash' markings on the tail. The national press immediately dubbed the team the 'Black Arrows', a name which became deservedly famous. When re-equipped with Lightnings, the standard rectangular-shaped markings were changed to a 'lightning flash' on the nose, centred on the roundel, while a stylized Squadron badge adorned the fin. In 1965, the new Lightning F 3s appeared in a more striking paint scheme. The yellow-outlined black 'lightning flash' remained on the nose, but the fuselage dorsal spine and the vertical tail surfaces were painted black, except for a yellow panel on which was superimposed a large Squadron badge, yellow on a black disc. The scheme was too flamboyant for the authorities, however, and in 1966 most of the black and yellow paint was removed, leaving the nose 'flash' intact and a much smaller version of the badge on the fin.

Squadron Phantoms retained the black 'lightning flash' on the nose, centred on a white disc within which was painted the unit badge. A somewhat toned down version of this scheme has survived a number of camouflage changes, including the current 'low-visibility' over-all grey, the tail marking now in outline form without a background disc. The RWR mounting was painted black with a yellow outline until 1985 when this marking was deleted.

Phantom FG 1 XV574 of No 111 Squadron in special markings — the CO's aircraft, 1987 (Military Aircraft Photographs).

No 115 Squadron

Badge
A dexter hand erased at the wrist holding a tiller — approved by HRH King George VI in February 1938. Presented by Air Commodore A.A.B. Thompson, Air Officer Commanding, No 3 Group, on 12 August 1938. The badge symbolized the importance of accurate navigation and a steady course.

Motto
Despite the elements

History
No 115 Squadron was formed at Catterick on 1 December 1917 from a nucleus provided by No 52 Training Squadron, specifically to operate the Handley Page 0/400 long-range night bomber. No aircraft or pilots were immediately available, so personnel were dispersed amongst other units until April 1918 when the unit reformed at Netheravon. In July, the Squadron moved to Castle Bromwich, was brought up to strength and mobilized, arriving in France on

1 September to join the Independent Force. Operations started on the night of 16-17 September, and by 5-6 November, when the Squadron's 15th and last raid was mounted, a total of 26 tons of bombs had been dropped for the loss of one aircraft. The Squadron remained in France until 4 March 1919 when it returned to the United Kingdom and disbanded on 18 October.

No 115 Squadron reformed on 15 June 1937 using 'B' Flight of No 38 Squadron as a basis. At first Hendons, borrowed from its parent, were flown, but Harrows began to arrive at the end of the month and the Squadron was soon operational on the aircraft. Conversion to Wellingtons started in April 1939 and antishipping sorties commenced in October, changed during May 1940 to land targets first in Norway and then in the Low Countries as part of Bomber Command's desperate efforts to stem the German advance into France. Attacks on German industrial targets commenced in June and continued for the next five years, No 115 Squadron remaining a 'main force' Bomber Command unit throughout. Hercules-engined Lancaster IIs were received in March 1943, replaced a year later by the more common Merlin-powered variants, and it was to be September 1949 before these were exchanged for Lincolns.

The Lincolns' career with No 115 Squadron was short, for the unit was officially disbanded on 1 March 1950 and the crews sent to America to convert to the B-29 Washington. The Squadron reformed at Marham on 13 June 1950, the first aircraft arriving in August. An impressive machine in appearance, the Washington was a technical nightmare, and it was with relief that they were replaced by Canberras in February 1954.

Lancaster B 1 PA181 of No 115 Squadron in 1945, but after the end of the war, for no guns are being carried and the serial is painted under the wings (D. West).

Argosy E 1 Omega *at Gibraltar in November 1975, the 'hand on tiller' badge and blue and yellow 'ILS' chevrons painted beneath the cockpit windows.*

The Squadron had a quiet time on Canberras, being one of the few Bomber Command units with the aircraft which did not take part in the Suez operation, though as a precautionary measure it did move to Cyprus in December 1956. Returning to Marham a month later, the Squadron disbanded on 1 June 1957.

Just over a year later, the Squadron reformed at Watton — by renumbering No 116 Squadron! Controlled by No 90 Group, the Squadron was tasked with the checking and calibration of RAF airfield radio and radar installations throughout the United Kingdom, Germany and parts of the Middle East. Varsities, supplemented by Valettas for a time, were used, one aircraft going as far as Gan in the Indian Ocean to calibrate the new ILS, while others found themselves checking equipment on warships. The Inspector of Radio Services' Hastings, appropriately named *Iris*, joined the Squadron in April 1967, but its days were numbered, for it was replaced by an Argosy in November 1968. Other Argosys had already started to replace the Varsity in February, but it was a slow change-over not completed until August 1970.

The 'Whistling Wheelbarrows' faithfully carried out the calibration tasks for ten years, until finally replaced by the more economical Andover in January 1978. Ten years later these sprightly ex-transports are still performing this mundane but vital task, the Squadron having moved to Benson on 7 January 1983 to operate its special E 3 variant alongside the aircraft of the Queen's Flight.

Standard

Granted by HRH Queen Elizabeth II and promulgated on 20 November 1963. Presented by Air Chief Marshal The Earl of Bandon GBE CB CVO DSO at Watton on 30 September 1966.

Battle Honours

*Independent Force & Germany 1918
*Channel & North Sea 1939-1943
*Norway 1940
France & Low Countries 1940
*German Ports 1940-1945
*Ruhr 1940-1945
*Fortress Europe 1940-1944
Invasion Ports 1940
*Berlin 1940-1944
Biscay Ports 1940-1943
Baltic 1943
*Normandy 1944
France & Germany 1944-1945
Rhine

*Denotes Honours emblazoned on Standard

Affiliation

No 218 Squadron — linked as No 115/218 Squadron from February 1949 to February 1950, and June 1950 until 1955.

Aircraft insignia and markings

Bomber squadrons did not carry unit markings during the First World War, but when No 115 Squadron received its Harrows in June 1937 they adopted the current style of identification, the numerals '115' being painted on the fuselage forward of the roundel. A single letter aft of the roundel identified the individual aircraft.

Following the Munich Crisis of 1938, the code letters 'BU' were allotted to No 115 Squadron and probably employed on Harrows. Certainly the 'BU' code

was used on Wellingtons, changed to 'KO' in September 1939, in both cases painted on the aircraft aft of the fuselage roundel. The same code was used on Lancasters of 'A' and 'B' Flights, supplemented by 'A4' on 'C' Flight aircraft when it first formed in November 1943. This Flight was used as a nucleus for No 195 Squadron in October 1944, and the code went with it. The new 'C' Flight adopted 'IL' until August 1945 when the Squadron reverted to two-Flight strength. After the war, the 'KO' code was retained on Lancasters, Lincolns and Washingtons, painted on the rear fuselage of the latter, with the individual letter moved to the fin.

Canberras of the Squadron were unmarked except for black-painted wing-tip tanks, but when the unit reformed for calibration work with Varsities, these were a little more distinctive, carrying the yellow Signals Command trim line down the full length of the fuselage and individual letters. Argosys had a stylized blue and yellow ILS beam on the fin with the Roman numerals 'CXV' superimposed in red, and similar markings were initially used on Andovers. Since they have been repainted in 'high-visibility' red/grey/white colours, however, the unit markings have been revised and now consist of a Squadron badge on a white disc flanked by the blue and yellow chevron, repositioned on the forward fuselage beneath the pilot's cockpit windows.

During May 1982, one of the Andovers was named *Guy Devas* by Group Captain W.G. Devas who commanded the Squadron in 1944 — a dedication for and by a person still alive is believed to be a unique occasion. In May 1984, the Wellingford coat of arms was painted on all the aircraft.

No 120 Squadron

Badge
Standing on a demi terrestrial globe, a falcon close — approved by HRH King George VI in August 1944 and presented by Air Marshal Sir John Baker KCB MC DFC, Air Officer Commanding-in-Chief, Coastal Command, on 12 July 1949. The falcon commemorates the Squadron's time in Iceland and the unit's predatory instinct.

Motto
Endurance

History
Officially formed on 1 January 1918, it was the 18th of that month before personnel started assembling at Cramlington, Northumberland. Equipped with the DH 9 day bomber, the unit was intended as a reinforcement for the Independent Force in France, but the Armistice was signed before No 120 became operational and the Squadron remained in limbo.

When it was decided to extend the continental mail

Left *Andover E 3 XS640 of No 115 Squadron landing at Brize Norton in October 1979* (J. Bartholomew).

Right *The mainstay of No 120 Squadron for many years was the Shackleton MR 3. WR989 was one of the first received by the unit in 1958.*

service operated by RAF squadrons, No 120 was moved to Hawkinge and on 1 March 1919 four DH 9s of 'B' Flight flew the first schedules to Maisoncelle in France. A DH 10 twin-engined bomber was used experimentally during May, but it was the single-engined DH 9 and DH 9As which continued in service, moving to Lympne in July when the route was extended to Cologne. By August, British occupation forces had been much reduced, however, and the much smaller commitment was handed over to civil aviation, No 120 Squadron ceasing mail flights on 24 August and disbanding on 21 October 1919.

The Squadron reformed on 2 June 1941 at Nutts Corner, Northern Ireland, with the express purpose of closing the 'Atlantic Gap', the area of mid-ocean in which U-boats could operate without fear of interference from land-based anti-submarine aircraft. No 120 was equipped with special long-range Liberator aircraft which, after the usual teething troubles, became very successful.

The Squadron moved west to Ballykelly on 21 July 1942, and after several sightings and attacks scored the first confirmed success on 12 October when *U-597* was sunk by depth charges. A detachment was operated from Iceland from September 1942, the whole Squadron moving there during April 1943, 'A' Flight operating from Reykjavik and 'B' Flight from Meeks Field (later renamed Keflavik). In the first six weeks of flying from Iceland, four more U-boats were sunk and by the end of 1943 the Battle of the Atlantic was nearly won. In March 1944, No 120 returned to Ballykelly and joined Coastal Command's massive anti-U-boat operations in support of Operation 'Overlord', the Normandy invasion. The Squadron

ended the war as the RAF's top-scoring anti-submarine unit, destroying 14 U-boats outright, having shares in the destruction of three more, and damaging eight.

Despite this outstanding record, No 120 Squadron was disbanded on 4 June 1945, but reformed again on 1 October 1946 when No 160, recently returned to the United Kingdom from Ceylon with Liberators, was renumbered at Leuchars. A number of Lancaster ASR 3s had already been received by No 160 Squadron, and these were used for training while three Liberators remained operational for SAR duty. By the end of February 1947, conversion was complete and the last Liberators left in June. A detachment was sent to Ein Shemer, Palestine, in November 1947, the crews engaged on searches for illegal immigrant ships until February 1948 when they returned to Leuchars. The Squadron moved further north to Kinloss in February 1950, and a year later received the first Shackletons to enter RAF service. Intensive flying trials of the new aircraft occupied the summer of 1951, the Squadron then settling down to working it up operationally.

A move to Aldergrove was made in April 1952 and three Shackleton 2s joined the Mk 1s a year later. The odd system whereby the squadrons operated a mixture of aircraft was rationalized in 1954 when No 120 reverted to Mk 1s, changing to Mk 2s in October 1956, and two years later to the radically different Shackleton Mk 3.

On 1 April 1959, the Squadron returned to Kinloss and, apart from detachments, has stayed there ever since, the Shackletons being replaced by Nimrods in February 1971. In January 1977, a new role was added to the anti-submarine, surface surveillance and SAR tasks, that of patrolling the United Kingdom 200-mile fishery limits, flown by the Squadron in rotation with other No 18 Group Nimrod units until October 1981, when the task was taken over by the Ministry of Agriculture, Fisheries and Food, using Islander and Dornier Do 228 aircraft.

During 1981, the crews converted to the up-dated Nimrod MR 2, using air-to-air refuelling to carry out long-range patrols over the Southern Atlantic from Ascension Island during the recovery of the Falkland Islands. No 120 Squadron still flies this excellent maritime aircraft as part of the Kinloss Wing, operating within No 18 Group, Strike Command.

Standard

Granted by HRH King George VI and promulgated on 27 March 1952. Presented by HRH Queen Elizabeth II at Kinloss on 14 August 1961. The usual requirement for 25 years continuous service was waived in view of the Squadron's outstanding war achievements.

A new Standard was presented by HRH The Prince Philip, Duke of Edinburgh KG KT OM GBE QSO at Kinloss in July 1988.

Battle Honours

*Atlantic 1941-1945
*Biscay 1941-1944
*Arctic
*Channel & North Sea 1941-1945
South Atlantic 1982

*Denotes Honours emblazoned on Standard

Mascots

Icelandic falcons — two stuffed birds were presented by Mr D.D. MacRae of Forres and Mrs M.D. Fergson of Pitlochry.

Affiliation

No 220 Squadron — linked as No 120/220 Squadron from February 1949 until September 1951.

Memorial

A stained glass window in the Anglican Church of St Columba, Kinloss, was commissioned by the Squadron to commemorate their 65th anniversary. It was completed in 1983 and dedicated in April 1984.

Aircraft insignia and markings

No unit markings were carried by No 120 Squadron aircraft during 1918-19. When reformed in 1941, the Squadron's Liberators were usually coded 'OH', painted on the rear fuselage, with an individual letter forward of the roundel, though some just used an aircraft letter. In August 1943, a numeral probably replaced the unit code letters, but during July 1944 the Squadron reverted to 'OH' until disbandment. When renumbered from No 160 Squadron, the latter unit's code 'BS' was retained and used on Liberators and Lancasters.

When Shackletons were received, the Squadron was allotted the 18 Group unit code letter 'A', each aircraft also carrying an individual letter in light sea grey. In 1956, following repainting of the aircraft in

Right *Nimrod MR 2P of the Kinloss Wing, used by Nos 120, 201 and 206 Squadrons as required, July 1987.*

Below left *Shackleton MR 2 WG532 'F' of No 120 Squadron in Cuba during 1958. Maritime aircraft get around much more than is generally realized.*

over-all dark slate grey, the Squadron number '120' replaced the earlier markings. Painted in white-edged red on the rear fuselage, the unit marking was balanced by an individual letter on the nose. After an incident in the Red Sea area involving another Shackleton squadron, 'Royal Air Force' was painted in white on the rear fuselage and the '120' was moved forward and slightly decreased in size. A Squadron badge appeared on the forward fuselage and a 'falcon' emblem on the fins.

When the aircraft were 'pooled' at Kinloss during the late 1960s, unit markings were removed from Shackleton 3s and have not re-appeared on Nimrods except for special occasions, usually overseas detachments, when 'CXX' has sometimes been painted on the fin.

No 151 Squadron

Badge

On a hurt an owl affrontée, wings elevated alighting on a seax — approved by HRH King George VI in May 1937. The owl represents the night fighter role, while the seax is derived from the Arms of Essex to commemorate North Weald, the Squadron base when the badge was being designed.

Motto

Foy pour devoir — 'Fidelity into duty'

History

Formed at Hainault Farm on 12 June 1918 by transferring a Flight from Nos 44, 78 and 112 (Home Defence) Squadrons to the new unit, its purpose was to provide night fighter defence against the extensive attacks being made on British bases in France. Equipped with Camels, the first Flight crossed the Channel on 16 June and by the end of the month the complete Squadron was operational in the Abbeville area. Its first success came on 23 July, and in August No 151 went over to the offensive pioneering the 'intruder' operations of the Second World War by loitering in the vicinity of German airfields at night awaiting the return of their bombers. By the Armistice, they had claimed the destruction of 26 enemy aircraft at night, a considerable feat in a machine without location aids and acknowledged to be difficult to fly in daylight, never mind in the dark. The Squadron remained in France until February 1919, then returned to the United Kingdom and disbanded at Gullane on 10 September.

Seventeen years later, on 4 August 1936, No 151 Squadron reformed using a Flight from No 56 Squadron as a nucleus. Brand new Gauntlet IIs were received in October, and were still in use when the Munich Crisis of 1938 erupted. Soon afterwards Hurricanes began to arrive, but it was March 1939 before the last Gauntlet was despatched to No 602 Squadron and the unit was again declared operational.

When the Second World War began, No 151 Squadron was still at North Weald and flew sector patrols uneventfully until May 1940 when detachments at Manston started operating over France to assist Air Component and Advanced Air Striking Force units struggling with the Luftwaffe onslaught during Germany's thrust into France. During the Dunkirk evacuation, the Squadron helped cover the beaches

Left Hurricane 'L' of No 151 Squadron at Sealand in August 1939, coded 'GG'. The Squadron badge can just be discerned in the white 'spearhead' on the fin (H.A.G. Smith).

Right Meteor NF 11 WM223 proudly displays St Andrews crosses on the fuselage during the early 1950s (RAF Museum P12934).

Below right A fully-armed Hawk T 1A of No 2 Tactical Weapons Unit, Chivenor, over the Taw Estuary, North Devon. XX337 carries the current 'shadow' No 151 Squadron. (British Aerospace plc (Kingston) 8702525).

and then defended coastal convoys while awaiting the inevitable Battle of Britain. Severely mauled during the Battle, the unit was withdrawn north on 1 September, and, when night raids started, transferred to nocturnal activity, receiving some AI-equipped Defiants in December to operate alongside black-painted Hurricanes.

The Squadron had some success by maintaining a patrol line, but none at all in attempted co-operation with Turbinlite-equipped Havocs of 1453 Flight. When these efforts were abandoned in January 1942, the Hurricanes left and the unit flew only Defiants until April when conversion to Mosquito night fighters began. By the time the last Defiant left in July, the first success with the Mosquito had been gained and these continued into 1943 when the Squadron started intruder sorties over the Continent. In April, No 151 moved from Wittering to Colerne and started detachments in Cornwall to extend the range of patrols over the notorious Bay of Biscay, where Ju 88s were making a nuisance of themselves.

Further moves were made in response to German fighter-bomber raids on East Anglian airfields and renewed attacks on London, but by March 1944 the Squadron was back in the south-west flying 'Instep' patrols over the Bay and 'Rangers' over France. Back in East Anglia in October 1944, the Squadron concentrated on intruder and high-level bomber support operations throughout the winter months until the end of the European war. The inevitable post-war run-down saw No 151 Squadron disbanding on 10 October 1946.

Five years later, on 15 September 1951, the Squadron reformed at Leuchars as a Vampire night fighter unit in 12 Group. The operational NF 10s started to arrive in February 1952, and the unit was finally up to strength by December. The Vampire was merely a stopgap, however, and in March 1953 the Squadron

converted to Meteor NF 11s, replaced in turn by Venom NF 3s in July 1955. Never a popular aircraft, the Venoms were superseded by Javelins in May 1951, and at last the unit had an effective aircraft with which to tackle the increasing threat from long-range Soviet bombers penetrating the northern air defence region.

More cuts in the strength of Fighter Command were on their way, and on 19 September 1961 No 151 Squadron was disbanded once more. It was not for long, however, for on 1 January 1962 the Signals Development Squadron of the Central Signals Establishment at Watton was re-designated as No 151 Squadron. Tasked by Signals Command on various electronic countermeasures training and development duties, the Squadron was divided into four Flights, 'A' with Varsities, 'B' flying Lincolns, 'C' Canberras and an unnamed Flight operating a couple of Hastings, one of them 'Iris'. The Lincolns were withdrawn just before the unit was renumbered No 97 Squadron on 25 May 1963.

Eighteen years later, on 21 September 1981, one of the training squadrons of No 2 Tactical Weapons Unit, Chivenor, was designated No 151 (Shadow) Squadron and given a reserve air defence role with Hawks. The aircraft have been equipped to carry two Sidewinder air-to-air missiles on underwing pylons in addition to the standard gun pod under the fuselage, the Squadron operating alongside the other four reserve Hawk units and providing a significant low-level fair-weather addition to the UK air defence front-line strength.

Standard
Not granted.

Battle Honours
Not determined (only applicable when a standard is granted).

Mascots

Two owls — these gifts to the Leuchars-based Javelin night fighter unit were handed over to the reformed Squadron at Watton in January 1962. Their subsequent fate is unknown.

Affiliation

No 23 Squadron — linked as No 23/151 Squadron from February 1949 to September 1951.

Aircraft insignia and markings

The Squadron's Camels carried a horizontal white stripe along the full length of the fuselage sides. The Gauntlets had the official marking of a black bar edged top and bottom by light blue bars on each side of the fuselage roundel and across the upper mainplane between the roundels. In September and October 1938, the aircraft were camouflaged and coloured markings were replaced by two-letter unit codes for identification. It is believed that 'TV' was allotted to No 151 Squadron, and that it was carried on some Gauntlets though replaced by 'GG' when Hurricanes arrived.

At the outbreak of war in September 1939, the unit code was changed to 'DZ', a combination retained until 1946. On reformation at Leuchars, the Scottish connection was emphasized by the adoption of a St Andrew's cross, a white cross on a blue background. Outlined in black, it was painted on each side of the boom roundel of Vampires and Venoms and on the fuselage of Meteors. Coloured nose-wheel doors denoted the Flight, and also carried the individual aircraft letter in white.

On the Javelin, a single St Andrew's cross was carried on the fin on which the aircraft letter was also painted, but on Hawks the same markings reverted to the fuselage, positioned on each side of the roundel. On the 'low-visibility' grey-camouflaged aircraft, the markings were miniaturized and in pale colours, a single aircraft letter appearing on the fin.

No 201 Squadron

Badge

A seagull, wings elevated and addorsed — approved by HRH King Edward VIII in May 1936 and presented by Air Marshal Sir Arthur Longmore KCB DSO during August 1936. This was an officially approved version of a badge long in use by the Squadron.

Motto

Hic et ubique — 'Here and everywhere'

History

No 201 Squadron came into being on 1 April 1918 as a result of the amalgamation of the RNAS and RFC to form the RAF. It had previously been No 1 Squadron, RNAS, which originally formed at Fort Grange, Gosport, on 16 October 1914 for operations in France with the Army. Almost immediately, the unit was re-styled No 1 (Naval) Squadron, and with four Bristol Scouts a detachment was formed at Newcastle for coastal reconnaissance. In December, Avro 504s and Sopwith Tabloids were received, and four of the former went to Dover as a local defence Flight. The rest of the Squadron, apart from 'C' Flight at Newcastle, moved to Dover and took part in attacks on Bruges before crossing to France on 26 February 1915 with Avro 504s, a Vickers Gunbus and a two-seater Bristol.

Operations were varied and included reconnaissance, photography, artillery spotting and bombing, mainly in the Ostend/Zeebrugge area. The scouts on strength were also used for attacks on German airships, and it was while on his way to bomb the sheds at Berchem St Agathe on the night of 6-7 June that Flight Sub Lieutenant R.A.J. Warneford sighted *LZ37*. He caught up with it near Bruges and, climbing above the vast envelope, released his six 20 lb

Sunderland GR V DP198 moored in the Thames off the Tower of London, boldly announcing its unit by number and badge (RAF Pembroke Dock).

Shackleton MR 3 XF710 'K' of No 201 Squadron 'on patrol'. The 'seagull' emblem is painted on the white shield on the fin (Hawker Siddeley Aviation A2/2).

bombs. There was a violent explosion which turned the flimsy Morane monoplane on to its back. Regaining control, Warneford saw the airship on the ground in flames, but then suffered engine failure and had to force land in enemy territory. He repaired the engine and took off only to be forced down again in thick fog near Cap Gris Nez. He was immediately awarded the Victoria Cross for this fearless solo attack.

In August 1915, the RNAS was reorganized and the Squadron was renamed No 1 Wing. Returning briefly to Dover, it was soon back in France to continue its all-purpose existence with an extraordinary variety of aircraft. Another reorganization in March 1916 saw Nos 1 and 2 Flights of No 1 Wing becoming 'A' Squadron, the Flights flying two-seater Nieuports for reconnaissance work and single-seaters for fighting duties. A third Flight, equipped with twin-engined Caudrons bombers, joined the unit for several weeks, but from June 1916 'A' Squadron was slowly re-equipped with Sopwith Triplanes. On 6 December, the unit designation officially reverted to No 1 Squadron, RNAS. Heavily engaged in the mass dogfights so much a feature of the period, the Triplanes were also used for ground strafing until November when the attachment to the RFC ceased and No 1 returned to the United Kingdom for re-equipment.

Fully worked up on Camels, No 1 (Naval) returned to France in February 1918 and was soon embroiled in savage air fighting during Germany's spring offensive. Becoming No 201 Squadron in April, the unit concentrated its main effort on ground attack work, though it was a classic dogfight which resulted in the award of the Squadron's second VC. Attached to the Squadron for refresher flying, Major W.G. Barker

DSO MC attacked and shot down an enemy two-seater during the morning of 27 October while out alone in his personal Snipe. He was immediately attacked by a Fokker biplane which he promptly despatched. Now in the middle of a formation of Fokkers attacking him from all directions, he was seriously wounded and lost consciousness. Recovering, he picked out one of his attackers which went down in flames. He again fainted, recovered, and shot down another before crossing over the lines and crash-landing, badly wounded in both legs and with his left arm shattered. It was a remarkable performance!

After the Armistice, No 201 Squadron remained in France but handed over its aircraft to No 203 Squadron and was reduced to cadre on 23 January 1919. Returning to the United Kingdom on 15 February, the Squadron was officially disbanded on the last day of the year.

As the end of the 1920s drew near, the rather low-key flying boat element of the RAF was reorganized and strengthened, No 480 (Coastal Reconnaissance) Flight at Calshot being re-designated No 201 Squadron on 1 January 1929. Equipped with the excellent Southampton, No 201 Squadron was soon well established, the highlight of each year's activity being the annual 'cruise'. In April 1936, the first London flying boat replacement was collected and the Squadron was completely re-equipped by the end of the year. Annual 'cruises' continued until 1938, but the following year more serious things were afoot and No 201 found itself at Sullom Voe in the Shetlands with six Londons on strength. Patrols across the Norway-Shetland 'gap' commenced on 4 September 1939, but in November the Squadron moved to Invergordon to receive Sunderlands.

Back in the Shetlands, the priority was anti-submarine patrols over the North Atlantic, but reconnaissance of northern Norway was a secondary and very dangerous task, continued until a move was made to Castle Archdale, Northern Ireland, in October 1941. With D-Day approaching, No 201 Squadron went to Pembroke Dock in March 1944 to assist in the successful English Channel blockade which virtually prevented U-boat movement in the invasion area. Back at Castle Archdale in November, the Squadron resumed Atlantic patrols, the last being despatched on 3 June 1945. It was also the last wartime patrol by Coastal Command, Royal Air Force.

Retained after the war, No 201 remained at Castle Archdale until August 1945 when a move was made to Pembroke Dock, followed by another to Calshot in March 1946. Trials on the replacement Seaford flying boat were made, but the Sunderland soldiered on, the Squadron taking part in the Berlin Airlift in 1948 flying from the Elbe near Hamburg to the Havel See in Berlin. Operations in support of the North Greenland Expedition were another hazardous peacetime mission, but the days of the flying boat were numbered and on 28 February 1957 the Squadron disbanded.

No 201 Squadron reformed at St Mawgan on 1 October 1958 by renumbering No 220 which had spent the previous few months on intensive flying trials of the new Mk 3 version of the Shackleton maritime reconnaissance aircraft. Used for anti-submarine, shipping surveillance and air sea rescue work, the aircraft, the landplane equivalent of the Sunderland, was operated by No 201 Squadron for the next 12 years during which the unit moved to Kinloss to counter the increasing Soviet threat in northern waters.

In October 1970, the Squadron received the first of the Nimrod replacements and has flown the 'Mighty Hunter' from Kinloss for the past 18 years, upgrading to the much improved Mk 2 variant in 1981. Using its flight refuelling capability, the Squadron took part in the Falklands campaign of 1982.

Standard

Granted by HRH King George VI and promulgated on 27 March 1952. Presented by Air Vice Marshal G.W. Tuttle CB DFC FRAeS, Air Officer Commanding, No 19 Group, at Pembroke Dock on 16 December 1955. The Standard was unique in embodying the Croix de Guerre, presented to the Squadron after action in support of the French Army during 1917.

A new Standard was presented by HRH The Prince Philip, Duke of Edinburgh, KG KT OM GBE QSO at Kinloss on 9 November 1984. Prince Philip is Honorary Air Commodore, Kinloss.

The old Standard was laid up in the town church of St Peter Port, Guernsey, on 17 March 1985.

Battle Honours

*Western Front 1915-1918
*Arras
*Ypres 1917
*Somme 1918
Amiens
Hindenburg Line
Channel & North Sea 1939-1945
*Norway 1940
*Atlantic 1941-1945
*Bismarck
Biscay 1941-1945
*Normandy
South Atlantic 1982

*Denotes Honours emblazoned on Standard

Nimrods have carried Squadron markings for special occasions. At Greenham Common in June 1981, Nimrod MR 1 XV252 has the No 201 Squadron 'seagull' on the fin.

Nimrod MR 2P XV239 of the Kinloss wing in July 1987 — a 'pooled' aircraft drawn on by Nos 120, 201 and 206 Squadrons as required, and therefore carrying a Station badge.

Affiliation

Guernsey — officially affiliated in April 1939 as part of the Municipal Liaison Scheme. Since the war, the liaison has been fostered and a No 201 Squadron room is a feature of the Castle Cornet Museum in Guernsey. In 1978, the Squadron also became affiliated with HMS *Guernsey*.

Memorial

A stained glass window featuring the Croix de Guerre, No 201 Squadron badge and the crest of Guernsey, in the Station church, Kinloss, was dedicated on 8 November 1984.

Aircraft insignia and markings

It is unlikely that the Squadron used a unit marking until the Triplane was in service, but during late 1917 two short vertical white bars were painted on the rear fuselage sides and an individual number was used to distinguish the aircraft. Soon after their Camels arrived in France, the Squadron adopted a single vertical white stripe positioned aft of the fuselage roundel.

When reformed in 1929, the Southamptons had the four numerals of their serials painted in black on the nose, but Londons adopted individual aircraft letters. After the Munich Crisis, the unit code 'VQ' was allocated and carried, changed to 'ZM' in September 1939. Coastal Command dropped the two-letter code system in August 1943 and introduced a single numeral, No 201 Squadron adopting '1' which identified the unit within the Castle Archdale Wing. Individual aircraft code letters were also carried.

In July 1944, the code letters returned, No 201 Squadron being given 'NS'; this was used on Sunderlands until 1951, when the single letter 'A' was

introduced as the unit marking, supplemented by the Squadron badge on the forward hull. In 1956, another change was made, the Squadron number appearing on the rear fuselage of Shackleton 3s in white-edged red until aircraft at Kinloss were 'pooled' during the mid-sixties.

Nimrods have remained unmarked except on special occasions when badges, or a representation of the 'seagull' emblem, have been used — but soon removed.

No 202 Squadron

Badge

A mallard alighting — approved by HRH King George VI in December 1937. The badge highlighted the unit's long association with water and flying boats.

Motto

Semper vigilate — 'Be always vigilant'

History

No 202 Squadron can trace its origins back to the early days of the Royal Naval Air Service, first forming as No 2 Squadron, RNAS, at Eastchurch on 17 October 1914. Equipped with a motley collection of aircraft, it moved to Dover in February 1915 for operations against Belgian ports, but was also tasked with providing anti-Zeppelin patrols. In June 1915, the RNAS was reorganized and No 2 Squadron was swallowed up by No 2 Wing.

Another reorganization resulted in No 2 Squadron reforming from 'B' Squadron of No 1 Wing on 5 November 1916 at Dunkirk. The Squadron was basically equipped with Farman F40s which were used for reconnaissance over the Belgian Coast, but also had a number of Sopwith Pups and 1½-strutters on strength for escort duties. The opposition gradually strengthened, and it was with relief that the first DH 4s arrived in March 1917. The last of the 1½-strutters left in November, and, fully equipped with one type of aircraft at last, the Squadron continued its spotting, reconnaissance and bombing tasks over southern Belgium, even after becoming No 202 Squadron, RAF, on 1 April 1918.

A few DH 9s were received in May 1918, but they were soon returned to the Depot and operations with DH 4s intensified during the final stages of the advance into Belgium. Soon after the Armistice, the DH 4s were dispersed amongst other squadrons and in March 1919 No 202's cadre moved to the United Kingdom for disbandment on 22 January 1920.

No 202 Squadron reformed on 9 April 1920 at Alexandria, Egypt. Equipped with Short 184 seaplanes, the Squadron was intended for co-operation duties with the Mediterranean Fleet, but inter-service rivalries and further economies resulted in disbandment on 16 May 1921.

RAF maritime activity in the Mediterranean was confined to the seaplane station at Kalafrana and its resident 481 Flight for the next eight years, but on 1 January 1929 the Flight was upgraded and became No 202 (Flying Boat) Squadron. The same six Fairey IIID floatplanes already at Kalafrana remained in service until July 1930 when IIIFs started to arrive, and it was to be May 1935 before flying boats appeared on Squadron strength in the form of the excellent Scapa. A 'cruise' to West Africa by two of these 'boats' proved something of a saga, however, and the Squadron were ready for the sturdy London replacements which arrived in September 1937.

Protective patrols were flown during a tense period of the Spanish Civil War and the Squadron was placed on a war footing during the Munich Crisis, but both passed off without incident. Re-equipment with Sunderlands started in April 1939 but plans changed, the eagerly anticipated aircraft were withdrawn, and No 202 entered the Second World War still flying Londons.

Within days, the Squadron was operating from Gibraltar harbour, the Londons supplemented by a number of Swordfish floatplanes which were formally taken over from No 3 Anti-Aircraft Co-operation Unit during October 1940. Clashes with Vichy forces increased the Squadron's problems, but armed patrols continued and in April 1941 the first Catalinas were received, the last patrol by a London being on 4 June. The Catalinas, supplemented by a number of Sunderlands from December 1941 to September 1942, carried out anti-submarine patrols over the convoy routes.

Hectic activity during Operation 'Torch', the invasion of North Africa during the autumn of 1942, gradually slackened over the next two years and on 3 September 1944 No 202 Squadron was transferred to Castle Archdale, Lough Erne, Northern Ireland. Now equipped with 'Leigh-Light' Catalinas, the Squadron was soon in the thick of Atlantic anti-submarine operations concentrating on areas immediately west of Ireland until the end of the European war. With plenty of Sunderlands now available, Catalina-equipped units were short-lived, No 202 Squadron disbanding on 12 June 1945.

On 1 October 1946, No 518 Squadron, a meteorological reconnaissance unit, was renumbered No 202 at Aldergrove. Equipped with specially modified Halifax 6 aircraft, the Squadron flew out over the Atlantic on daily 'Bismuth' sorties checking the weather at various altitudes on a predetermined track. Four years later, Hastings Met 1 aircraft re-equipped the Squadron, and remained in operation until their job was taken over by weather satellites. During the last few years before disbandment on 31 July 1964,

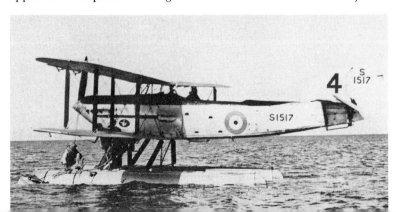

A Fairey IIIF of No 202 Squadron moored of Calafrana, Malta, during the early 1930s. Could that be an early representation of the 'mallard' badge on the forward fuselage?

Hastings Met 1 TG567 in the dark slate-grey colour scheme used in the early 1960s.

A Sea King HAR 3 of No 202 Squadron completes a display in July 1983 with a flypast streaming the RAF Ensign.

the Squadron also acted in the transport role for Coastal Command.

Once again the Squadron was not inactive for long, No 228 Squadron at Leconfield being renumbered No 202 a month later. Equipped with Whirlwind HAR 10s, No 202 was now a short-range search and rescue unit operating detached Flights of two helicopters at strategic positions along the east coast of the United Kingdom. The Squadron was soon in the news, and has deservedly remained in it ever since, for a series of outstanding rescues at sea and on land.

From January 1976, the Squadron HQ has been situated at Finningley where the Sea King HAR 3 started to replace the elderly Whirlwind in 1978. The new helicopter provided an immediate quantum leap in capability resulting in a re-arrangement of the detached Flights around the United Kingdom — these are now at Boulmer, Brawdy, Coltishall, Leconfield and Lossiemouth. Amongst the best known of RAF units by the general public, No 202 Squadron really does warrant news media descriptions such as 'Angels of Mercy' and proves it almost daily.

Standard

Granted by HRH King George VI and promulgated on 27 March 1952. Presented by Air Chief Marshal Sir Douglas Evill at Aldergrove on 6 September 1957.

Sir Douglas had been the Squadron Commanding Officer in 1916.

A new Standard was presented by His Excellency the Governor of Gibraltar, Air Chief Marshal Sir Peter Terry GCB AFC at Finningley on 16 June 1987.

Battle Honours

*Western Front 1916-1918
*Atlantic 1939-1945
*Mediterranean 1940-1943
*North Africa 1942-1943
*Biscay 1942-1944

*Denotes Honours emblazoned on Standard

Aircraft insignia and markings

No 2 Squadron, RNAS, did not use official markings, but by 1918 many of the DH 4s were gaily, but individually, painted. Soon after transferring to the RAF, the Commanding Officer was ordered to remove such markings and the unit's aircraft were then restricted to red and white wheel discs and carefully painted individual aircraft letters on the sides of the engine cowling.

When the Squadron reformed in 1929, the Fairey IIIDs retained the single-numeral identification used by 481 Flight, and this was continued on IIIFs, some of which also carried an unofficial unit badge on the sides of the forward fuselage. Scapas also had the numeral identification painted on the fin, replaced by a letter on Londons.

Following the Munich Crisis, the Squadron was allotted the code letter 'JU', but it is doubtful whether they were carried. The wartime code 'TQ' was in use from September 1939, painted in light grey forward of the fuselage roundel with an individual letter aft. Both London and Swordfish aircraft used 'TQ', replaced on re-equipment with Catalinas by 'AX', applied in dull red just forward of the side observation cupolas. Sunderlands also used the 'AX' code until the deletion of unit markings on Mediterranean-based maritime aircraft at the end of 1942. On moving to the United Kingdom in 1944, codes were re-introduced, 'TJ' being painted on the Squadron's Catalina IVs.

When reformed from No 518 Squadron, the former unit's code 'Y3' was retained on Halifaxes and Hastings until 1951 when the unit code 'A' was introduced, an 18 Group allotment. In the late 1950s, the codes were dropped completely and replaced by a black '202' on a white disc on the fin. The individual aircraft letter appeared on the tip of the nose, also within a white disc. During the early 'sixties, the number '202' was transferred to the rear fuselage and painted in red with a thin white edging, a large 'mallard' badge appearing on the fin.

The all-yellow Whirlwinds had the 'mallard' emblem on the tail rotor pylon within a white disc. The bird was white, brown and dark green with bright yellow beak and feet. A similar marking on Sea Kings has been moved to the forward fuselage just aft of the pilot's cockpit.

No 206 Squadron

Badge
An octopus — approved by HRH King George VI in January 1938 and presented by Air Vice Marshal H.M. Cave-Brown-Cave DSO DFC AFC, Air Officer Commanding, No 16 Group, on 11 March 1938. The octopus, a very active creature, indicated the Squadron's vigorous approach to challenge.

Motto
Nihil nos effugit — 'Naught escapes us'

History
No 206 Squadron, RAF, was originally formed for bombing duties in France as No 6 Squadron, RNAS, on 1 January 1918 at Dover from personnel of No 11 Squadron, RNAS, and the Walmer Defence Flight. An earlier No 6 Squadron, RNAS, formed late in 1916 and disbanded in August 1917, had been a fighter unit and had no direct connection with the 1918 unit.

No 6 Squadron, RNAS, crossed to France on 14 January 1918 with DH 4s, but these aircraft were only used for training, operationally-equipped DH 9s being received the following month. Used for both bombing and reconnaissance duty, the Squadron started operations on 9 March concentrating on German naval facilities in Belgium. At the end of the month the Squadron transferred from 5 Wing RNAS to the 11th (Army) Wing, RFC, and the following day became No 206 Squadron, RAF. Re-allocating as the 2nd Army's reconnaissance squadron, No 206 concentrated on photographic work until September when it was heavily involved in the final Western Front offensive as a bomber unit, claiming the dropping of 5¼ tons of bombs in a single day as a record.

After the Armistice, the Squadron moved into Germany and operated part of the air mail service from December 1918 until May 1919, when it returned to France. Less than a month later, the Squadron was despatched to Egypt, arriving at Helwan on 27 June still equipped with DH 9s. On 1 February 1920, the unit was renumbered No 47 Squadron and it was to be 16 years before No 206 reformed — on 15 June 1936, at Manston using 'C' Flight, No 48 Squadron, as a nucleus. Equipped with Anson general reconnaissance aircraft, the unit moved to Bircham Newton the following month and spent the next 12 months as an advanced training unit for newly fledged pilots.

No 206 Squadron commenced North Sea patrols on 1 September 1939 and for the next few months was very active, managing the signal feat of shooting down an attacking He 115 floatplane and hitting a U-boat. The latter probably only received a shaking, so ineffective was the 100 lb anti-submarine bomb, but it was a good start. Re-equipment with Hudsons commenced in March 1940, and the Squadron roamed all over the North Sea until moving to St Eval in July 1941 for operations in the south-west approaches.

The unit transferred to Aldergrove in August, but the official base meant little, for aircraft were

One of the first Shackleton MR 1s to dispense with the dorsal turret. 'V' of No 206 Squadron at St Eval late in 1954.

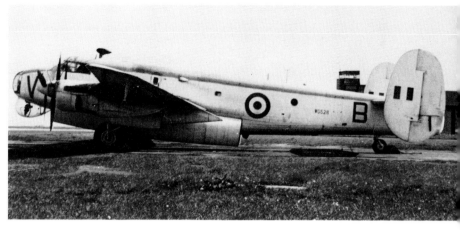

detached to forward airfields as required for particular operations. Conversion to four-engined Fortress IIs started in July 1942, this aircraft proving very effective over the Atlantic, especially following a move to Lagens in the Azores during October 1943. This allowed convoy coverage much further south than had previously been practicable.

The Squadron returned to the United Kingdom in April 1944 for re-equipment with Liberators, this extremely able anti-submarine aircraft being used on the 'Channel Stop' operation during June before being transferred to the dangerous Norwegian coastal areas. The arrival of Leigh Light-equipped Liberators in November meant a change to night operations, which continued until the end of the war in Europe.

During June 1945, the Squadron transferred to Transport Command and flew from Oakington on the long haul to India, their Liberators taking out freight and, after the end of the war, returning with POWs and United Kingdom-bound troops. The Squadron disbanded on 25 April 1946, but reformed on 17 November 1947, again in the transport role and flew Yorks during the Berlin Airlift from July 1948 until disbanded at the end of August 1949. Reformed at Waterbeach in November 1949, the Squadron flew Yorks again on the long-range Transport Command routes until disbanded on 20 February 1950.

Two and half years later, No 206 Squadron reappeared in Coastal Command, reforming on 27 September 1952 from a nucleus provided by No 224 Squadron and equipped with Shackleton MR 1 aircraft. Flying from St Eval, the Squadron provided reconnaissance and rescue cover over the western approaches in addition to detachments for a variety of tasks ranging from Recce/SAR during the 1956-58 nuclear tests off Christmas Island to goodwill 'show the flag' visits. For about a year, 1953-54, the Squadron was equipped with a mixture of Shackleton MR 1 and MR 2 aircraft, but then reverted to

Mk 1s until January 1958 when the first of the radically different Mk 3s was received. After considerable 'teething troubles', the latter aircraft settled down and were flown by the Squadron from St Mawgan and Kinloss until the arrival of the Nimrod in November 1970.

Upgraded to Mk 2 standard during 1981-82, these superb maritime reconnaissance aircraft have been flown from Kinloss by the Squadron for the past 18 years. During that time they have participated in exercises and operations all over the world, not least during the recovery of the Falkland Islands.

Standard

Granted by HRH Queen Elizabeth II and promulgated on 20 November 1963. Presented by HRH The Princess Margaret, Countess of Snowdon, CI GCVO at Kinloss on 28 July 1966.

Battle Honours

*Western Front 1916-1918
*Arras 1917
Lys
*Channel & North Sea 1939-1945
*Atlantic 1939, 1941-1945
*Dunkirk
Invasion Ports 1940
*Fortress Europe 1940, 1942
German Ports 1940, 1942
*Biscay 1941, 1943-1944
*Bismarck
Baltic 1945
South Atlantic 1982

*Denotes Honours emblazoned on Standard

Aircraft insignia and markings

No unit markings were carried during the First World War, or in Egypt during 1919-20. Ansons initially car-

Above *Shackleton MR 3 WR978 on detachment in Malta. The 'octopus' badge is prominent on the fin in addition to the standard use of the Squadron number during the 1960s.*

Left *Nimrod MR 2 XV235 of the Kinloss Wing in July 1987. No 206 Squadron draws on the Wing aircraft 'pool' as required.*

ried the numerals '206' on the fuselage sides aft of the roundel, changed to the code letters 'WD' after the Munich Crisis and 'VX' on the outbreak of war. Ansons and Hudsons both used 'VX', but the Fortresses at first merely used individual aircraft letters, supplemented by the base Squadron identification numeral '1' in August 1943. By the time the Liberators were received in 1944, the numeral scheme had been abandoned and the code 'PQ' was allotted and probably retained throughout later Coastal and Transport Command service.

Yorks did not carry markings, but when reformed with Shackletons the 19 Group coded letter 'B' was employed, painted on the fuselage just forward of the tailplane, with the aircraft letter on the nose. In 1956, the markings on Coastal Command aircraft reverted to the pre-war style, the Squadron number being painted on the rear fuselage in dull red edged in white. Some time after the Mk 3 Shackletons were received, an 'octopus' emblem was added, painted on the fins in red on a white disc. When the aircraft were centralized at Kinloss, the unit markings were removed and have only re-appeared on Nimrods for particular occasions, and then only in the form of fin-mounted emblems.

No 208 Squadron

Badge

A sphinx affrontée — approved by HRH King George in October 1937 and presented by Air Marshal C.T. Maclean CB DSO MC on 11 February 1938. The Gizah Sphinx commemorated the Squadron's long association with Egypt during the 1920s and 1930s. An unofficial 'winged eye' badge had been in use from July 1930 until 1937.

Motto

Vigilant

History

No 208 Squadron originated in the Royal Naval Air Service as No 8 Squadron, first formed at Dunkirk on 26 October 1916 from units of the Dunkirk Command. Consisting of three Flights, one each of Nieuport Scouts, Pups and 1½-strutters, the Squadron immediately transferred to RFC control and was attached to the 5th Brigade RFC for operations from Le Vert Galant near Amiens.

During February 1917, the unit re-equipped with Sopwith Triplanes and proved very successful with this agile machine. Replacement Bentley-engined Camels continued the protection of artillery-spotting RE 8s until the unit was withdrawn for a short rest at Walmer, Kent. Returning to the Western Front in March 1918, the unit was just in time for the German spring offensive and was re-designated 'in the field' as No 208 Squadron, RAF.

The first few days of No 208 Squadron's existence were difficult, culminating on 9 April with the deliberate destruction of 16 Camels to prevent them falling into the hands of the enemy as Allied troops fell back. Reformed at Serny, the Squadron was re-equipped within days and morale rose rapidly as successes mounted, the Camels being used for offensive patrols and ground attack work during the final offensive which brought about total German collapse. Re-equipment with Snipes had just started at the Armistice, and it was with these aircraft that No 208 Squadron joined the occupation forces in Germany. The unit remained until September 1919, then withdrew to the United Kingdom and disbanded at Netheravon on 7 November.

The Squadron reformed on 1 February 1920 at Ismailia, Egypt, by renumbering No 113 Squadron. The inherited RE 8s were replaced by Bristol Fighters in November, this versatile aircraft being used for army co-operation duties. In September, No 208 went to Turkey for a year as part of the British force sent in response to the Nationalist unrest sweeping the country. On return to Egypt, the Squadron settled down into a long association with Army units in the Canal Zone, receiving replacements for their aged

'Brisfits' in the form of the Atlas during May 1930. These were supplanted by the more popular Audax in August 1935, joined by a number of Demons during September. The latter were transferred to the newly-formed No 64 Squadron in March 1936, but the Audax soldiered on until January 1939 when Lysanders were received.

Following the entry of Italy into the war on the side of Germany, No 208 Squadron commenced operations over the Western Desert in June 1940. Hurricanes joined the Lysanders in November to provide a tactical reconnaissance element, and both were very active during the advance through Cyrenaica (now Libya). Events in Greece forced a redistribution of forces in the Middle East and No 208 Squadron moved there on 1 April 1941. Immediately forced on to the defensive, the Squadron had to withdraw to Crete on the 24th and the remnants were back in Egypt by the end of the month.

No 208 Squadron re-grouped in Palestine and took part in operations over Syria before returning to the Western Desert in October 1941, still employed on tactical and photo reconnaissance. The Lysanders were plainly obsolete, but were not replaced by Tomahawks until May 1942, just in time for Rommel's big push forward to El Alamein. In September, the Tomahawks were relinquished and the Squadron became an all-Hurricane unit, moving in January 1943 to Iraq. During April came re-designation as No 208 (Fighter Reconnaissance) Squadron, and training continued in Syria and Palestine. Spitfires were received in December, but it was March 1944 before the Squadron was in Italy and back on fighter and ground attack operations.

After the German surrender, the Squadron stayed in Italy until July 1945, when a move to Palestine soon found it in the midst of increasing Jewish terrorist activity and Arab counteraction. On 22 May 1948, the unit became the victim of an unprovoked attack by Egyptian Air Force Spitfires on Ramat David airfield, and then, following a transfer to the Canal Zone in November, all four aircraft on a border patrol failed to return on 7 January 1945. They had been

Spitfire LF IX PV 117 of No 208 Squadron carrying the 'RG' code authorized for use throughout the Second World War, but little used.

Hunter FGA 9 XE611 in December 1966 at Muharraq. The markings, originally in chevron form on Hunters, are again in 'bar' form but raised on the fuselage to avoid damage from an engine vent.

Buccaneer S 2 XV863 in April 1987, the ornate 'winged eye' used as an emblem in the 1930s on the fin while the more familiar blue and yellow chevrons adorn the nose.

'bounced' by Israeli Spitfires and shot down. Clearly the Squadron was in a 'cannot win' situation.

Still a fighter-reconnaissance squadron, No 208 received Meteor 9s in March 1951, and took them to Malta in January 1956 following the British withdrawal from the Canal Zone. Two years later, No 34 Squadron disbanded at Tangmere and their Hunter 5s and nine of the pilots formed a new No 208 Squadron which moved to Cyprus in March with new Hunter 6s. Again the Squadron found itself the subject of terrorist attack — this time from Cypriots. A surprise disbandment came on 30 March 1959, but the following day No 142 Squadron at Eastleigh, Kenya, flying Venom 4s, was renumbered No 208.

A year later the Venoms were disposed of locally and the majority of the Squadron personnel left for the United Kingdom and conversion to Hunter FGA 9s. These were flown to Nairobi in June 1960, but spent much of the next 15 months on detachment, including a short-notice move to Kuwait in July 1961 when that country was threatened by its neighbour,

Iraq. Leaving in October, it had a spell in Bahrain before transferring to Khormaksar where No 208 joined the Strike Wing for operations in the Aden Protectorate. In June 1964, the Squadron moved to Muharraq in support of British forces in the Gulf area, remaining until disbanded on 10 September 1971.

On 1 March 1974, No 208 Squadron reformed at Honington with Buccaneers for low-level strike operations, moving to Lossiemouth in 1983 where it now forms a Maritime Strike Wing with No 12 Squadron, operating in 18 Group, Strike Command.

Standard

Granted by HRH King George VI and promulgated on 9 September 1943. Presented by Air Vice Marshal Sir Geoffrey Bromet KBE CB DSO RAF (Retd) at Abu Suier on 18 November 1955. Sir Geoffrey had been the first Squadron Commander.

A new Standard was presented by Air Marshal Sir Humphrey Edwards-Jones KCB CBE DFC AFC BA

RAF (Retd), President of the Naval 8/208 Squadron Association, at Lossiemouth on 1 June 1984.

The old Standard was laid up in St Clement Danes Church on 27 October 1985.

Battle Honours

*Western Front 1916-1918
*Arras
*Ypres 1917
Lys
*Somme 1918
*Egypt & Libya 1940-1942
Iraq 1941
*Greece 1941
Syria 1941
*El Alamein
*Italy 1944-1945
Gustav Line
Gothic Line

*Denotes Honours emblazoned on Standard

Aircraft insignia and markings

Triplanes and Camels of 'Naval Eight' carried a white disc aft of the fuselage roundel, changed in March 1918 on Camels to two white bars inclined inwards at the top and positioned forward of the fuselage roundel. Similar markings were retained on Snipes.

Bristol Fighters in the Middle East had a white disc on the fin, originally with cartoon characters painted on them, but later replaced by card suits which were sometimes repeated under the lower mainplanes. The Atlas carried a 'flying eye' motif across the rudder, but the Audax replacements appear to have remained unmarked in No 208 Squadron service, even after the Munich Crisis when the unit code 'GA' was officially allocated. This code was painted on Lysanders early in 1939, but changed to 'RG' at the outbreak of war in September. In practice, the 'RG' code was little used until 1945 when Spitfire IXs formed the Squadron equipment. During 1941-42, Hurricanes had an unofficial white 'lightning flash' on each side of the fuselage roundel, but from 1943 until 1945 most Squadron aircraft were unmarked. After the war, Spitfire XVIIIs continued the use of the 'RG' code and also featured a unit badge on the sides of the engine cowlings.

Meteor FR 9s only carried individual aircraft letters at first, but in 1953 Fighter Command-type coloured markings reached the Middle East and No 208 Squadron adopted blue/yellow/blue bars on each side of the roundel. Hunter 6s also featured the 'bar' markings, as did Venoms, the latter re-introducing the 1920s playing card emblem on tip-tanks. Hunter FGA 9s had the blue and yellow markings on the nose, re-shaped as an 'arrowhead' on which was superimposed a badge on a white disc.

Buccaneers retain the 'arrowhead' on the nose forward of the roundel, and on the fin carry the 'winged eye' emblem last seen on Atlas aircraft of the 1930s. In 1984, the single aircraft letter on the fin was suffixed by 'S' (derived from the sphinx on the badge) to denote the Squadron, but the letters were removed in 1987 during the period of frequent swopping of aircraft whilst a major modification programme was under way.

No 216 Squadron

Badge

An eagle, wings elevated, holding in the claws a bomb — approved by HRH King Edward VIII in May 1936. The badge was the official version of an emblem in use for a number of years.

Motto

CCXVI dona ferens — '216 bearing gifts'

History

No 216 Squadron is a direct descendant of 'A' Squadron, RNAS, which formed at Manston on 5 October 1917 with four Handley Page 0/100 twin-engined bombers. Further aircraft brought the strength up to 12 which were flown to France on 17 October for strategic night bomber operations. Re-designated No 16 Squadron, RNAS, on 8 January 1918, the unit joined the RAF on 1 April as No 216 Squadron, and soon afterwards some of the first 0/400s in service were received.

In June, No 216 became part of the Independent Force commanded by Major General H. Trenchard and dedicated to the destruction of the German munitions industry. Raids were regularly mounted on Ruhr towns, the last on the night of 10 November when an 0/400 bombed Metz and an 0/100 attacked Frescaty airfield. Within weeks of the Armistice, No 216 Squadron was at Marquise flying the Valenciennes-Namur sector of the official mail service set up for the occupation forces. In January, the service was extended to Cologne, but operations

Valentia KR2793 at Aden in June 1939 already camouflaged but still with the bomb-carrying 'eagle' badge on the nose (D.L. Webb).

ceased in May 1919 when the Squadron prepared for a move to the Middle East, flying its 0/400s to Egypt.

Although officially still a bomber squadron, No 216 soon found itself operating as a transport unit flying both passengers and mail between Egypt and Palestine. During 1921, the DH 10 slowly replaced the ponderous 0/400, the last of which left in October. The new aircraft helped pioneer the Cairo to Baghdad mail service which was continued by the Vimys received in June 1922. Despite cramped accommodation, these aircraft were retained until January 1926 when Victorias arrived just as Imperial Airways took over the mail route. The roomy fuselage of the Victoria much enhanced the Squadron's ability to provide troop carrying, casualty evacuation and supply dropping facilities for the Army, but they also pioneered a trans-African route in 1930 and flew it until it was taken over commercially in 1936.

During April 1931, the unit was officially redesignated No 216 (Bomber Transport) Squadron, which certainly described its operations more accurately, and in February 1935 re-equipment with Valentias began, though it was little more than an updated Victoria! Bombing training was increased during the Abyssinian Crisis, and continued with Bombays when these monoplanes partially re-equipped the Squadron in November 1939.

When Italy entered the War in June 1940, the Bombays were used for bombing while Valentias continued transport work until finally relinquished in October 1941. A detachment at Khartoum operated the West Africa route pioneered ten years earlier, while the main Squadron was active in the evacuation from Greece and in the support of beleaguered Habbaniya. Freight and passenger services were also

flown, and in December six DH 86As were taken on strength for casualty evacuation duty. The latter transferred to No 117 Squadron in March 1942, and in July a Flight of Hudsons joined No 216. Dakotas were received in March 1943, resulting in the departure of the Hudsons in April, and the trusty Bombays in June, when the Squadron took on the dual tasks of 'scheduled' services and airborne forces operations.

Detachments increased during 1944, 15 Dakotas going to India for air supply over Imphal and the re-supply of Chindit forces operating behind enemy lines. Later in the year, the Squadron supported Tito's partisans in Yugoslavia. The Squadron finished the war still officially based in Egypt, but with detachments as far apart as Nairobi and Karachi.

By September 1945, the Squadron had settled down to route flying, though in 1946 paratroop training was reintroduced. Valetta replacements started arriving in November 1949 to continue operations as part of the Middle East Transport Wing, but with the run-down of British forces in the Canal Zone, No 216 Squadron transferred to the United Kingdom in November 1955 and joined Transport Command. The Valettas were disposed of and the Squadron started preparing for the introduction of the Comet jet-powered transport into RAF service at Lyneham. The first Comet arrived on 7 June 1956, and deliveries continued for a year during which the aircraft established itself on Transport Command routes and had started its long VIP and VVIP passenger career by transporting the Queen from Marham to Leuchars.

By 1960, Britannias had taken over much of the routine route flying, and No 216 concentrated on the

VIP task and other 'special' flights. The first of five Comet 4s arrived at Lyneham during February 1962, and with these fine aircraft No 216 returned to the long-range scheduled routes, the smaller Comets being confined to the UK-Mediterranean sectors until withdrawn in April 1967. With the VC 10s of No 10 Squadron now in full operation, the Comet 4 was also withdrawn from Air Support routes and used exclusively for VIP, standby, and operational detachment support, until the aircraft was withdrawn and the Squadron disbanded on 30 June 1975, after 58 years of unbroken service.

No 216 Squadron was officially reformed on 1 July 1979 in a very different role, that of maritime strike in support of the Royal Navy. Buccaneers were received and the Squadron was about to become operational when a fatigue problem grounded all aircraft in the 'fleet'. When cleared, the number of available Buccaneers was reduced, and at Lossiemouth in August 1980 the unit became known as No 12 Squadron (North), and was merged fully when the No 12 (South) element joined them.

Although not formally acknowledged, No 216 Squadron ceased to exist as an independent unit, and when re-established on 1 November 1984 it was again a transport squadron, with the mighty Tristar. Initial deliveries were passenger transport versions, but later dual purpose transport/tankers were delivered for use on the long haul to the Falkland Islands and the air-refuelling of fighter/bomber detachments and UK-based interceptors over the North and Arctic seas.

Standard

Granted by HRH King George VI and promulgated on 9 September 1943. Presented by Air Chief Marshal Sir Donald Hardman GBE KCB DFC at Lyneham on 24 May 1957.

The Standard was laid up in the RAF College Chapel, Cranwell, from July 1975 until November 1984.

A new Standard was presented by Air Chief Marshal Sir Peter Harding KCB CBIM FRAeS at Brize Norton on 24 June 1988.

Battle Honours

*Independent Force & Germany 1917-1918
*Egypt & Libya 1940-1942
*Greece 1940-1941
*Syria 1941
*El Alamein
El Hamma
*North Africa 1943
Mediterranean 1943
Manipur 1944
*North Burma 1944
*South East Europe 1944-1945

*Denotes Honours emblazoned on Standard

Aircraft insignia and markings

Unit markings were not generally carried by bomber aircraft during the First World War, and No 216 Squadron's 0/100s and 0/400s were no exception.

In the Middle East, some of the 0/400s were individually named, but the first unit markings appeared on DH 10s, which were soon adorned with playing card suit emblems and even a swastika (which

Though No 216 Squadron's Buccaneer era was short-lived, a few aircraft did display the 'eagle' emblem. Here is XV332 at Honington in November 1979.

Tristar K 1 ZD951 of No 216 Squadron at St Mawgan in August 1987, with a 'warlike' eagle emblem on the fin.

did not then have today's connotations). The replacement Vimys had individual aircraft numerals painted under the wings, but Victorias relied on a black fuselage band for identification until near the end of their careers, when single-letter codes were painted on the nose and rear fuselage. Valentias also employed individual aircraft letters, but in Flight colours, and had a Squadron badge on the nose. After the Munich Crisis of 1938, they were hastily camouflaged and had the newly allotted unit code 'VT' painted on them. Following the outbreak of war, the code was changed to 'SH', used by both Valentias and Bombays, but when Hudsons arrived they received the code 'LQ'.

The markings on Dakotas were confined to individual aircraft letters, initially single but, during 1944, changed to double letters. The Squadron code letters 'GH' were in use from about 1947, but when Valettas were received they were unmarked except for a dark blue fuselage cheat line and the 'last three' of their serials on the fin. Comets were painted in standard Transport Command colours, and from 1959 onwards received individual names on the forward fuselage of Mk 2s.

When the Squadron reformed with Buccaneers, they carried an 'eagle' emblem on the engine nacelles and this has also appeared on the fins of the current Tristar tanker/transports, the 'eagle' in brown with an orange and brown tail and bomb.

The Comet 2s were named as follows:

XK669	*Taurus*	XK670	*Corvus*	XK671	*Aquila*
XK695	*Perseus*	XK696	*Orion*	XK697	*Cygnus*
XK698	*Pegasus*	XK699	*Sagittarius*		
XK715	*Columba*	XK716	*Cepheus*		

No 230 Squadron

Badge

In front of a palm tree eradicated, a tiger passant guardant — approved by HRH King George VI in February 1937. The badge commemorated the Squadron's association with Malaya, the traveller's palm being a reference to the long flights so often undertaken while the tiger is said to have been inspired by the label on the bottles of a local Singaporean brew.

Motto

Kita chari jauh (Malay) — 'We search far'

History

No 230 Squadron formed at Felixstowe in August 1918 from an amalgamation of 327 and 328 Flights, both equipped with F2A flying boats. The Squadron operated over the North Sea on maritime reconnaissance duties, which meant anti-Zeppelin, anti-shipping and anti-U-boat patrols. In September, 487 Flight, flying Camels from nearby Butley landing ground, was added to the strength for escort duty. After the Armistice, the Squadron remained at Felixstowe and a few F5 boats were received during 1920. These were taken to Calshot in May 1922 where the Squadron was renamed No 480 Flight on 1 April 1923.

Reformed on 1 December 1934 at Pembroke Dock, the Squadron was without aircraft until the first Singapore III arrived in April 1935. After an accelerated work-up, the unit flew to Egypt during September as part of the build-up which followed Italy's attack on Abyssinia. Returning to Pembroke Dock in August 1936, the Squadron set off for the Far East three months later with five 'boats'. After visiting Hong Kong, No 230 made its headquarters at Seletar, Singapore, where Sunderlands were received during June 1938. Following the declaration of war in Europe, patrols were flown over the Indian Ocean and a detachment was formed at Trincomalee, Ceylon. The whole Squadron settled at Koggala in February 1940 before returning to Egypt in May to fly anti-submarine patrols over the Mediterranean.

Operations were stepped up when Italy entered the war in June, and during October the Squadron got involved in the Greek campaign, flying troops and freight to and from Egypt. By January 1941, the Squadron was covering Aegean convoys and was engaged in the evacuation of Greece, Yugoslavia and Crete, gaining a Flight of Dornier Do 22 floatplanes

in the process, ex-Yugoslav machines which were kept operational until February 1942.

In January 1943 came a move to East Africa for patrols over the Indian Ocean. The unit returned to Ceylon in February 1944 and a year later had a detachment at Calcutta for freight and 'casevac' flights to and from Burma. The whole Squadron moved to Akyab, Burma, in April, and resumed maritime work by attacking Japanese coastal shipping.

The Squadron triumphantly returned to Singapore in December 1945, but four months later was back in the United Kingdom, settling at Calshot during September 1946 after short periods at Pembroke Dock and Castle Archdale. Co-operation exercises with the Home Fleet were the main task, until July 1948 when the Squadron joined the Berlin Airlift to fly freight into the besieged city from Hamburg. Relieved after five months, the Squadron moved to Pembroke Dock in February 1949, its normal maritime activities interrupted by the 1952 British North Greenland Expedition, a detachment to Greece, and an exercise in Singapore. The days of the flying boat were numbered, however, and on 28 February 1957 the Squadron disbanded at Pembroke Dock.

No 230 Squadron reformed on 1 September 1958 by renumbering No 215 Squadron at Dishforth. Equipped with single-engined Pioneers, the Squadron was now engaged on army support work and moved to Cyprus during November for a six-month tour. At Upavon from April 1959, the Squadron was partially re-equipped with Twin Pioneers which it

Sunderland 1 L2160 in the Far East moored to a river boat soon after arrival in 1938. Just aft of the Malay inscription on the nose is an outline No 230 Squadron badge within a six-pointed star (RAF Museum P9875).

Whirlwind HAR 10 XR395 'R' in July 1969. Just in case the 'tiger's head' on the cabin door shield is not recognition enough, '230' is painted beneath it.

took to the Camaroons in September 1960 for internal security work, while the Pioneer Flight went to Northern Ireland for border patrols.

Reunited at Odiham in August 1962, the Squadron received Whirlwind 10s, taking these helicopters to Germany in January 1963 to provide front-line support for the BAOR. Returning to the UK in 1965, the whole unit moved almost immediately to Labuan for operations during the Indonesian 'confrontation'. Back at Odiham in November 1966, the Squadron continued its intermittent detachments to Cyprus in support of United Nations forces until December 1971, when No 84 Squadron took over. No 230 then became the RAF's second Puma-equipped squadron, and continued in the Army support role with rotational detachments to Northern Ireland, Cyprus and Belize, until returning the Germany during January 1981 to replace No 18 Squadron.

Despite the return of No 18 Squadron in May 1983, No 230 has remained in Germany, its Pumas nominally based at Gutersloh but more usually detached with units of 1 British Corps of the Rhine Army, or on winter survival training in Bavaria.

Standard

Granted by HRH Queen Elizabeth II and promulgated on 17 October 1956. Presented by HRH The Duke of Gloucester at Odiham on 26 October 1962.

Battle Honours

*Home Waters 1918
*Mediterranean 1940-1943
*Eastern Waters 1943-1945
*North Burma 1944
*Burma 1945

*Denotes Honours emblazoned on Standard

Affiliation

No 240 Squadron — linked as No 230/240 Sqn from February 1949 to June 1952.

Nickname

'The Tigers' — elected a full member of the exclusive group of NATO squadrons which have a 'tiger' motif as their emblem, despite the Squadron's non-fighter pedigree.

Aircraft insignia and markings

Flying boats at Felixstowe were painted in bizarre colour schemes during the First World War, but no squadron markings were carried.

The Singapores equipping the Squadron in 1934 were also unmarked, except for an individual letter in black on the hull beneath the cockpit side windows. The code 'FV' was allotted after the Munich Crisis of 1938 but was almost certainly not carried on either Singapores or the replacement Sunderlands. The wartime allocation 'NM' was used from September 1939 until the unit went to East Africa early in 1943. For the remainder of the war, the Sunderlands only carried individual letters, but on return to the United Kingdom in 1946 the code '4X' was introduced and a unit badge appeared on the side of the forward hull. In 1951, the single code 'B' replaced the '4X', in turn dropped in favour of the Squadron number '230' in 1956. This was painted in black forward of the hull roundel with the individual letter aft.

Pioneers carried a single aircraft letter identification on the rear fuselage, this being moved to the fins of 'Twin Pins' and just forward of the boom on Whirlwind 10s. The latter also had a black five-sided shield painted on the forward fuselage with a tiger head and the numerals '230' on it in yellow. Pumas introduced

Puma HC1 XW229 *at Leuchars in May 1978. The official 'tiger's head' badge of No 230 Squadron is beneath the cockpit windows, and another 'tiger' emblem is on the cabin door!*

a two-letter code, the individual letter prefixed by the unit identification 'D', painted on the tail boom. The Squadron badge is painted on a turquoise disc on the main cabin doors, the 'palm tree' light green and the 'tiger' yellow and black. A white and gold tiger has been used on occasion, and for the 'Tiger Meet' aircraft have been painted overall in 'tiger stripes'.

No 234 Squadron

Badge

A dragon rampant, flames issuing from the mouth — approved by HRH King George VI in August 1940. The dragon indicated the fighting role of the Squadron and the flames commemorated the Spitfire, in use at the time.

Motto

Ignem mortemque despuimus — 'We spit fire and death'

History

Formed in August 1918 from the ex-RNAS units on

Tresco, Isles of Scilly, No 234 Squadron had a mixed complement of Curtiss H 12 and Felixstowe F2A and F3 flying boats. Patrols out into the Atlantic and up the English Channel continued until the Armistice, the last convoy escort being on 10 November. The unit then slowly wound down and disbandment came on 15 May 1919.

No 234 Squadron was reformed 30 years later, at Leconfield on 30 October 1939, for shipping protection duties. Its first aircraft, Magister trainers, were soon supplemented by a strange mixture of Blenheim IFs, Tutors, Gauntlets and a Battle, on which work-up was attempted. Fortunately, Spitfires were received in March 1940 and the Squadron became operational during May as a day fighter unit. It was August before No 234 became involved in the Battle of Britain, but by the end of the month it was 10 Group's highest scoring squadron. Afterwards, the Squadron reverted to convoy escort work until 1942 when fighter sweeps over France and bomber escorts became the main task.

During September 1943, most of the personnel were posted to Australia to form No 549 Squadron, and it was virtually a new No 234 which emerged at Hutton Cranswick in October. Still flying Spitfires, the Squadron flew more convoy escorts until early 1944 when offensive operations over France and the Low Countries became the priority. For fighter-bomber work during the battle for Normandy, the unit joined 85 Group but remained based in the United Kingdom, receiving Mustangs during September 1944 for long-range escort of Bomber Command's 'heavies' engaged in daylight raids on Germany.

Following the German surrender in May 1945, the Squadron re-equipped with Spitfire IXs during

Above *Hunter F 4s of 229 OCU in 'shadow' No 234 Squadron markings on the Chivenor flight line during 1958. The intricate design of red diamonds on a black background flanking the red 'dragon' badge is similar to that used in Germany when the unit was operational (via W. Taylor).*

Left *Some Hawk T 1As were still in camouflage as late as October 1987. Their larger 'shadow' Squadron markings showed up well compared with the replacement miniaturized version (J.D.R. Rawlings).*

Above right *Hawk T 1A XX302 of No 1 Tactical Weapons Unit in 'shadow' No 234 Squadron markings and low-visibility camouflage.*

August, and the Meteor III in February 1946, only to be renumbered No 266 Squadron at the end of August. Six years later, on 1 August 1952, No 234 reformed as a Second Tactical Air Force fighter unit at Oldenburg, equipped with Vampires. Conversion to Sabres started in June 1953, but they were only operational for 18 months before Hunter 4s replaced them in May 1956. These fine aircraft lasted even less time, for, as part of a savage reduction in the strength of the RAF day fighter force in Germany, the Squadron disbanded on 15 July 1957.

Just over a year later, on 30 November 1958, No 234 Squadron made a surprise re-appearance as the 'shadow' number for part of 229 OCU, Chivenor.

On annual exercises, the OCU instructors practised their war role by detaching with their updated Hunter 6s and 9s to East coast airfields to provide day interception and ground attack support to the regular air defence squadrons. In September 1974, No 229 OCU was disbanded but the aircraft, instructors and 'shadow' squadrons moved to Brawdy to form the Tactical Weapons Unit (TWU).

The Hunter was phased out by No 234 (Shadow) Squadron in August 1978 and replaced by Hawks, these aircraft subsequently being modified for a secondary low-level interception role. The unit remains part of No 1 TWU at Brawdy, fully capable of providing a back-up for the front-line squadrons in time of tension or conflict.

Standard

Not granted.

Battle Honours

Not determined (only applicable when a Standard is granted).

Affiliation

'Madras Presidency' — the Squadron was adopted by the people of the Presidency of the Indian State of Madras in April 1940. In recognition of a monetary gift from the State nominally sufficient to purchase a squadron of Spitfires, the unit's title officially became No 234 (Madras Presidency) Squadron on 10 June 1941. Reference to Madras was dropped after India became a Republic.

Aircraft insignia and markings

No unit identification markings were carried by the flying boats at Tresco during the First World War. When reformed in 1939, the Squadron's Blenheims, and subsequently Spitfires, used the code 'AZ', the latter aircraft also sporting a white disc beneath the cockpit on the port side, on which was painted a Spitfire silhouette breaking up a swastika. Mustangs were also coded 'AZ', but this was changed to 'FX' when Spitfires returned in August 1945. Meteors also carried 'FX' prior to disbandment in September 1946.

In the Second Tactical Air Force, the Vampires of No 234 Squadron were identified by a black dragon stencilled on the nose and the unit code 'W', but the Sabres introduced black and red checks around the nose intake, the 'dragon' badge being moved to the fin where it was painted in red on a white disc. Late in 1955, the nose intake markings became yellow-edged red, and standard 'fighter style' black rectangles carrying a double row of eight red diamonds were painted on each side of the fuselage roundel. The same markings were retained on the Hunter but positioned on the nose flanking the Squadron 'dragon' badge.

The 229 OCU Hunters allocated to No 234 (Shadow) Squadron carried similar markings until transfer to Brawdy, where the aircraft were initially 'pooled'. The markings returned with the introduction of the Hawk, and now flank the fuselage roundel, in miniaturized form on 'low-visibility' grey-coloured aircraft. A 1 TWU badge adorns the nose of all Hawk T 1As at Brawdy.

No 360 Squadron

Badge
In front of a trident erect, a moth, wings displayed — approved by HRH Queen Elizabeth II in September 1973. The moth uses ultrasound to confuse predatory bats, a property analogous to the Squadron's electronic countermeasures role. The trident symbolizes the naval presence in the Squadron.

Motto
Confundemus — 'We shall throw into confusion'

History
Formed as the 'Joint RAF/RN Trials & Training Force' at Watton on 1 April 1966, the unit had the task of providing electronic countermeasures (ECM) training for RAF and Royal Navy crews of aircraft carrying airborne interception radar, air defence controllers, and ground and shipborne radar operators. The remaining personnel of No 831 Squadron, FAA, were transferred to the 'Force' on 16 May, and the early months were spent assessing the task and deciding how to tackle it whilst awaiting delivery of specially equipped Canberras. On 23 September, the unit officially became No 360 Squadron, a number chosen because it had no previous connotation with either the Royal Air Force or the Royal Navy.

On 10 October 1966, the Squadron took over 'B' Flight of No 97 Squadron and its Canberra 2, 4 and 6 aircraft. The first T 17 specially modified for the jamming task was delivered in December and ex-No 97 Squadron aircraft left during 1967 when the work-up phase was completed and sufficient 'spoofers' were on strength. On 2 January 1967, No 361 Squadron was provisionally formed and placed under the control of No 360 until sufficient crews and aircraft were available for it to deploy to the Far East. In the event this plan was cancelled, and No 361 was formally disbanded on 14 July, the crews joining No 360, a unit unusual in being 75 per cent funded by the RAF and 25 per cent by the Royal Navy, every fourth CO being a naval Commander.

The Squadron moved to Cottesmore in May 1969 and Wyton in June 1974. The unit is very active, taking part in all major United Kingdom and NATO exercises, and may be found, usually operating a pair of aircraft, on airfields the length and breadth of NATO. During 1987, six of the Squadron's twelve Canberras were updated to T 17A standard, the changes giving much greater jamming flexibility.

Standard
Not granted.

Battle Honours
None.

In glossy camouflage finish, Canberra T 17 WH665 sports the original form of No 360 Squadron marking on the fin in July 1971.

A modified Canberra T 17A in the latest 'hemp' colour being refuelled in May 1987. Yellow 'lightning flashes' across the red 'bars' on the fuselage and 360's 'moth and trident' badge on the fin are prominent.

Aircraft insignia and markings

Initially unmarked, the aircraft had a blue '360' crossed by a red 'lightning flash' on a white background painted on the fin during 1971. Early in 1975, the fin marking was changed to a representation of the Squadron badge, the moth having a brown and black body with pale yellow, light brown and white wings, while the trident was mid-blue shadowed with pale blue.

During December 1984, 'fighter-style' markings were added on each side of the fuselage roundel, red rectangles with diagonal yellow 'lightning flashes' across them. Earlier, the single aircraft identification letter on the fin had been joined by an 'E' prefix distinguishing the Squadron from other Canberra units at Wyton.

In 1987, maritime 'hemp' camouflage was adopted on the aircraft's upper surfaces, while the undersides remained light grey, the colourful Squadron markings being retained.

No 617 Squadron

Badge

On a roundel, a wall in fesse, fracted by three flashes of lightning in pile and issuant from the breach water proper — approved by HRH King George VI in March 1944. The broken dam is indicative of the successful attack on the dams in May 1943.

Motto

Après moi, le déluge — 'After me, the flood'

History

Unique amongst RAF squadrons in being specifically raised to undertake one operation, No 617 Squadron was formed at Scampton on 21 March 1943 equipped with Lancasters. The CO, Wing Commander Guy P. Gibson DSO DFC was given the unprecedented privilege of combing other squadrons for personnel so that he could form crews of the highest possible calibre. For several weeks, not even Gibson was told more than the barest details of the Squadron's mission, only that low-level flying over water at night was an essential, and intensive training to that end took place during April and early May.

When revealed, Operation 'Chastise' was breathtaking in concept — the breaching of three enormous dams, the Möhne, Eder and Sorpe, which together stored more than 300 million tons of water thought vital to German factories in the Ruhr valley. The plan involved the use of a specially designed mine which had to be dropped at precisely 60 ft and at exactly 220 mph. Modified Lancasters arrived in May and 19 of them took off during the late evening of the 16th and attacked early the next morning. Both the Möhne and Eder were successfully breached but the Sorpe, and a fourth dam, the Schwelme, survived. Wg Cdr Gibson, who repeatedly flew over the Möhne and Eder dams to draw fire away from the attacking aircraft, received the Victoria Cross for his gallantry. Thirty-two other members of the Squadron were also decorated but the cost was high, eight Lancasters and their crews being lost during the night.

It was decided to keep the Squadron in existence for special operations, many of which employed the

Above *After the war, No 617 Squadron went to India for a short spell using Lancaster B 7 aircraft coded 'KC' and painted in the 'Far East' colours of white upper surfaces and black undersides* (RAF Museum P2769).

Left *Vulcans were in No 617 Squadron service for many years during which a variety of unit markings were employed before finally settling on the representation of the unit's badge illustrated here on* XJ783, *May 1980.*

enormous 12,000 lb 'Tallboy' and the 22,000 lb 'Grand Slam' bombs. Under Wg Cdr G.L. Cheshire DSO DFC, the Squadron also became expert at target marking, and he too received the Victoria Cross — not for one isolated act of courage but for literally years of operational flying during which he invariably led from the front at great personal risk.

The Squadron remained in Bomber Command after the war, receiving Lincolns in September 1946 and Canberras during January 1952. In 1955, the Squadron went out to Malaya for operations against communist terrorists, but on 15 December that same

year it was disbanded. Two and a half years later, on 1 May 1958, the Squadron reformed at Scampton with Vulcan B1s, replaced by the Blue Steel-equipped Vulcan 2 in September 1961. When the Blue Steel 'stand-off' bomb was withdrawn in 1968, the Squadron continued to operate the Vulcan in the long-range strike role until disbanded on 31 December 1981.

A year later it re-appeared as a Tornado GR 1 strike squadron at Marham, and has gone from strength to strength, proving outstandingly successful in the prestigious USAF Bombing Competition

A rather drab Tornado GR 1 of No 617 Squadron at St Mawgan in August 1987. The unit's current markings flank the fuselage roundel and are repeated on the tip of the tail.

by taking every major prize for which it was eligible in 1984. The Squadron is still at Marham operating as part of No 1 Group, Strike Command.

Standard

Granted by HRH King George VI and promulgated on 27 March 1952. Presented by HRH Queen Elizabeth the Queen Mother at Scampton on 14 May 1959. A plaque set in the ground by the hangars at Scampton commemorates the presentation.

A new standard was presented by HRH Queen Elizabeth the Queen Mother at Marham on 13 January 1988 (nearly 30 years after she had performed the original ceremony).

Battle Honours

*Fortress Europe 1943-1944
*The Dams
*France & Germany 1944-1945
*Biscay Ports 1944
*Normandy 1944
*Tirpitz
*Channel & North Sea 1944-1945
*German Ports 1945

*Denotes Honours emblazoned on Standard

Nickname

'The Dambusters'

Memorial

The grave of Wing Commander Gibson's labrador, 'Nigger', who was killed on the eve of the attack on the Ruhr dams, is situated outside No 2 Hangar, RAF Scampton.

A 10 ft high 'dam', symbolically broken in the middle, was unveiled on 17 May 1987 in the village of Woodhall Spa, near Horncastle, Lincolnshire, dedicated to the men of No 617 Squadron. (A scale model of the Möhne Dam was presented to the Squadron by the Post Office Savings Department Branch of the RAF Association during November 1955.)

Aircraft insignia and markings

The original 'Dambuster' Lancasters carried the unit code 'AJ', which was retained on standard Lancaster replacements. An additional Flight used the letters 'KC' and B1 (Special) Lancasters modified to carry 'Grand Slam' bombs were identified by the use of the code 'YZ'.

After the war, Lancasters and Lincolns used the code 'KC', but Canberras of the Binbrook Wing all sported a 'lightning flash' on the sides of the nose,

The magnificent memorial erected in Woodhall Spa during 1987 to commemorate the members of the Squadron who lost their lives during the Second World War (Mrs K. Bartholomew).

No 617 Squadron aircraft identifiable by the colour — dark blue, edged in gold. Vulcan B1 markings were restrained, No 617's aircraft carrying no identification except a small Squadron badge on the fuselage sides beneath the pilot's cockpit. On anti-flash white-painted Vulcan B2s, three pale pink 'lightning flashes' appeared on the fin, but when the V-Force changed to the low-level role and aircraft were camouflaged, the markings were not immediately restored. A few aircraft sported 'Dayglo' red 'lightning flashes' cut from plastic sheet, but these were not weather resistant and were replaced in 1972 by a white diamond with a pale blue outline, red flashes, yellow 'dam walls' and black 'waves' — a representation of the Squadron badge.

Tornados re-introduced the 'lightning flash' on top of the fin in the form of a red flash on a black background, and on black bars on each side of the fuselage roundel. Individual aircraft codes were in black, edged in red, changed early in 1983 from numbers to letters. The code letters in use are those employed by the original 'Dambuster' Lancasters.

Glossary and abbreviations

A&AEE	Aeroplane & Armament Experimental Establishment
ADC	Aide-de-camp
AFC	Air Force Cross
AI	Airborne Interception (radar)
'Anti-Diver'	Anti V1 flying bomb
'Art Obs'	Artillery observation
ASR	Air-sea rescue
AVM	Air Vice Marshal
BA	Bachelor of Arts
BAFO	British Air Force of Occupation
BEF	British Expeditionary Force
'Big Ack'	Nickname for Armstrong Whitworth FK 8
Bismuth	Codename for a meteorological flight over the Atlantic on prescribed tracks
'Black Buck'	Codename for a series of Vulcan bomber sorties over the Falkland Islands, 1982
'Brisfit'	Nickname for Bristol F2B Fighter
Cadre	The basic 'skeleton' of a squadron
CB	Companion of the order of the Bath
CBE	Commander of the Order of the British Empire
'Chopper'	Jargon term for a helicopter
CI	Order of the Crown of India
C-in-C	Commander-in-Chief
CMG	Companion of the Order of St Michael & St George
CO	Commanding Officer
'Col Pol'	Colonian Policing
Co-op	Co-operation
'Corporate'	Codename for the operation to recover the Falkland Islands, 1982
'Crusader'	Codename for operation in the Western Desert, 1941.
CVO	Commander of the Victorian Order
DFC	Distinguished Flying Cross
DL	Deputy Lieutenant
DSC	Distinguished Service Cross
DSO	Companion of the Distinguished Service Order
Echelon	Component of a squadron
'Eindekker'	Fokker E1 monoplane
FBIM	Fellow of the British Institute of Management
'Firedog'	Codename for the operation in Malaya against communist guerrillas
'Flaming Coffin'	Nickname for the De Havilland 4
Flt	Flight
FRAeS	Fellow of the Royal Aeronautical Society
GBE	Knight Grand Cross of the Order of the British Empire
GCB	Knight Grand Cross of the Order of the Bath
GCMG	Knight Grand Cross of the Order of St Michael & St George
GCVO	Knight Grand Cross of the Royal Victorian Order
'Grand Slam'	Codename for a 22,000 lb bomb
'Harry Tate'	Nickname for the RE 8
HRH	His (Her) Royal Highness
Impressed	Term applied to civil aircraft taken over by the Government in time of war
Intruder	Offensive night operation to a fixed point or specified enemy target

'Jag'	Jargon for Jaguar aircraft
KBE	Knight Commander of the Order of the British Empire
KCB	Knight Commander of the Order of the Bath
KCVO	Knight Commander of the Royal Victorian Order
KG	Knight of the Garter
KT	Knight of the Thistle
Leigh Light	Trainable searchlight fitted to an anti-submarine aircraft
MA	Master of Arts
MC	Military Cross
Met	Meteorological
MM	Military Medal
'Muskateer'	Codename for the Anglo-French operation against Egypt in 1956
MVO	Member of the Royal Victorian Order
NATO	North Atlantic Treaty Organization
'Ninak'	Nickname for the De Havilland 9A
'Nivo'	Dark green night bomber camouflage paint of the 1920s
OBE	Officer of the Order of the British Empire
OCU	Operational Conversion Unit
OM	Member of the Order of Merit
OTU	Operational Training Unit
'Overlord'	Codename for the Allied invasion of Europe, 1944
'Phoney War'	Jargon for the period of relative inactivity in France during the winter of 1939-40
'Plainfare'	Codename for the operation to supply Berlin from the air during the Russian blockade, 1948-49
QSO	Queens Service Order (New Zealand)
RAAF	Royal Australian Air Force
RAF	Royal Air Force
RCAF	Royal Canadian Air Force
RFC	Royal Flying Corps
'Rhubarb'	Low-level strike operation against targets in occupied Europe
RNAS	Royal Naval Air Service
RNZAF	Royal New Zealand Air Force
'Rover'	Armed patrol searching for enemy shipping
RWR	Radar Warning Receiver
SAAF	South African Air Force
SAC	Strategic Air Command (USAF)
SEAC	South East Asia Command
SEATO	South East Asia Treaty Organization
Sqn	Squadron
Strafe	Air-to-ground attack on troops and installations
Tac/R	Tactical reconnaissance
TAF	Tactical Air Force
'Tall Boy'	Codename for a 12,000 lb bomb
'Tiger Force'	Codename for the British bomber organization for operations against Japan, 1945
'Turbinlite'	Airborne searchlight for night fighter operations
UDI	Unilateral Declaration of Independence
VC	Victoria Cross
VIP	Very Important Person
VVIP	Very Very Important Person
'Whistling Wheelbarrow'	Nickname for the Argosy C1 transport

Appendix I:
Order of Battle—Squadrons

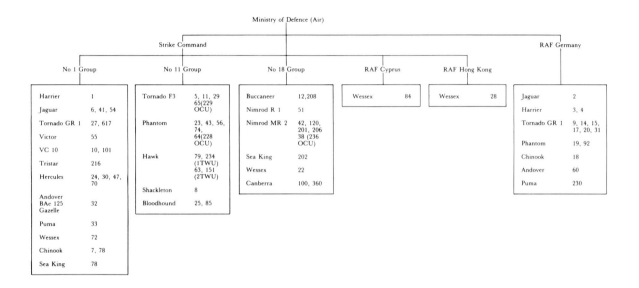

Ministry of Defence (Air)

Strike Command

RAF Germany

No 1 Group		No 11 Group		No 18 Group		RAF Cyprus		RAF Hong Kong		RAF Germany	
Harrier	1	Tornado F3	5, 11, 29 65(229 OCU)	Buccaneer	12,208	Wessex	84	Wessex	28	Jaguar	2
Jaguar	6, 41, 54			Nimrod R 1	51					Harrier	3, 4
Tornado GR 1	27, 617	Phantom	23, 43, 56, 74, 64(228 OCU)	Nimrod MR 2	42, 120, 201, 206 38 (236 OCU)					Tornado GR 1	9, 14, 15, 17, 20, 31
Victor	55										
VC 10	10, 101									Phantom	19, 92
Tristar	216	Hawk	79, 234 (1TWU) 63, 151 (2TWU)	Sea King	202					Chinook	18
Hercules	24, 30, 47, 70			Wessex	22					Andover	60
				Canberra	100, 360					Puma	230
Andover BAe 125 Gazelle	32	Shackleton	8								
Puma	33	Bloodhound	25, 85								
Wessex	72										
Chinook	7, 78										
Sea King	78										

Appendix II:
Heraldic terms

Addorsed	Wings spread, back to back
Affrontée	Full fronted
Base	Bottom of display
Bend	Diagonal partition or display
Charged	Placed on
Close	With closed wings
Conjoined	Joined together
Couped	Neck cut off straight
Cubit arm	Arm cut off at the elbow
Demi	Half
Dexter	To the left, looking at the shield
Displayed	Affrontée, head turned, wings and legs spread
Eradicated	Uprooted with roots showing
Erased	Torn off (usually at the neck)
Fess	Horizontal partition or display
Fimbriated	With an edge of a different tincture
Fracted	With fruit
Guardant	Head towards the observer
Hurt	Blue disc
Issuant	Proceeding from (as an animal issuing from the base of the badge)
Mask	Face of an animal affrontée
Mullet	Five-pointed star shape
Ogress	Circle (roundel) usually carried on a shield
Pale	Vertical partition or display
Passant	Walking, with three paws on the ground
Pile	Wedge shape
Plate	White roundel
Potent	Crutch (often a cross with the four arms ending in a crutch-like form)
Quadrat(e)	Square superimposed on the junction of a cross
Queued	Two tails with a common root
Rampant	Erect in profile with hind paws on the ground
Salient	Applied to a wild beast standing on both hind feet and about to spring at its prey
Saltire	Diagonal cross
Seax	Scimitar with a notch on the back of the blade
Torteaux	Red roundel
Voided	Centre removed (the void is usually the same shape as the object)
Volant	Flying horizontally

Appendix III:
RAF Battle Honours

First World War

Promulgated in February 1947:

Aegean 1915-1918
For operations in the Aegean area against German and Turkish land, sea and air forces, including the Dardenelles, the Gallipoli Campaign and various operations over the Aegean Sea and against Turkish coastal targets.

Arabia 1916-1917
For operations over Arabia in support of the Arab revolt against the Turks.

East Africa 1915-1917
For operations over German East Africa during its conquest from the enemy, by aircraft either based in the country or operating from exterior seaplane bases.

Egypt 1914-1917
For operations by squadrons based in Egypt during the Turkish advance on the Suez Canal across Sinai; and for operations in the Western Desert against the Senussi.

Home Defence 1916-1918
For interception duty against enemy aircraft and Zeppelins raiding Great Britain.

Home Waters 1914-1918
For operations over home waters, whether by land-based or carrier-borne aircraft.

Independent Force & Germany 1914-1919 (originally two separate Honours, but amalgamated in March 1952)
For squadrons based in France as part of the Independent Force, and for operations over Germany, whether by squadrons based in France or carrier-borne aircraft.

Italian Front & Adriatic 1917-1918 (originally two separate Honours, but amalgamated in March 1952)
For operations over the Trentino and neigbouring areas in support of the Allied Armies on the Italian Front; and for operations over the Adriatic and attacks on targets on the Dalmatian coast.

Macedonia 1916-1918
For operations in support of Allied Forces at Salonika and in the advance on, and defeat of, the Bulgarian armies in Macedonia and adjoining territories.

Mesopotamia 1915-1918
For operations over Mesopotamia and Persia in the liberation of Mesopotamia from the Turks.

Palestine 1916-1918
For operations over Palestine, Transjordan and Syria, in the liberation of those territories from the Turks.

South West Africa 1915
For operations by South African personnel during the conquest of German South West Africa.

In addition, individual Army battle honours were selected by the Air Council and awarded to squadrons which had intimately participated in land battles. Twenty were promulgated in April 1951 as follows:

Amiens
Ansac
Arras 1917
Cambrai 1917
Gaza

Helles
Hindenburg Line
Isonzo
Loos
Lys
Meriddo
Mons
Neuve Chappelle
Piave
Somme 1916
Somme 1918
Suvla
Vittorio Veneto
Ypres 1915
Ypres 1917

Two more were approved retrospectively in January 1964:
Marne 1918
Messines 1917

Inter-War

A list of honours were promulgated in February 1947 covering local wars, mainly in the Middle East and India, awarded to squadrons which, after scrutiny of their records, it was considered took a notable part. Such honours were not eligible for emblazonment on Standards. They were:

Aden 1928	Northern Kurdistan 1932
Aden 1929	North Russia 1918-1919
Aden 1934	North West Frontier
Afghanistan 1919-1920	1930-1931
Burma 1930-1932	North West Frontier
Iraq 1919-1920	1935-1939
Iraq 1923-1925	North West Persia 1920
Iraq 1928-1929	Palestine 1936-1939
Kurdistan 1919	Somaliland 1920
Kurdistan 1922-1924	South Persia 1918-1919
Kurdistan 1930-1931	South Russia 1919-1920
Mahsud 1919-1920	Sudan 1920
Mohmand 1927	Transjordan 1924
Mohmand 1933	Waziristan 1919-1925

Second World War

Promulgated in February 1947:

Anzio & Nettuno	For operations in support of the Allied landings in Italy, 9-16 September 1943.
Arakan 1942-1944	For operations by fighter, bomber and transport squadrons in support of the first and second Arakan campaigns, November 1942 to February 1943 and November 1943 to March 1944.
Arnhem	For squadrons participating in the operations of the Allied Airborne Army, 17-26 September 1944.
Arctic 1940-1945	For operations over the Arctic by squadrons of Coastal Command based in Iceland, Russia and the Shetlands.
Atlantic 1939-1945	For operations by aircraft of Coastal Command and others employed in the coastal role over the Atlantic Ocean from the outbreak of war to VE Day.
Baltic 1939-1945	For operations over the Baltic and its approaches by squadrons of Bomber and Coastal Commands from the outbreak of war to VE Day.
Battle of Britain 1940	For interception operations by fighter squadrons over Britain, August to October 1940.
Berlin 1940-1945	For bombardment of Berlin by aircraft of Bomber Command.
Biscay 1940-1945	For operations over the Bay of Biscay by aircraft of Coastal and Fighter Commands, and of Bomber Command loaned to Coastal Command between the fall of France and VE Day, 25 June 1940 to 8 May 1945.
Biscay Ports 1940-1945	For operations over the Bay of Biscay ports from the fall of France to VE Day.
Bismarck	For operations by aircraft of Coastal command associated with the action against the *Bismarck*, 24-29 May 1941.
Burma 1941-1942	For operations in defence of Rangoon and in support of British Forces during the Japanese invasion of Burma, December 1941 to May 1942.
Burma 1944-1945	For operations during the 14th Army's advance from Imphal to Rangoon, the coastal amphibious

assaults, and the Battle of Pegu Yomas, August 1944 to August 1945.

Ceylon 1942 — For operations against Japanese aircraft and naval units by squadrons based in Ceylon during the Japanese attacks of April 1942.

Channel & North Sea 1939-1945 — For ship attack, anti-submarine and mining operations over the English Channel and North Sea from the outbreak of war to VE Day.

Dieppe — For squadrons participating in the combined operations against Dieppe on 19 August 1942.

Dunkirk — For operations covering the evacuation of the British Expeditionary Force and the French from Dunkirk, 26 May to 4 June 1940.

East Africa 1940-1941 — For operations over Kenya, the Sudan, Abyssinia, Italian Somaliland, British Somaliland, Eritrea and the Red Sea during the campaign which resulted in the conquest of Italian East Africa, 10 June 1940 to 27 November 1941.

Eastern Waters 1941-1945 — For operations over waters east of the Mediterranean and Red Sea including the Indian Ocean, Bay of Bengal, Java Sea and South China Sea throughout the war with Japan.

Egypt & Libya 1940-1943 — For operations in the defence of Egypt and the conquest of Libya, from the outbreak of war against Italy to the retreat of the Axis Forces into Tunisia, 10 June 1940 to 6 February 1943.

El Alamein — For operations during the retreat to El Alamein and subsequent actions, June to November 1942.

El Hamma — For operations at El Hamma in support of the Battle of the Mareth Line by squadrons operationally controlled by Air Headquarters, Western Desert, 20-24 March 1943.

Fortress Europe 1940-1944 — For operations by aircraft based in the British Isles against targets in Germany, Italy and enemy-occupied Europe, from the fall of France to the invasion of Normandy.

France & Germany 1944-1945 — For operations over France, Belgium, Holland and Germany during the liberation of north-west Europe and the advance into the enemy's homeland, from the start of air action preparatory to the invasion of France to VE Day, April 1944 to 8 May 1945.

France & Low Countries 1939-1940 — For operations in France and the Low Countries between the outbreak of war and the fall of France, 3 September 1939 to 25 June 1940.

German Ports 1940-1945 — For bombardment of the German ports by aircraft of Bomber and Coastal Commands.

Greece 1940-1941 — For operations over Albania and Greece during the Italian and German invasion, whether carried out by squadrons based in Greece or operating from external bases, 28 October 1940 to 30 April 1941.

Gothic Line — For operations in support of the breaching of the Gothic Line, August to September 1944.

Gustav Line — For squadrons participating in the operations against the Gustav Line, May 1944.

Habbaniya — For units engaged in the defence of Habbaniya, 30 April to 6 May 1941.

Home Defence 1940-1945 — For interception operations after the Battle of Britain, in defence of Great Britain and Northern Ireland against enemy aircraft and flying bombs, November

Invasion Ports 1940	For bombing operations against German-occupied Channel ports, to dislocate enemy preparations for the invasion of England.
Iraq 1941	For operations in the defeat of Rashid Ali's rebellion, 2-31 May 1941.
Italy 1943-1945	For operations over Italy.
Madagascar 1942	For operations by squadrons of the South African Air Force during and after the landings in Madagascar.
Manipur 1944	For operations in support of the besieged forces at Imphal, March to July 1944.
Malaya 1941-1942	For operations against the Japanese in Malaya, Sumatra and Java from 8 December 1941 to 12 March 1942.
Malta 1940-1942	For squadrons participating in defensive, offensive and reconnaissance operations from Malta during the period of enemy action against the island, 10 June 1940 to 31 December 1942.
Mediterranean 1940-1943	For operations over Italy, Sicily and the Mediterranean and Aegean Seas by aircraft based in the Mediterranean area between 10 June 1940 and 30 June 1943.
Meuse Bridges	For squadrons participating in bombing operations against crossings of the Meuse during the German breakthrough between Sedan and Dinant, 12-14 May 1940.
Normandy 1944	For operations supporting the Allied landings in Normandy, the establishment of the lodgement area and the subsequent breakthrough, June to August 1944.
North Africa 1942-1943	For operations in connection with the campaign in French North Africa from the initial landings in Algeria to the expulsion of the Axis Powers from Tunisia, 8 November 1942 to 13 May 1943.
North Burma 1943-1944	For the supply by air of General Wingate's first long-range penetration into North Burma, February to June 1943; and for the air supply and support of his second expedition, 5 March to 26 June 1944.
Norway 1940	For operations over Norway during the German invasion, 9 April to 9 June 1940. Applicable to squadrons based in Norway and those operating from home bases.
Pacific 1941-1945	For operations against the Japanese in the Pacific theatre throughout the war with Japan, 8 December 1941 to 15 August 1945.
Rhine	For operations in support of the battle for the Rhine crossing, 8 February to 24 March 1945.
Ruhr 1940-1945	For bombardment of the Ruhr by aircraft of Bomber Command.
Russia 1941-1945	For operations from Russian bases.
Salerno	For operations in support of the Allied landings in Italy, 9-16 September 1943.
Sicily 1943	For operations in furtherance of the conquest of Sicily by aircraft based in Africa, Malta and Sicily, 1 July to 17 August 1943.
South East Europe 1942-1945	For operations over Yugoslavia, Hungary, Romania, Bulgaria and Greece.
Special Operations	For operations by squadrons regularly assigned to special duties, the succour of resistance movements in enemy-occupied countries by dropping supplies and by introducing and evacuating personnel by air from the formation of the first special duty flight, 20 August 1940, after the fall of France, to VE and VJ

	Days respectively.	**Post-Second World War**	
Syria 1941	For operations over Syria during the campaign against the Vichy French, 8 June to 12 July 1941.	Korea 1950-1953	Limited to the three RAF Sunderland squadrons which flew patrols during the Korean War but were not involved in confrontation with the enemy. Not authorized to be emblazoned.
The Dams	For squadrons participating in the operations for breaching the Möhne, Eder, Serpe and Kembs Dams, May 1943 to October 1944.		
Tirpitz	For operations resulting in the sinking of *Tirpitz*.	South Atlantic 1982	For service in latitudes between 35 and 60 South during the period 2 April to 14 June 1982. Three of the 15 RAF squadrons involved (Nos 1, 18 and 63 (Regiment) Squadrons) have the right of emblazonment.
Walcheren	For operations in support of the capture of the island of Walcheren, 3 October to 9 November 1944.		

Appendix IV:
Representative current
Inter-Squadron Trophies

Aird Whyte Challenge Trophy

A silver rose bowl, approximately 11 ins (28 cm) in diameter and 6 ins (15 cm) high, standing on an ebonite plinth, the Aird Whyte Challenge Trophy had originally been presented to a Mr C.S.R. Palmer by the Institute of Civil Engineers. He gave it to his grandson, Sergeant H.F. Aird Whyte, an air gunner who was reported missing, believed drowned, on 4 November 1943 when the Catalina of 302 Ferry Training Unit in which he was flying was engaged in combat and shot down over the Firth of Lorne.

In 1951, the rose bowl was given by Sergeant Aird Whyte's mother to Coastal Command as an inter-squadron gunnery cup, later changed to gunnery and anti-submarine bombing. With changes in aircraft and tactics, the annual competition evolved into a full scale day and night anti-submarine competition, one crew from each squadron and the OCU being selected to take part. Traditionally the winning crew represents the RAF in the Fincastle Trophy.

Winners

1951 210 Sqn	1964 42 Sqn	1977 206 Sqn
1952 120 Sqn	1965 224 Sqn	1978 201 Sqn
1953 120 Sqn	1966 224 Sqn	1979 201 Sqn
1954 206 Sqn	1967 206 Sqn	1980 120 Sqn
1955 201 Sqn	1968 210 Sqn	1981 201 Sqn
1956 120 Sqn	1969 201 Sqn	1982 Not awarded +
1957 206 Sqn	1970 Not awarded*	1983 42 Sqn
1958 Not awarded	1971 201 Sqn	1984 236 OCU
1959 Not awarded	1972 120 Sqn	1985 120 Sqn
1960 224 Sqn	1973 203 Sqn	1986 236 OCU
1961 203 Sqn	1974 206 Sqn	1987 201 Sqn
1962 224 Sqn	1975 201 Sqn	1988 201 Sqn
1963 120 Sqn	1976 201 Sqn	

*Due to Nimrod re-equipment programme
+ Operation 'Corporate'

Dacre Trophy

Consisting of three bronze archers on a bronze dais fixed to a marble base and mounted on a wooden plinth, the Dacre Trophy was presented to Fighter Command on 30 August 1951 by Air Commodore and Mrs Dacre in memory of their son, Flying Officer K.F. Dacre DFC, killed on operations over Germany in a No 605 Squadron Mosquito.

Originally awarded to the regular fighter squadron declared the most effective in weapons training, the requirements have been broadened and the winner is now the 11 Group unit judged to have obtained the best all-round results on armament practice camp, missile practice camp, readiness and reaction exercises, tactical evaluation, flight safety and aircraft recognition.

Winners

1952/53 74 Sqn	1962/63 92 Sqn	1975/76 56 Sqn
1953/54 19 Sqn	1963/64 64 Sqn	1976/77 43 Sqn
1954/55 Not awarded	1964/65 19 Sqn	1977/78 56 Sqn
	1965/66 92 Sqn	1978/79 5 Sqn
1955/56 19 Sqn	1966/67 23 Sqn	1979/80 23 Sqn
1956/57 64 Sqn	1967/68 5 Sqn	1980/81 56 Sqn
1957/58 63 Sqn	1968/69 23 Sqn	1981/82 111 Sqn
1958/59 63 Sqn	1969/70 11 Sqn	1982/83 43 Sqn
1959/60 66 Sqn	1970/71 5 Sqn	1983/84 29 Sqn
1960/61 Not awarded	1971/72 5 Sqn	1984/85 56 Sqn
	1972/73 11 Sqn	1985/86 56 Sqn
1961/62 Not awarded	1973/74 29 Sqn	1986/87 111 Sqn
	1974/75 23 Sqn	

Salmond Trophy

This trophy was presented by Sir Geoffrey Salmond, Air Officer Commanding, RAF India, in 1930 as the 'RAF India, Sir Geoffrey Salmond Bombing Cup' for annual competition between army co-operation squadrons in the sub-Continent.

After the Second World War, the Trophy was allocated to Bomber Command for competition between Canberra squadrons and then, in 1959, was transferred to RAF Germany for award to the winner of a LABS Canberra contest. Changes to the rules allowed other types of aircraft to compete from 1971.

Winners

1930 5 Sqn	1964 213 Sqn	1974 No contest
1931 5 Sqn	1965 213 Sqn	1975 14 Sqn
1932 5 Sqn	1966 3 Sqn	1976 14 Sqn
1933 31 Sqn	1967 3 Sqn	1977 14 Sqn
1934 5 Sqn	1968 213 Sqn	1978 16 Sqn
1935 31 Sqn	1969 213 Sqn	1979 16 Sqn
1936-54 No contest	1970 16 Sqn	1980-85 No contest
1955 83 Sqn	1971 3 Sqn	1986 9 Sqn
1956-62 No contest	1972 14 Sqn	1987 31 Sqn
1963 213 Sqn	1973 31 Sqn	

Seed Trophy

The origins of this magnificent silver trophy, which features birds, animals and aircraft, is uncertain, but it is thought to have been intended for presentation to Miss Amy Johnson on her return from her famous solo flight to Australia in 1930. If this is correct, it was not awarded, but was bequeathed to Mr Clifford Seed in 1977 and he presented it to the RAF on 10 May 1979. It is awarded annually to the fighter squadron in 11 Group, Strike Command, producing the best results in air-to-air gunnery at the armament practice camp, a weighting factor being applied to take account of differing types of aircraft.

Winners

1978/79 111 Sqn	1982/83 43 Sqn	1986/87 229 OCU
1979/80 43 Sqn	1983/84 5 Sqn	
1980/81 111 Sqn	1984/85 43 Sqn	
1981/82 Not awarded	1985/86 5 Sqn	

Index

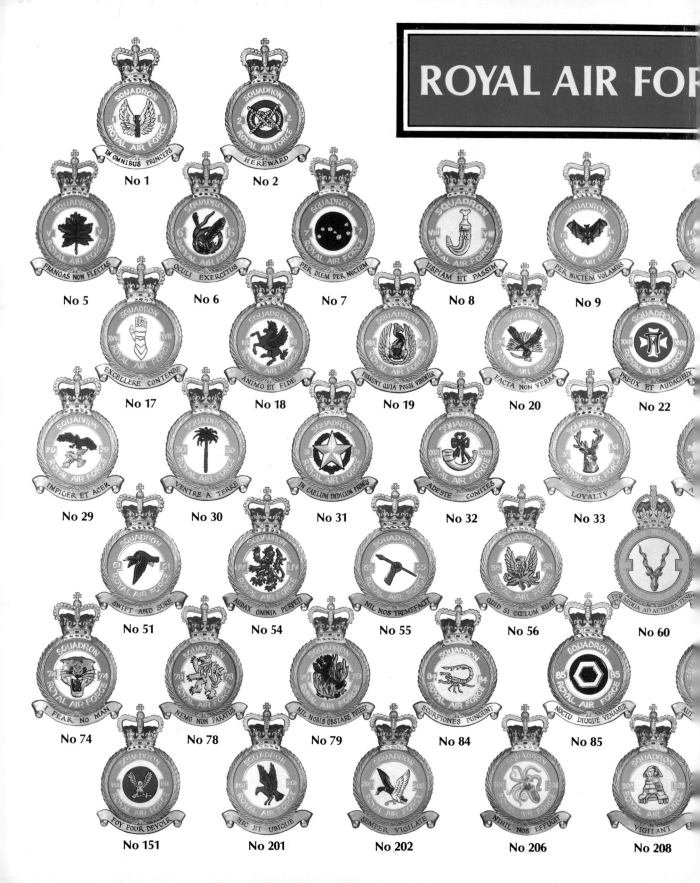

No 1

No 2

No 5

No 6

No 7

No 8

No 9

No 17

No 18

No 19

No 20

No 22

No 29

No 30

No 31

No 32

No 33

No 51

No 54

No 55

No 56

No 60

No 74

No 78

No 79

No 84

No 85

No 151

No 201

No 202

No 206

No 208